D0398383

RUNNING WITH RAVEN

ALSO BY LAURA LEE HUTTENBACH

*The Boy Is Gone: Conversations
with a Mau Mau General*

BISCAYNE BAY

47th St

Alton Rd

Collins Ave

F

◀ To Miami

41st St

Julia Tuttle Causeway

ATLANTIC OCEAN

35th St

E

MIAMI BEACH

Lincoln Rd

D

15th St

C

Espanola Way

B

A → F → A = 8 Miles

South Beach

Collins Ave

Ocean Drive

MacArthur Causeway

5th St

Fifth Street Lifeguard Stand

Alton Rd

Raven's Running Routes

1 - Back and Forth North
🏁 → B → A → B → A → C → 🏁

2 - 35th Street
🏁 → B → A → E → 🏁

South Pointe Dr

3 - Back and Forth South
🏁 → A → B → A → D → A → 🏁

GOVERNMENT CUT

A

FISHER ISLAND

4 - 47th Street
🏁 → A → F → 🏁

Map by Brian Edward Balsley, GISP

RUNNING WITH RAVEN

The Amazing Story of One Man,
His Passion, and the Community
He Inspired

LAURA LEE HUTTENBACH

CITADEL BOOKS
Kensington Publishing Corp.
www.kensingtonbooks.com

CITADEL PRESS BOOKS are published by

Kensington Publishing Corp.
119 West 40th Street
New York, NY 10018

All Kensington titles, imprints, and distributed lines are available at special quantity discounts for bulk purchases for sales promotions, premiums, fundraising, educational, or institutional use.

Special book excerpts or customized printings can also be created to fit specific needs. For details, write or phone the office of the Kensington sales manager: Kensington Publishing Corp., 119 West 40th Street, New York, NY 10018, attn: Sales Department; phone 1-800-221-2647.

CITADEL PRESS and the Citadel logo are Reg. U.S. Pat. & TM Off.

ISBN-13: 978-0-8065-3842-6
ISBN-10: 0-8065-3842-2

First Printing: May 2017

10 9 8 7 6 5 4 3 2 1

Printed in the United States of America

First Electronic Edition: May 2017

ISBN-13: 978-0-8065-3844-0
ISBN-10: 0-8065-3844-9

*For my siblings—Pat, Eric, and Marisa—for making sure
I am never more than myself, and for making me believe
that myself is enough, maybe sometimes too much.*

For Mary Beth Koeth, for how you help us see the world.

For Mitchell Kaplan, for the way you honor books and writers.

And for Raven Runners, for every eight miles and these stories.

CONTENTS

Raven's Community,
A Selection of Characters

Along with Raven and Laura Lee "White Lightning," more than twenty-five hundred people have run with Raven through these pages, including:

Miracle, Raven's longtime girlfriend, is a professor at FIU, a pool player, fisherman, runner, and a swimmer. Her greatest fear is of entrapment, while Raven's is of abandonment.

Mary Cooper is Raven's mother. Her second husband, **the Eagle**, with white hair and a pointy nose, became Raven's nemesis.

Bulldog was an outgoing boxer at the famed 5th Street Gym, where Muhammad Ali trained. Together with Bulldog's best friend, **Killer**, the boxers convinced Raven to run.

The Astrologer, twenty-one years his senior, was Raven's first serious girlfriend, from 1975 to 1988. She was big into working out and loved Christmas and psychics. The Astrologer suggested that Raven should keep a list of runners.

Coyote, a poet, harmonica player, and male nurse, was the first person to run eight miles with Raven in 1977.

Yul, an avid arm wrestler—bald and with a speech impediment—was the third runner to complete eight miles with Raven in 1982.

Placard Man, a Raven Run coach, was a well-liked, germophobic homeless man who carried around handwritten public service announcements on cardboard. Raven received his mail.

Gringo, a former land baron in Spain, has run over fifteen hundred times with Raven, including in eighty-six-mph wind during Hurricane Irene, but today can't bear to see Raven running in so much pain.

Taxman, a 63-year-old socialist and accountant, has logged the most runs (1,959) with Raven. Conservative runners call him "Comrade Tax." His wife, Lasagna Lady, is a Raven Run coach.

Dizzy Issie, a middle school principal and ultramarathoner who came from Cuba in 1967 on the Freedom Flights, met his wife and best friend on the Raven Run. He is ranked number two.

Poutine, named for her favorite Canadian dish, holds the female record for 143 consecutive runs and swims.

Hurdler, a law professor and former steeplechaser, earned his nickname jumping over every trashcan on the beach, which came to 572 cans.

Creve Coeur, a bodybuilder and federal marshal from Creve Coeur, Missouri, with more than four hundred runs, asked Raven to marry him and his wife, Hollywood Flasher, in an intimate ceremony over eight miles in 2009.

Butcher started running with Raven after getting released from prison for drug trafficking. In 2013, he ran with Raven two hundred consecutive days, which he says saved his life.

WHAT IS IT ABOUT RAVEN?

ROBERT "RAVEN" KRAFT is a 65-year-old songwriter who runs eight miles every day, without exception, in the sands of Miami Beach, and he's been doing that every single day for the last forty-one years.

Seriously. He hasn't missed one sunset.

It's common for people to dismiss Raven's content by his packaging, because, I'll admit, he is a strange-looking fellow. For his running uniform, he is shirtless in short black shorts, one black glove, a black headband, black socks, and running shoes that don't have to be black. Nearsighted, he wears aviators that turn dark in the light, and when he's not wearing them, he squints like Clint Eastwood. He combs his longish black hair into a wave that breaks across his scalp. The ends of his mullet curl with sweat. He cuts his own hair and trims his white beard, dyeing black his mustache and chinstraps that frame his thin chapped lips with a dark heart. Scoliosis, sciatica, and spinal stenosis have caught up to his running pace, so he can't stand up straight. A deeply tanned torso covered by a forest of chest hair slouches over his caved-in abdominals, turning his body into a five-foot-ten apostrophe. When he runs, his right foot lands heavier than his left, giving him the gait of a graceful pirate with a peg leg. He wears his pain on his wrinkled face, and it's not pretty. He is not a person with whom you'd expect to relate or from whom you'd expect to learn. Most people think he is homeless. If I didn't know him, I'd probably cross the street.

But people from every American state and all over the world flock to meet him. Over twenty-five hundred people—ages 6 to 80—have run eight miles with him, earning a nickname and a spot on his esteemed runner's list. The top three runners—Taxman, Dizzy, and Gringo—all have over sixteen hundred runs on the books (that Raven meticulously keeps). Raven hasn't run alone in over a decade.

What is it about this man that makes people from everywhere come to his South Beach sandbox? Besides a nickname, what do you get from Raven?

In seeking the answer to that question, I—White Lightning—have run over a thousand miles with Raven. I've attended Raven Run events like the Annual Awards banquet in January, the Spring Picnic, and Raven's Birthday Dinner on October 17. I've recorded hundreds of hours of interviews with him at his apartment, and I've talked to him on the phone for much longer. I have written this book. But *my* problem is that I'm generally drawn to obsessive, offbeat types who can tell a good story about a place that is unfamiliar to me. In this way, Raven is definitely my type.

To figure out the source of Raven's magnetism, I started asking Raven Runners two questions: Why did you first come to run with Raven? And, why did you come back? In response, I heard eight common refrains, each of which will be explored in the eight parts of this book.

For example, when Amy, a pretty 40-year-old woman from Denver, moved to Miami Beach, she had trouble finding friends. "My biggest complaint was that there was no community," she said, expressing a common frustration for residents new to the Beach. "The city was so transient." Her colleagues at the Miami Design Preservation League—the organization that promotes and protects the Art Deco of South Beach—suggested that she run with Raven. On her second attempt in July 2009, she completed all eight and became Preservationist. "This run was so important to me," she recalled on a run in 2014. "First it was the challenge of eight miles. Then it was the social group and community. Then it was the physicality. I got so strong." She started doing half-marathons. "I gained so much confidence," she continued. "For my job, I had to be outgoing and raise money and meet people, but that wasn't the real Amy. I have social anxiety. But when you meet people running, it creates this intimacy. Maybe it's because you're looking forward, rather than directly at the person next to you. You just feel comfortable sharing things you're going through." Preservationist has over two hundred runs with Raven. She named some of her best friends—All-American, Troublemaker, Seaside Sparrow, Juris Prudence, and Expresso. "Every day I know where Raven is," she said. "He's the most constant thing in my life."

At the Raven Run Annual Awards banquet one January, I was sitting across from Green Thumb, a kind, 69-year-old real estate agent. He sports a white beard and a tan face, and he tends to the South Beach community garden. "I have to say, you always meet interesting people with Raven," he observed. "You never meet, like, a consultant." That night, when Raven was trying to induct a runner called Firecracker into the Hall of Shame—a controversial practice among us—she protested and launched into a fiery tirade. Green Thumb and I just looked at each other and shrugged. To us, the memorable and colorful characters are a real draw. To Raven, they are unavoidable because the run is free and open to anyone and everyone (unless—I'll go into this later—you are one of six banned people who got violent and threatened to kill Raven). For accepting everyone, sometimes Raven pays a price.

Many runners gave me attributes that they admired about Raven. "I aspire for that kind of singular dedication and focus," said Unoffendable, a 50-year-old marketing professional and

Vikings fan. "Today's *woulda-coulda-shoulda* society embraces excuses. Raven refuses, be it weather, age, health, whatever." Before he moved from Miami to Texas in 2014, Unoffendable completed twenty-two "partials"—four-mile runs—in a row. "That opened my eyes a bit," he said. "When I tell his story I usually challenge the listener to think of the last time he skipped sleep (party or study) or food (usually illness), and this dude runs eight on the sand. I mean he is more dedicated to his run than we are to basic needs."

Raven knows where he is supposed to be every day, and he has no desire to be elsewhere. He is clear on his purpose in life—to give strangers and friends eight miles to belong and make connections. He finds it meaningful. Purpose and authenticity rub off—not necessarily because you share the same purpose or because you are like that person—but because you have a purpose or you want a purpose, and you want people to accept you when you are being yourself. That's what Raven encourages—to be healthy, to do what you say, and to be true.

"I could not think of a person nor an event of any kind which seemed as predictably dependable as Raven and his daily run," remarked Shoe Guy, a former Eastbay Shoe executive who has 693 runs with Raven. Through him, he has made great new friends and recruited his own family to experience eight miles. "If you find something special like the Raven Run, it grows in value when you share it with people you love," said Shoe Guy. "My girlfriend, part Native American, became 'Moccasin.' My three sons became 'Shoe Horn,' 'Midsole,' and 'Cleats.' And finally, my daughter-in-law, a lovely former ballerina prone to an occasional fall became 'Slipper.' "

What surprised me most by the answers I received from Raven Runners on why they run with Raven was how little they related to running. "While we are all runners, it's not really about 'the run,' " observed Canuck, an attorney from Toronto who has over two hundred runs with Raven. "It is the people who have made this run into the special thing that it is." Raven offers everyone consistency and structure in an American city whose appearance and identity are continuously changing. Unlikely relationships sparked over eight miles now span the globe.

Raven's girlfriend of the last nineteen years, Miracle, is a professor of black-and-white print photography at Florida International University, specializing in pictures of Florida wildlife. She knows the scientific name for every plant, though she has trouble remembering doctors' appointments. She is willowy with long blond hair, which she brushes frequently, and plays in a pool league under her other pseudonym, Miami Slim. One of the most eloquent people I know, Miracle believes Raven fulfills two profound needs in people: "In our culture today there's this need for the kind of myth that people used to have and we don't have anymore," she told me on the phone while she was driving to class. "I mean nobody believes in the Man of Steel. People want something that they can believe in. I think Raven is that thing. No matter where you are in the world, you know there's this superhuman guy doing something that's just impossible to imagine." She cleared her throat. "And the other thing that I think is universal to our species is a need for knowing where your place is. You call it roots or home, but that sense of where you belong is extremely important. If you know anyone that doesn't have that, you know how cursed they are because they spend a lifetime of wandering and searching. They may never find it. The fact that Raven is doing this in one place, he has that. I think people who want to hear the stories from him, it's not just about entertainment, it's about connecting to the idea of a sense of place. You can call it regional, even local, even limited to an eight-mile stretch, but it's an idea that extends into the heart of every human being. When they touch Raven, they touch the myth and the sense of place simultaneously."

I first met Raven on a weekend afternoon in May 2011, three months after moving to Miami Beach from my hometown of Atlanta. I was lying out in the sand with my friend

Jessie, an attorney who played volleyball with me at the University of Virginia, and Raven happened to stop right in front of my beach towel. "Hey," I said. "I've passed you running on the beach. You're the Raven."

"I know," he replied, adjusting his black headband. "I remember you. I've probably been running since before you were born. When's your birthday?"

"August first, 1982."

"That was a Sunday," he said. *It was?* "They were dredging the beach, and I was running under the old pier when a wave washed ashore. I veered to the right to miss the wave and went headfirst into a concrete piling."

"Were you okay?" I asked.

Reaching behind his neck, Raven delicately pressed water from the end of his mullet. "I cracked my head open," he said. "A lifeguard drove me to the hospital, and I got eighteen stitches." The doctor told him he'd had a concussion and needed to stay the night for observation. "But instead I went back to the Beach to finish my eight miles," continued Raven. "I even made it to work that night. I was a security guard."

"That's not a positive association with my birthday," I said.

"Actually it turned out real positive," he said. "Somebody called the *Herald,* and they ran my story inside the Neighbors section—the Raven Run's first press!"

Water was dripping off his chest hair. "Did you just get done running?" I asked.

"No, I went swimming. I run in the evening. You should come with us. Meet at the Fifth Street lifeguard stand at five thirty."

Before I could think it through, the words left my lips. "What day?"

Any day. Every day. There was no weather hotline, no confirmation number. If Raven was alive, he'd be running. "I'll start thinking of a nickname for you," he continued. "But you have to finish the eight."

Jessie, lying in a bikini on the towel next to me, popped up. "Do you have a White Lightning yet?" she asked.

"No," said Raven, pointing at me. "Is that what people call you?"

It wasn't, really. It was what a homeless man standing on the corner of 5th and Ocean had called me on the way to the beach that afternoon. After looking me up and down in one fell motion, the man proclaimed, "Good afternoon, White Lightning." Jessie and I—normally immune to the street commentary of Miami Beach—burst out laughing and had been talking about it ever since.

"Well you're white, Southern, and you look fast," concluded Raven, smoothing his salt-and-pepper beard. "George Jones does a great version of that song. It's an idea, White Lightning."

That Tuesday, in front of the blue and yellow lifeguard stand, a dozen sweaty runners were chatting and stretching. Raven recognized me immediately. "Glad you came," he said. "You ready? It's almost time for roll call." A minute later, falling in line behind our leader, the flock headed south to Government Cut, at the end of the island.

With the fanfare of a wrestling ring announcer, Raven introduced the runners in attendance. "Right here, on my left, if you have a boss you don't like, have him hire Chapter 11." The rest of the group clapped as Chapter 11, a 77-year-old former mechanic wearing two knee braces, gave a nod. Chapter 11's résumé lists five airlines, two boatyards, and a restaurant as places of employment that went belly-up. "Now, behind me, he's the man who's always right—even when he's wrong, or left, it's the Strategist!" The runners clapped again for the attorney in his 40s. "From Canada, with the record of one hundred forty-three consecutive runs and swims, she knows *the road is long*—Poutine!"

At the end of roll call, Raven introduced me. "We got Laura Lee from Georgia here. Everyone say hi."

Though the Miami summer was just gearing up, the thermometer registered in the upper eighties. By mile two, the gum in my mouth had dissolved. I craved water. The sand shifted underneath me and sucked in every step. It was way harder than Raven made it look. At Government Cut, we U-turned and ran fourteen blocks north, where we U-turned again and repeated the sandy loop.

As we ran together, I asked the questions most every first-time runner asks, and he answered in a matter-of-fact way, like he had fielded them a thousand times before, which he had. He spoke in the crystal-clear voice of a radio announcer. It was like running with a podcast.

Because he had run the exact same path every day since 1975, Raven could give a unique history of Miami Beach—a long spit of sand, hotels, and old shingled bungalows on the margin of a great new international city. He began the streak when the town was known as "God's Waiting Room," wall to wall with retirement homes and old people. Then came the Cocaine Cowboys, the Mariel Boatlift, *Miami Vice,* models, Versace, and world-class conventions like Art Basel and Ultra Music Festival. The man had run through the ruination and rebirth of South Beach—from old white Jews to the Ellis Island of Latin America and the Caribbean—remembering every detail and person who'd crossed his path along the way. I love learning history like this—peering out the window from a unique local's perspective.

As a traveler, I couldn't imagine staying in one place for my entire life. "So you've really never taken a vacation?" I asked.

"Why would I want to go on vacation?" he said, nodding to the west, to the pink clouds sucking in the last orange drops of sunshine. "I live in paradise. When you don't wanna leave a place, staying ain't hard to do."

Around mile six, Raven turned to me. "I can tell you're going to make eight miles. You live up to White Lightning. You okay with that?"

* * *

RAVEN CALLED TUESDAYS "Story Hour with White Lightning." (I learned that the lifeguards had their own nickname for me, Miss Tuesday. "Before your time there was an actress called Tuesday Weld," Raven explained. "You kind of look like her. I told the lifeguards your dance card was full, but they still like Tuesdays.") In the two-plus hours it took Raven to run eight miles, we usually got through three or four vignettes. Some days, Raven arrived with character profiles prepared; other times the scenery or passersby inspired the tale. Stories came with meticulous details, down to the day and time. People had rich descriptions. Dialogues were full and lively. I knew not only the make and model and color of the car people drove but what song was playing on the radio when conversations took place. He told me birthdays and unique habits. His memory was exceptional, like *Rainman*.

The Miami Beach he had grown up in was completely different from the city I know today. "Miami's probably changed more in the last forty years than any other American city," said Raven. "And I know we say this kind of stuff all the time, but they just don't make characters like they used to."

About his early years, as Robert Kraft, before becoming the Raven, he was reticent, so I suggested we meet for our first interview at a Starbucks in South Beach one Friday night in 2011. Wearing his unbuttoned black Levi's jacket and chest hair, Raven felt the eyes of every customer in the shop. "I think they're trying to figure us out," said Raven, pointing to an Italian family of four staring at our table. Then background music stole his focus. "This was a hit when I was in high school," he said, singing along to "What Becomes of the Brokenhearted." Almost everyone there looked like someone he knew, and he pointed out the resemblance. When Starbucks closed, we hadn't gotten far.

"Would you be more comfortable if we talk at your apartment?" I asked.

"I think so, White Lightning," he said. "But I have to warn you, it's a little messy."

The next night, sitting on the ripped cushion of his black leather couch, Raven was articulate and methodical. Next to him, stacked higher than his head, red and blue plastic crates overflowed with records, cassettes, and old newspapers. Shoeboxes stuffed with letters teetered on top. A cut-out picture of Johnny Cash, wearing his trademark black button-down shirt, was taped to the wall above Raven's first record player, which, he bragged, "worked perfectly up until about twenty years ago." Below that, he has pinned a Nixon bumper sticker saved from the 1968 campaign. He loves Nixon. Posters of Waylon Jennings and baseball player Ron "The Penguin" Cey stared down at us from their walls. Every lampshade was crooked, and the shelves leaned to one side. The air was stale with a touch of mildew, like a basement filled with running shoes.

He lives alone in a two-bedroom South Beach basement apartment on Ocean Drive between 3rd and 4th Streets, two blocks from the Atlantic. He calls himself a collector, but most people who have been inside use the word "hoarder." He has every letter that anyone has written to him. Every thing is a memory, and he can't throw away experiences. "I think that comes from my childhood," he explains. "We didn't have much, so everything I got I cherished." Hoarding is also an antidote to his terrible fear of abandonment. "It's like if I have my things here," he says, "I won't be alone." His main collections represent his biggest obsessions—music, running, South Beach history, and baseball.

His living room was the setting for our recorded interviews, which usually took place before the run between noon and two o'clock, when he left for the outdoor gym on 9th Street to do pull-ups. Raven preferred to meet after the run, between eight thirty and midnight. For these sessions, we would end eating a Klondike bar or ice cream, then he would walk me to my car and ask me to call him when I arrived home safely. "You gotta be careful, White Lightning," he told me. "There are a lot of strange characters out there."

Raven is a collector of things and people. He doesn't like anyone to be forgotten. In the cast of his life, it is hard to distinguish between an extra and a supporting role, because one meeting with a stranger could change him forever. One interview in particular illustrates this point. Raven was telling me about Jovial Joe, a former Merchant Marine from Boston who looked like a tiny, toothless Kirk Douglas, smiling a gummy smile. As a young man, Jovial Joe used to throw back beers with John F. Kennedy, who was born the same year in 1917. By the time Raven met him, he was retired and passed his days extracting magazines and newspapers from the beach trashcans. "What kind of magazines do you like?" Jovial Joe had asked

Raven told him, "Anything with sports or music." The next morning, a collection of periodicals, freshly plucked from the garbage, was hanging in a plastic grocery sack from Raven's bicycle handlebars. If Jovial Joe found a magazine that he thought would be of extreme interest, he delivered it by hand to the lifeguard stand. The ritual went on for years until one week, Raven didn't get any deliveries.

When Raven called the Clinton Hotel, Jovial Joe's winter residence, the receptionist told him that Joe had had a heart attack and died. Raven's next call was to the funeral home, which hadn't located any family. Together with his neighbor and temporary German roommate named Angelica, Raven planned Jovial Joe's funeral service.

"Angelica was bawling her eyes out," Raven told me. "She didn't even know Jovial Joe." At the reception, the funeral director handed Raven the urn. "He had no relatives in the whole world," explained Raven. "So here I am signing for everything." Raven decided to sprinkle Joe's ashes on the beach, where he was most jovial.

I liked this story. Raven had given Joe a family and vice

versa. As I smiled, Raven pointed to a dark, wooden box on the shelf directly behind his head. He patted it twice. "He's right in there," he said. "That's Joe."

I stopped smiling. "Don't get nervous," said Raven. "I never had the heart to put him on the beach." In his possession, Raven has all that remains of a man society never knew. "Every time something nice happens, I say, 'Jovial Joe's looking out for me.' I felt good he was here."

An appropriate response didn't come to mind, so, to fill the silence, I asked, "Did the funeral home provide the box?"

"Yeah, they just handed it to me."

I wrote down "box provided" in my notebook. "Is it locked?"

"Yeah," he said. "I never opened it."

I also noted, "Locked," with an asterisk.

NEARLY EVERY RUNNER told me that the first time they ran with Raven, they ran out of curiosity. They came to him with admiration or disbelief, and they always came with questions. But when I asked runners why they came back, most everyone's response touched on a feeling of family, of community, of belonging to something real. They used words like "surprised" and "shocked" when they discovered that Raven, down deep, was someone they liked.

"I was shocked what a genuine good guy Raven was," wrote Dimples, who lives in New Jersey. "Two years later, I returned for my second run. When Raven arrived, he greeted me with, 'Hey, Dimples! How are you? You look like you lost some weight from the last time you were here? Your birthday is October ninth, right?' Shocked and surprised, I responded yes. And off we went for my second run." Raven makes people feel special when he remembers them. They feel like they are worth remembering.

Canuck told me, "I quickly learned that what I first thought was a bit of a freak of a guy was one of the nicest, if not the nicest, person I have ever met. And that really has nothing to do with running."

Picadillo wrote to me, "I met the legend but I also got to know a man with a kind heart, a loving humor, and a strong spirit. That's that guy you want as a running partner."

In all honesty, it is hard to run with Raven now. The pace is excruciatingly slow, and it's hard to watch him hurt. "His pain can be hell on him and on people who care about him," wrote Shoe Guy. "Rather than diminish his impressiveness, this condition only adds to the respect we should have for him. I find that my own aging body doesn't allow me to get out as much as I might like, but I realize that I am just human, not Raven."

So runners new and old continue showing up to honor Raven and what he's given us.

What started as a New Year's resolution in 1975 has outlasted the presidencies of Gerald Ford, Jimmy Carter, Ronald Reagan, two Bushes, Bill Clinton, and Barack Obama. Raven has covered more than 120,000 miles—that's a trip around the world, almost five times. "I had no idea what I was getting into," Raven told me. "I built my whole world, my whole life, around that run."

At the end of one three-hour interview, Raven inhaled deeply and stood up from the sofa. He winced as his stiff skeleton straightened out and his swollen, arthritic joints readjusted. His face twisted again as he sat back down on the couch. He leaned forward. "The whole thing is about redemption," he said. "From the beginning, I was just trying to save myself on the run. That's all. But now people tell me I've saved others, so I guess I've got something to be proud of."

RUNNING WITH RAVEN

I
PERMANENCE

As was said once by our friends Jacques and Macbeth, we are
poor players, strutting and fretting our hour on the stage, each
with our entrances and exits. We all expect to be at the center
of this little play, and each I think is drawn to things, people,
events which seem greater than the quotidian experience
we cycle through. The Man represents, to a degree, the
transcendence, the magnificence that we all expect and
aspire to, but simply don't have the discipline to accomplish
or foolishness to really try. Out, out brief candle? The Raven
pushes back mightily against that, because he will always be
there tomorrow, and tomorrow, and tomorrow . . .
—Evictor, 175 runs

It is reassuring to know that in such a transient society there
is a connection and consistency to someone or something
similar to the rotation of the earth around its axis, night and
day, or its orbit around the sun. Do you think Raven rotates
around South Beach? Or South Beach around Raven?
—Picadillo, 5 runs

I may be the only thing that hasn't changed around here in
the last forty years.
—Raven, over 15,000 eight-mile runs

ONE

Paint It Black

Looking around at the fortress of clutter that wreathes his private life, it's hard to connect this Raven with the spirited raconteur who, every day, assembles a diverse bunch of individuals in the name of community and exercise. His followers would be surprised to discover that, as a boy, their leader was painfully shy. "If I had to describe my childhood in one word, it would be 'lonely,' " says Raven.

To judge if a person has risen or fallen, we must know from where he came.

Raven was born Robert A. Kraft on October 17, 1950, in Richmond, Virginia, to Mary and Walter Kraft. When he was 4, his parents divorced, and his father went to California, where he remarried seven times.

The *Silver Meteor* train delivered Robert, Mary, and her mother to Miami Beach in 1955, right before he started kindergarten at South Beach Elementary. Mary always told him, "Children should be seen and not heard," and Robert listened. He had little interaction with kids his age. "We used to call it God's Waiting Room," Raven says. "Old people would just be out on the porch, waiting to die. In the summer, you could roll a bowling ball down Ocean Drive and not hit one person."

He hated school. When he was made to repeat first grade, his teacher wrote on his report card: *Robert has trouble social-*

izing. When he's spoken to, he just nods. His best friends were on baseball cards that he kept in his front pockets. He loved the Dodgers. Players taught him lessons in geography, statistics, math, history, and reading. "I'd memorize everything on the card. I'd look up where they were from. That was my education."

He still remembers these statistics. Once, on a run with me, Sleazebuster, and a guy called Y2K, Raven recited every single World Series—where it was played, who played, and other fun facts—since 1960. Then Sleazebuster said, "Can I give you my test? I'm trying to think of the roster, and I'm missing some names in the outfield. I got Pee Wee Reese, Junior Gilliam, Gil Hodges, Carl Furillo, Duke Snider—who am I forgetting?"

Asking for the 1955 Brooklyn Dodgers roster from Raven was like inquiring what he ate for dinner. "Jackie Robinson moved to third base," began Raven. "You had the platoon in the outfield—Sandy Amoros or Shotgun Shuba. Catcher was Roy Campanella. Ace pitchers were Johnny Podres, Carl Erskine, and Don Newcombe," said Raven. "But Junior Gilliam was my favorite."

Raven's favorite school days fell on Jewish high holidays, when pretty much all of his classmates and his teacher were at synagogue. "It was great," he recalls. "We basically had a free day with a sub. We never got homework." Before 1959, he knew only two Cubans at school, brothers named Ernie and Pompy Santella. So this is why, when I asked Raven how Cuban immigration affected Miami Beach, he answered, "Well it made the Jewish holidays a lot less fun."

After Castro and the Revolution, Robert's classes started filling up with *exiliados,* many of whom did not observe the Jewish holy days. Teachers assigned homework on Rosh Hashana, and Robert was upset.

A SINGLE MOM, Mary got a job working at a candy store, where Robert would sit at the counter after school sipping a Yoo-hoo while she rang people up at the cash register. When he got bored, he wandered outside to a bus stop in front of Dillards Hotel. On a pad of paper, Robert kept track of cars that passed. There was something soothing about making lists. Chevys, Fords, and Plymouths got the most tick marks, while Nash Ambassadors, Hudson Hornets, a Packard, or a Henry J by Kaiser was slightly more exciting. He didn't care about Mercedes or VW Bugs; only American cars counted. He sketched windows and taillights and became obsessed with fins. "Back then you could tell right away what kind of car it was," says Raven wistfully. "Now they all look the same."

When Mary started working the graveyard shift at Al's Restaurant, a twenty-four-hour luncheonette and auto tag agency, life got harder. His grandmother had moved to her own apartment, and Robert, age 8, started spending his nights alone. In the morning, he lay awake frozen in bed, hugging his pillow like a friend, until he heard his mother's high heels clicking up the wooden steps to their apartment. "I'd breathe and think, *Phew, thank God. I'm going to get fed, I can live another day*," says Raven. "I was terrified of being an orphan."

He calls himself a latchkey kid and often says, "If there's one thing my mother taught me, it's to always lock the door." (He still compulsively checks locks.) They were poor, too, living in the South Shore neighborhood—the southernmost point of the island—home to the housing projects, the city dump, the bus terminal, Mendelson's Kosher Meat Market, the MacArthur Milk Factory, and the Royal Palm Ice Company. Today it's known as South Pointe or SoFi—South of Fifth—with high-rise condos like the Portofino that sell for millions.

Robert was excited when his mom started dating an older man with a car, but the happiness wore off quickly when "the Eagle" returned to his ways of drinking, gambling, and womanizing. After learning the good-for-nothing was going to become his stepfather, Robert, age 14, put on a black shirt. "I looked in the mirror and said, 'That's me. Other people can wear colors, but I'm only wearing black.' "

Mary married the Eagle on October 17, 1965—Robert's 15th

birthday. There was no honeymoon. Instead, the Eagle moved in to their one-bedroom at 745 Euclid, the Krafts' fifth home in a decade. (Mary and Robert had taken it as an omen to leave their previous apartment when, as they were listening to the Animals' "We Gotta Get Out of This Place," their roof caved in during a hurricane.)

On Thanksgiving, the Eagle took Mary out to dinner, and Robert ate a Lum's hotdog by himself. On Christmas, the Eagle invited his racetrack buddies over to play poker. Robert, as usual, was listening to FUN 790 AM on his transistor radio in the corner. The radio wasn't loud when the Eagle grunted, "Hey, turn that down." Robert didn't move.

Boozed up on Kentucky bourbon, the Eagle's friends prodded him. "Are you going to let your stepson treat you like that?" The Eagle shoved his chair away from the table and went after Robert with fists swinging. One punch to the chin took Robert by surprise before he fought back. "I was bigger than him by then," notes Raven. The Eagle's friends realized the same thing as they pounced on Robert, dragging him to the bedroom. They closed the door and held it shut.

Mary was crying. "Please let him out," she said. "He's going to break down the door."

But Robert sat down to catch his breath. With his back against the wall, he lowered his head between his knees and silently made a promise: *If the Eagle ever lays another hand on me or my mom again, I'll kill him.*

HE WAS LOSING HIS FAMILY, and the world didn't care. His classmates were running down hallways singing gibberish like "Wooly Bully." That didn't speak to Robert. How could it speak to anyone? The Beatles were no better. "I Want to Hold Your Hand" and "She Loves You"—it was bubblegum music, songs that stuck in your head but had no substance. "She loves you, yeah, yeah, yeah?" says Raven dismissively. "I mean, come on. Girls are going crazy over this stupid stuff?" The boys were acting just as foolish, cutting bangs and doing fake British accents to sound like Paul McCartney and John Lennon. The whole thing pissed Raven off. It was another reminder that he was different, an outcast who didn't like the Beatles, because *How could someone not like the Beatles?*

One song changed his life, and it lasted six minutes. When Bob Dylan asked, "How does it feel," Robert knew. "Like a Rolling Stone" told the story about an outcast who lost love because the girl didn't think he was good enough, then her tables turned. "I always thought I wasn't good enough for anyone," says Raven. "That song spoke to me. Loud." When I asked Raven what exactly it was about the song that spoke to him, he looked at me like I was covered in purple spots. "I mean, have you *heard* it?" he asked.

Someone—not just someone but *Bob Dylan*—felt the same way he did. And a nation was buying Dylan's single and singing his story, connecting the down and out. There were a lot more outcasts in the world than Robert knew in junior high. Just by asking *how does it feel*, the song, he hoped, encouraged empathy. "Dylan wasn't just I loved her and lost her," says Raven. "It was about hard living. It had a message. It made you think."

"Like a Rolling Stone" reassured him in a misery-loves-company way, but it also gave Robert a purpose: If Dylan's message was resonating with people, maybe his own experience was worth something. If he could get paid for it, even better, but the important thing was to pick up the pen. "I didn't think my life was going to get any better," says Raven. "But if I could say something people related to and give them hope that they're not alone in this tough world, I wanted to try. It's always good to know you're not alone."

In the last week of ninth grade, a popular kid—a yearbook editor—stopped Robert in the hallway. "You want to know what you got for our class superlative?" *He had gotten a superlative?* "Yup," the boy continued, "we voted, and you got

Most Likely to Commit a Murder." Robert looked down and walked away.

"I've had that in my head my whole life," says Raven.

In the junior high auditorium at the end-of-the-year ceremony, Robert was waiting for the principal to call his name for Perfect Attendance, the only award he ever strived for. But Robert Kraft wasn't called, because, according to school records, he'd missed more than half a day. (Regarding that day, Raven says he had gone to the hospital after a rusty fishhook on the pier gave him blood poisoning. But he swears he was back at school before one.) "I was so upset. I wanted that award, that recognition, so bad," says Raven. "Encouragement is important to a kid, and nobody encouraged me."

That fall, he started tenth grade at Beach High, a bigger school than Ida M. Fisher Junior High, and a twenty-block walk from his grandmother's apartment, where he moved to escape the Eagle. As classmates were dropped off in Cadillacs, Robert arrived in a black Ban-Lon shirt soaked in sweat. Upperclassmen bullied him. "They'd shout, 'You're Paint It Black,' from the Rolling Stones," says Raven.

Shortly after his 16th birthday in gym class, Robert was playing football on a wet field. The quarterback, who was a senior, told him to go long and deliberately sent him to a puddle. As Robert reached up to catch the pass, his feet slipped, and he landed in the mud. Everyone folded over in laughter, and Robert looked to the teacher for help, but he did nothing. "I thought, *That ain't right*," says Raven.

The next day he dropped out.

TWO

ONLY DADDY THAT'LL
WALK THE LINE

In May 2013, Raven and I went for a bike ride in South Beach. We left from his apartment on Ocean Drive and 3rd Street, with me on a Deco Bike—a Miami Beach rental—and Raven on his black Schwinn Beach Cruiser. As usual, his chest hair poured out of his unbuttoned black Levi's jacket, which covered his shoelace belt. I was wearing jean cutoffs, a tank top, and flip-flops, with my blond hair pulled back in a ponytail. "I want to show you exactly where things happened," he had told me during our interviews.

Before we took a pedal from his driveway, Raven announced, "You know those two killers from *In Cold Blood*? They stayed there." He pointed across the street, to 335 Ocean Drive, which are low-rise condos. "It used to be called the Somerset Hotel. My mom and I would go next door to pay our rent, so we must've passed by when the killers were there." Raven was 9 years old during the Christmas of 1959 when Richard Hickock and Perry Smith hid out in Miami Beach. A few days after their South Beach vacation the two were arrested in Las Vegas, and later sentenced to death by hanging for murdering a family of four in Kansas.

"And that building next to it, 329 Ocean," Raven continued, "that's where George P. Lenart took the famous cowboy actor Lash LaRue to Alcoholics Anonymous." George P. Lenart was an old Beach character who looked like Ernest Hemingway with a bushy white beard and a notebook in hand. George swore he wrote better than Hemingway, but nobody had discovered him. Raven actually kept some of George's writings, which went like this:

7:23—Sitting at McDonald's, oh I gotta pee.
7:27—The eggs are no good, I'm going to return them.

Around George's waist, a rope held up his pants and functioned as a beer holster. Homeless, George would often get arrested for public drunkenness. Upon his release, he penned protest letters to the courts. "Dear Screwed-Up, Incompetent Judge Jones," began one. Raven had told me the story about George and Lash LaRue, but I'd forgotten where they met.

"They met at the Playhouse Bar, and George invited him to the AA meeting," answered Raven. "You ready, White Lightning? Let's get started."

As Lamborghinis and Teslas cruised by and young couples in bikinis passed on the sidewalk, heads turned to look at us. "They're trying to figure out how an old guy like me is with a pretty young woman like you," observed Raven. "They probably think I have a lot of money or something." The plastic grocery bag covering his ripped bicycle seat crinkled in the wind, and the tire wobbled from side to side as he gripped the rusty handlebars and pushed the bike across the street.

For Raven, every avenue is a stroll down memory lane. Every block triggers a scene. Familiar faces are everywhere. The past surrounds him. As we were making our way south, a man stopped us on the bike. "How you doing, Raven?" he said. "When are you running today?" The man, Jesse, was a boat captain who grew up in Miami Beach in the 1970s. He looked at me.

"This is White Lightning," said Raven. "She's writing my bio."

"Oh, that's great," he said. "Boy this place has really changed.

I would've never dreamed it could turn into what it is today. Back then it was just like a small surfing community, where everyone knew each other. Then, it went from a retirement community to a crime zone overnight."

"Oh, in the eighties, it was bad," said Raven. "No way you would've lived here, White Lightning. It was too dangerous."

We continued, with Raven narrating the tour along the way. "This is where the old band shell used to be. My grandmother came here for the old people dances. They'd play music from the old country, like the waltz." Now, electronic music thumped out of the speakers above our heads. If you want to get a drink at Nikki Beach Club, a vodka soda costs about twenty bucks.

Raven pointed toward the water. "That was the old pier where I'd write songs and I met Bulldog and Killer. Over there was the dog track." We pedaled toward Government Cut. "Fisher Island didn't exist. That was all trees. Even here, by the rocks, this area was lined with Australian Pines. I used to take girls here on dates. It was really romantic."

His bike slowed. "Uh-oh," he said, "here's an old-timer." He nodded toward a barefoot man wearing khaki cargo pants, an orange shirt, and reflector glasses, standing on a bench. Short with a big goofy grin, the man looked like the actor Martin Short. Raven introduced us. "White Lightning, meet Dave the Wave. Dave used to hang out with Goliath."

Goliath was another beach character, a bodybuilder from Coney Island who once appeared on *The Ed Sullivan Show* and *The Tonight Show* with his hand-balancing partner, David. At sunset, Goliath and his girlfriend, Suzanne, would strut down the beach wearing long purple robes. When they got to the rocks at the end, they dropped the robes. Their naked bodies absorbed the final rays of sun. Dave the Wave joined them.

"Yeah," said Dave the Wave. "We'd just sit on the rocks and smoke herb and talk to people about Jesus, totally naked. We'd say Jesus died for our sins so we could be free and guilt doesn't exist." Dave the Wave had just come from dropping his mom off at work. "She's eighty-nine," he said, "and still working. We got the blessings of Abraham—health, wealth, and happiness."

They shuffled through a few other characters like Holy Joe, who preached and handed out Bibles every Sunday on South Beach. "Nothing would stop Holy Joe. People would be throwing dead fish at him, or seaweed, but he'd just keep going. I saw some kids toss him in the ocean once. He'd come right out, reading from the Gospel saying I forgive you." Dave looked at me. "You know the Gospel?"

"Yes," I said.

"It's the Good News," he said. Dave took over Holy Joe's mission for a few moments before he told me about the times when enormous bales of marijuana would float ashore in Miami Beach. "I knew this one guy who was trying to become a lifeguard, and he used to drive an '88 Oldsmobile. A week later, I see him driving a real nice Chevy Conversion van. I knew there had to be a story there." His friend had found five bales of marijuana and sold it for $30,000. He took the money to the Chevy dealership and bought the van with cash.

I had to check my Deco Bike back into the system, so Raven and I parted ways with Dave the Wave. Riding to the bike stand, a white pickup truck with a surfboard in the back pulled up next to us. "Raven!" said an older man. "You still running?"

"Yes, I am," said Raven. "You still surfing?"

"Trying to," he said. "You gotta keep active because it's harder to hit a moving target, you know?"

"I know," said Raven.

When we traded in my bike, Raven looked to the west, where three luxurious high-rises creep out of Biscayne Bay. "Michael Martin, Tommy Waters, and the Bruiser lived there," he said, as he pointed to the Apogee Building, which now stands on the plot of land that used to contain the modest homes of three friends from elementary school. "There used to be seven drab three-story buildings," continued Raven. "That one there, on the right, the Yacht Club—that used to be the city dump." In his lifetime, the dump had turned into the Yacht Club.

We finished the day's tour on the corner of 5th Street and Washington, where the old, famous 5th Street Gym once stood. Today it's a Walgreens. "No more sawdust and punching bags," said Raven. "I tell you, White Lightning, I may be the only thing that hasn't changed around here."

TO HIS RUNNERS, Raven now represents a sense of permanence and stability he lacked in his youth. Evictor was 46 years old in 2009 when he first ran with Raven on Memorial Day weekend "having never voluntarily run more than a few hundred meters at once since junior high cross-country," he clarified in an email, "when I first realized that running is simply boring pain, the very worst type." His neighbor, a runner called Firecracker, invited him to run with "her eccentric friend" Raven, which she called "a cathartic experience." Evictor agreed to try it out and run a few miles, but he had to be in West Palm Beach for an event that night, so he said he couldn't make all eight. "I figured I'd say hi, jog a couple three miles with them, and head out in plenty of time."

Evictor's description continued: "Hot sunny day, huge crowds all seemingly shouting out this guy's (Raven's) name, giving him high fives, et cetera. Met Dizzy, Hollywood Flasher, Creve Coeur, Tortuga, Poutine, Chapter 11, Gringo, Hurricane, and a few others I'm forgetting now." He started talking to Raven about St. Louis, his hometown, and before he knew it they were at mile three. "I really didn't want to stop [and] admit failure; however, I also realized it was very hot, and I was very tired and in some pain." He paced his run according to the sun, "slowing down in the delicious shade of the buildings below Fifth. Also, Dizzy and Tortuga were circling to the back of the pack, where I was, offering encouragement (shame?), and I doggedly continued." Along the way, Hurricane, a runner in his 80s, was asking him for legal advice on eviction-related issues "despite the fact that I've been involved in no more than four or five evictions in my entire legal career," clarified Evictor. By the end of the run, he had eight miles and a new nickname under his belt as the 869th runner on the list.

"I could hardly walk, more stumbled drunkenly to my car, numbed," he recalled. "By the time I got home, any thought to going out was overcome by my body's need for an immediate sitz bath, where I collapsed for about three hours. I limped pitifully for the rest of the week, and the next Sunday, figured I'd try it again. It became a habit after that, as my body adjusted to the weekly pounding."

Today he has 175 runs with Raven and believes that the "folks I've met have almost uniformly been some of the most interesting and kind people I've met since moving to Miami." On why Raven has such a powerful draw for people, Evictor wrote this: "As was said once by our friends Jacques and Macbeth, we are poor players, strutting and fretting our hour on the stage, each with our entrances and exits. We all expect to be at the center of this little play, and each I think is drawn to things, people, events which seem greater than the quotidian experience we cycle through. The Man represents, to a degree, the transcendence, the magnificence that we all expect and aspire to, but simply don't have the discipline to accomplish or foolishness to really try. *Out, out brief candle?* The Raven pushes back mightily against that, because he will always be there tomorrow, and tomorrow, and tomorrow . . ."

"BETWEEN SEVENTEEN AND TWENTY-FOUR—those seven years— I lived a lifetime," Raven told me, sitting in his living room. "I traveled. That's why I don't like traveling anymore. I did all that."

In 1968, Robert decided to surprise his dad with a visit in California. As Raven is generally skeptical of happy endings, I wondered how he rationalized going across the country to see his deadbeat dad who clearly wanted little to do with him.

"Maybe it was naïve," Raven said, shifting his eyes to his sneakers, "but I kept thinking that, you know, he's my father, and at some point he'll start acting like it."

The visit was a disaster. Walter berated him for dropping out of school. He refused to go to a Dodgers game. He bragged about giving money to the City of Hope charity. Then he fell asleep in his armchair. Forty-five years later, Raven wouldn't look me in the eye when he told this story. "I guess that's good he gave to charity, but start at home first, right?" said Raven. "In high school I didn't have enough money for bus fare." Raven got quiet. "My father didn't tell people I existed," he said. "He didn't even offer me a glass of water."

Raven would spend his life trying to gather a family that he didn't have—losing his father and always being afraid that his mother wasn't going to come home.

From Los Angeles, Robert went to Las Vegas to visit Richard Phillips, a friend from high school. For three months, Robert bussed tables at the Golden Nugget casino. On long walks in the desert, he searched for who he was and what he wanted to be. He wanted a job traveling and chasing stories. His mother encouraged him to become a professional card dealer—a croupier—but he was leaning toward moving to Montana or Texas and living on a ranch. "You know, live a simple life," Raven explained to me. "Bale hay. Take care of horses. Fix fences."

I asked if he had ever ridden a horse.

"Once," he answered, "a pony, when I was three. I didn't know how to do any of that. I was hoping to meet a woman who knew how to grow things." Also under consideration was life as a circus carny. "I figured I could meet a lot of characters that way," he said seriously.

But everything changed one night at the Golden Nugget when he heard Waylon Jennings crooning "Only Daddy That'll Walk the Line." Dressed in dark clothes and cowboy boots with slicked-back hair, Jennings personified cool. His music was rugged honky-tonk with a rock-and-roll bottom beat, influenced by his late mentor, Buddy Holly.

"Waylon was a totally new sound," recalls Raven. "The only guy doing that besides him was maybe Johnny Cash, and Waylon's voice was less talky, more my style."

That night, at the Golden Nugget, Robert made one goal: to write songs for Waylon Jennings.

A FEW MONTHS LATER he was back in South Beach doing day labor jobs and playing stickball, but in February 1970 he bought a Greyhound bus ticket to Nashville, where *The Johnny Cash Show* was filming its second season. Robert waited around back at the Ryman Auditorium to shake Cash's hand and slip him a lyrics sheet. "Security back then wasn't as tight," Raven recalls. "You could actually talk to people."

For songwriting inspiration, Robert visited the post office to study Most Wanted posters. "Fugitive on the Run" was one of the songs he penned in Music City. But the pressures of self-promotion in such a bustling industry town ate at Robert's soul, and he missed South Beach. "I had to be someone I wasn't," he remembers. "My stomach was always growling and churning. I think I had ulcers. I didn't feel right."

In one last effort, Robert pressed a new song into Cash's palm after another broadcast at the Ryman. Cash told Robert, "I'm writing all my own stuff now, buddy, but maybe this guy can help you out. He's a songwriter." Cash nodded to the man on his left, who Robert already knew. "I'll never forget it," he says. "Johnny turned and gave him my lyrics sheet. The guy seemed a little high or stoned or something. But he didn't say a word. He just took my song and stuck it in his right pocket." The lyrics sheet was untitled and without a copyright. "I just figured if he liked it, he would call me. I didn't know anything. I was so naïve."

SIX MONTHS LATER, back in South Beach, Robert was listening to his transistor radio when, from out of its speaker, came a brand-new Waylon Jennings song. It took Robert two lines before he recognized the words. *Wait a minute*, he thought. *I know those lyrics. I* wrote *those lyrics.*

He sprinted back to his mother's apartment and, fingers shaking, dialed the radio station, thinking, *This is it. I've finally made it.* The radio DJ picked up and before he could even say hello, Robert interrupted him. "Who wrote that Waylon Jennings song you just played?" he asked. "Who's the songwriter?"

The DJ told him the name, and it was not Robert Kraft.

Without proof except the carbon copy of the lyrics sheet, Robert had no recourse—and his downward spiral began. "I became very angry, with a hair-trigger temper," he recalls. "I felt like everybody was against me. My father had left, my mom married the Eagle, my song was stolen—everything. *Life was against me. I couldn't* trust anybody." As Robert tumbled into depression, his song climbed higher and higher on the Country Music charts. (On the record, Raven won't name the songwriter who was standing next to Johnny Cash, and I've honored this request.)

His outlet had become his torment. Someone else was going to get credit for the best thing he had ever done. That afternoon, a cloud as dark as his Levi's jacket settled overhead.

Suffering, some artists will tell you, can be an effective writing tool. But first you have to get past anger, and Robert couldn't do that. Rage isn't a useful emotion in country ballads. One of his songs from the era was titled, "I Hate You," and the chorus went, "I hate you, you're bad. You're evil, you make me sad."

"It wasn't my best work," concedes Raven. "But I was scared it was going to happen again, that someone would steal another song or even rip an idea from my head."

Mary, his mother, offered little sympathy. "Are you sure he stole your song?" she asked. She told him the same thing she always told him when he didn't feel well. "Well just don't think about it." Or, "Why don't you write a better one?"

Apathy, he decided, must be a healthier alternative to pain, and his 21st birthday presented him with legal anesthesia in the form of Boone's Farm Strawberry Hill.

RAVEN HASN'T TOUCHED ALCOHOL since 1990, and I wondered how long this drinking binge in his early 20s lasted. "Oh, let me tell you the worst," began Raven one night when we were sitting in his living room, sometime in the fall of 2012. As usual, he was on his couch in black jeans with a shoelace belt and no shirt. (He prefers to wear less than pay more for air-conditioning.)

One night in 1972, he drank three bottles of Boone's Farm and passed out in the gutter. When he came to, a tall man was standing over him. "I can picture him in my mind right now," said Raven. "Black hair, slicked back. New Jersey accent—one of those gambler mafia, Italian rough-talking guys. Straight out of *The Sopranos*." They would pass each other in the streets and sometimes waved as the man went between the dog track and the Playhouse bar. That night, standing over 21-year-old Raven in the gutter, the man spoke like he had a throat full of sawdust. "He says, 'You know, I've been watching you, and you're better than this. It's about time you straightened up,' " recalled Raven. "And I listened. I was like, *Hey thanks!* I said [to myself], by the end of the year I'm going to do everything I can not to get drunk."

"Let me get this straight," I said. "You quit drinking because an Italian mafia boss saw potential and told you to shape up."

"His name was Sal," said Raven, brushing the top of his thighs with his hands. "He was just one of the gamblers, probably *knew* the guys in the mafia, but he wasn't *in* that group." Raven doesn't know why, of all the drunken messed-up people in the neighborhood, Sal targeted him. "I guess he thought I was a good kid," explained Raven. "It made an impact. Sal never saw me drunk again."

Raven can't recall if he ever saw Sal again, period. While other people might have thought, *Look who's talking*, Raven just listened. Raven likes to keep it simple. He accepted that Sal had a valid point, and he didn't look for reasons to discount the wisdom. When it comes to the truth, Raven doesn't judge the vessel. "I saw I did foolish things when I drank, and I didn't feel good," he said. "And I saw other people making fools of themselves when they drank. I decided I didn't want to be a fool in that way." So he left it, just like that, because of a stranger named Sal.

From the gutter, a person has a lot of avenues for reform— God, rehab, school, or a career has set many a wayward persons on a straighter path—but Raven's redemption would come through two boxers named Bulldog and Killer, and it would take over twelve million steps.

II
AUTHENTICITY

Raven is unique in a world of domesticated clones and people
who struggle to fit in everywhere.
—Creve Coeur, 408 runs

I wouldn't want to join any club that would
have me as a member.
—Lobotomy, who was quoting Groucho Marx, 250 runs

You always meet interesting people with Raven.
You never meet, like, a consultant.
—Green Thumb, 460 runs

If someone was raggedy, I knew he had better stories.
A guy picking up garbage in an alley is always going to
have something more interesting to say than a guy going
back and forth from work. Someone wearing a suit and
tie was the last person I wanted to talk to.
—Raven

THREE

THE WORLD'S VERSION
OF SOMEBODY

When I first moved to Miami Beach in February 2011, a friend broke down the city to me like this: "If you *are* somebody, you go to New York. If you *want to be* somebody, you go to Los Angeles. If you want to be *somebody else*, you go to Miami."

Four years in this town have taught me that Maseratis can be rented, bodies contain fake parts, and plans are optional. It's a town to reinvent yourself. Most everyone is from another place. Nobody can tell you who you're supposed to be, because nobody knows you well enough to make the determination. To this stereotype, Raven is an anomaly. He arrives on time. He doesn't have a car, a driver's license, a passport, or a cell phone. In a city of jet-setters, Raven has never ridden in an airplane. He does what he says he'll do, and he hates it when people don't. He speaks only English. While electronic music thumps out of every souvenir shop, Raven idolizes the Man in Black, Johnny Cash. With Raven, you don't meet the club promoter who can get you into Liv, Set, Mynt, or Story. He would rather know a genuine asshole than a fake yuppie. Raven is, unabashedly, nobody but himself, and he likes to attract people who are similarly at ease in their own skin.

It's thrilling to be an insider in a group comprised of and led by outsiders. You want to congratulate people for being themselves in a world that's asking them only to be young, rich, and sexy. In Miami Beach, where appearances dictate status, Raven shouldn't be faring well. Many people who look weird in this city are weird. (Believe me, I've done *a lot* of research.) But Raven surprises everyone by being kind, intelligent, generous, and humble—and, yes, a little crazy, too. But aren't we all?

Trying to put my finger on one quality that consistently makes me like people that I meet with Raven, it's realness. While most everyone is telling you what they think you want to hear, Raven Runners speak their truth.

I've learned this many times, but one of my first lessons was on my second run with Raven in June 2011, when I met a lifeguard named Low Key. I asked him, in his eleven years on Beach Patrol, to tell me about his proudest save. I wanted a heroic story. He thought for a moment. "It was one of those weekends where the beach was just packed with bodies," he began. "I saw a big crowd of people standing around in the water, and I thought it was a fight. Then I saw one man holding on to something that looked like a big blob of gel, carrying it to shore."

Low Key paddled his board out to the man and realized the blob was an octopus, which he took from the man. "I paddled out to deeper waters," he continued, "and it wasn't moving the whole time. I thought it was dead. I put it under water and held it for a few seconds—still didn't move—until all of a sudden it puffed up like a balloon, turned around, and sprayed purple ink all over me. I was watching as it swam away and felt pretty good about myself when it turned around again and swam right back up to my board, poking its big head out of the water until I could see his eye. He held it there for a second, then swam away again. I think it was grateful. I think he knew I saved his life."

His proudest save was an octopus. His second-proudest save, he told me, was a pelican caught in a fishing line, which turned out to be a double-rescue because he also saved the fish.

"I wasn't expecting both of your proudest rescues to be animals," I remarked.

"Yeah," he said nodding. "A lot of times I like animals more than people. People can be such assholes, you know?"

IN 1972, AROUND THE SAME TIME as the gutter incident, Raven was leaning against the pier railing watching the parade of South Beach characters go by when Bulldog walked up to him. Bulldog was a fighter at the 5th Street Gym. He had curly reddish-brown hair and light Irish skin with cheeks that were always rosy from taking hits. His baby face was cherubic, but when he spoke his growl was anything but the voice of an angel. The tattoos on his arms, a bulldog and a shamrock, were symbols of his Marine Corps service in Vietnam, and he was always grunting, *Hoo-rah! Semper Fi!*

With no preface, Bulldog said to Robert, "Hey Johnny, you gettin' any grinding?" Grinding, in Bulldog's lingo, meant sex, and Johnny was an all-purpose nickname. You see, a conversation with Bulldog required a glossary: Men and women were things. Hair was moss. Eyes were globes. The nose was a snout. Mouth was jowls. Butt was ort. Legs were sticks or stumps. Teeth were jibs. Ears were "eee-s," and a hearing aid was an ear cock. Glasses were shades or cheaters. Hands were paws. Going to the bathroom was dropping gold. Going out to eat was "putting it down." Heart Attack was H-A. Elvis was E-P. Checking out the scene was a recon mission. Clothes were vines. Shoes were treads. Drunk was wasted or wine-soaked. Ugly was twisted. Drinking was sipping. The Marine Corps was the crotch. His home was a cage. "Yeah, I met this thing, she looks pretty good, her ort's a little sloppy," he would say about a date. "She didn't want to go in the ocean for the routine, so we took a drive in my short, and I went back to my cage."

"That thing you were talking to last week," continued Bulldog, "You getting' any grinding off her?" That "thing" was a young brunette called Little Bit who hung out at the pier. When Robert said no, Bulldog invited him to run. "Come on, Johnny," he said. "I gotta do my roadwork. You're with me."

"Roadwork" was a boxer's endurance training, running and shadowboxing for a few miles. It was more a command than an invitation. Barefoot and wearing jean cutoffs, Robert adjusted his spray-painted black cowboy hat and ran after Bulldog, who commenced his half-wave, nod, and "howyadoing" chant to everyone they passed—lifeguards, senior citizens, and pretty young tourists visiting grandparents.

Meanwhile, Robert couldn't breathe after a few steps. He felt weak from his diet of hot dogs and alcohol. He hadn't run a mile since high school PE, and the only running he liked to do was around the bases. On its own, the exercise seemed pointless—even wasteful. But that afternoon, Robert was just trying to keep up with Bulldog in the soft sand. "Come on, Johnny!" Bulldog barked over his shoulder. "You can do it." Robert decided that even if he dropped dead, he wasn't going to walk. He wanted to accomplish something. He *needed* to accomplish something.

Two miles later, heaving but moving, Robert finished behind Bulldog. Endorphins pumped through his body. His legs felt alive and strong, and Bulldog praised him. That day something changed in Robert's head. For the first time in as long as he could remember, he felt *good*.

He started joining Bulldog and Killer, Bulldog's best friend, for roadwork once or twice a week, for two or three miles. Killer trained with Angelo Dundee at the 5th Street Gym. Among those who follow boxing, the 5th Street Gym is as legendary as Angelo, who is best known for training Muhammad Ali, though he has stood in the corner for fourteen world champions: Carmen Basilio, Willie Pastrano, Ralph Dupas, Luis Rodriguez, Sugar Ramos, Jimmy Ellis, José Napoles, Michael Nunn, Adilson Rodrigues, George Scott, Pinklon Thomas, Slobodan Kacar, Sugar Ray Leonard, and George Foreman.

Before boxing, Killer had gone to clown school in Sarasota but dropped out due to a personal conflict with his instructor. He then tried stand-up comedy in Las Vegas, in between driving a taxi. Before he perfected making people laugh, he was drafted for Vietnam, and the Marine Corps turned him into a boxer. Bulldog and Killer used roadwork to troll for women on the beach and hit on anything with breasts under 70.

In his female conquests, Killer was aggressive. "If a girl didn't want to be with him, he'd walk away and say, 'Eh, she's a lesbian,' " recalls Raven. Then he moved to the next prospect, who was usually within earshot of the first. "I'd think, *She just saw you get shot down, you should go farther away.* But no, he hit on everybody." If Bulldog got shot down, he announced, "Who cares? I lost my pride years ago."

Raven admired Killer and Bulldog; they were confident, entertaining, and self-deprecating. They were themselves and proud of it. Rejection was a joke. On the run, Bulldog pointed to the few young tourists and encouraged Robert. "You can get that, Johnny. You gotta try." Slowly but less surely, he did start trying.

His fighter friends dubbed him the "Cowboy." He didn't particularly like the nickname, but he went along with it because it made him feel a part of something. "I learned from them," said Raven.

I MET KILLER IN FALL 2012 at the 5th Street lifeguard stand before the run. Raven had told me to be a little skeptical of his stories because Killer had a tendency to exaggerate. "He took a lot of punches," explained Raven.

The first thing Killer told me was: "The difference between me and Bulldog is that when I tell something, it's true. With Bulldog, it's about one percent truth, ninety-nine percent bullshit."

"What about Raven?" I asked, leaning against the lifeguard stand to stretch. "Does he tell the truth?"

"Raven?" repeated Killer in his New York accent. "Eh, he's too dumb to lie. He ain't got enough education."

Seaside Sparrow, a blond environmental lawyer in her 40s, laughed, catching Killer's attention. "Now she's gotta lie," he said, pointing to Seaside Sparrow. "If she didn't lie, she wouldn't be making a living. I was a paralegal. I know it."

"Environmental lawyers are usually on the right side," she said.

Killer shook his head. "Nah, nah. It's a misfortune of your profession."

Killer had come with his 28-year-old son, Danny, the third born of four children. Earlier that day, they visited Bulldog in a nursing home in Hollywood, reporting sadly that he was basically a vegetable.

Killer is five-ten, in great shape—especially for a man of 70, but also for a 30-year-old. "Raven says you're a writer, huh?" Killer asked me. "Well you need to read my books then." After his career as a professional boxer, Killer tried out several professions—from car salesman to real estate agent—but he has determined that writing is his calling. "If I tell you a story, and it's not in *South of South Beach*, it doesn't exist." That night he would give me a signed copy of *South of South Beach*, which is a self-published, 739-page tome, written under his real name, Keith Laufenberg.

When Killer listened, the left corner of his mouth curled up and the right corner went the other way, making it look like he doubted everyone. He shadowboxed mid-conversation and interrupted frequently. His smile was intimidating and bright; every other tooth was covered in gold. The nail on his ring finger was black. On a guy whose hand gestures would put an Italian to shame, the loose nail was noticeable. His ears curved out from his head like cauliflower and his nose spread across his face. Maybe it's because he loves himself so much you think you'd be crazy not to, but Killer is extremely likable.

Grunting as his hands dropped to the sand, Raven tried to relieve the pressure on the pinched nerve in his lower back. Killer looked at his friend and shook his head in an *ain't-it-sad* way. "The guy can't walk, but he can run," said Killer. "Man, you gotta rest one day."

"I rest every day for twenty-two hours," said Raven.

"Everything changes but you, Raven," he said, turning to me. "If he misses a day, he thinks he's gonna die. If he keeps going, he's gonna die. So I guess you got two ways to go. You're gonna die, or you're gonna die."

It was time for roll call. "On my far left," began Raven, "he's been known to put the pedal to the medal, changing gears—Hot Rod!" We clapped. "In the pink, she's an endangered species—the Seaside Sparrow!" Raven pointed at me. "She's not Moonshine, she's—White Lightning!" He nodded to the white-haired man, smiling broadly, in white glasses. "He never runs barefoot, but he will run with Moccasin [his girlfriend]—Shoe Guy!" Next was the shirtless man with more than a six-pack chiseled into his abs. "Eighty-five consecutive runs, out of the slaughterhouse, not afraid to get his hands bloody—the Butcher!

"Right here," said Raven, pointing to the man six months older than him, Rookie of the Year in 2004, "I'm sure he's on his way to Happy Hour, of course—some things don't change! A classic kind of guy—Classic Deluxe!" Raven smiled, turning to the five-foot-eleven brown-eyed photographer, "The prettiest rose from Texas—Yellow Rose!" A Mexican man with a toothy grin got ready to wave. "He's looking to find his lost piece of mind—Lobotomy!" Finally, it was time to introduce his longtime friend. "When he walked into the Fifth Street Gym, Muhammad Ali would shiver and go the other way—K.O. Killer! And he's got his son, Danny, here, who is attempting eight." A decade earlier, Danny had failed to finish but this time he was confident.

The day's route was Back-and-Forth-South: 5th Street south to the pier, up to Espanola (around 15th), back south to the pier, back north to Lincoln Road, back south to the pier, then finally finish at 5th. "Do you mind if I ask you a few questions?" I asked Killer.

"You can ask me all you want, man," he replied.

"When Raven first told you he was going to run every day," I said, "what did you think?"

"I thought he was full of shit."

THAT NIGHT, A GROUP OF US went for dinner at Boston Market. Killer showed up wearing the shirt Raven had given him—a sleeveless, thin, black nylon shirt that had RAVEN RUN on the front in neon green letters and a raven-looking bird. I asked, "How did running change Raven?"

"One thing it did is that he got too tired to chase as many women," said Killer.

"So running calmed him down?" I asked.

He tilted his head and looked at me. "You ran eight miles today, right? Did it calm you down a little? You might've wanted to go out dancing later, but not now. Maybe tomorrow night." When he first met Raven, Killer said, Raven didn't have an athletic bone in his body. He could barely make one or two miles. "Look," he continued, "the guy I knew was the Cowboy. That's what we called him, the Cowboy. He was real easygoing. He was not obsessive-compulsive. Now all of a sudden—when you run with him, he can tell you what step you're on—'we're on mile two, fifth block, two steps.' Has he ever done that for you? He can do that! That's not normal."

"It ain't normal," agreed Raven.

His son Danny jumped in. "There's a lot of schools of thought on exercise. There's guys who say you can work out seven days a week, and you can be fine. But there's other guys that say you have to take a rest day."

Removing the red straw from his fountain drink, Killer waved it around as he talked. "When you get older, man, you get older," he said.

Soon the restaurant was closing, and Killer was back to admonishing Raven for not taking a day off or cutting back his mileage. It saddens him to see his friend in pain, but he admits Raven is better now than when he started the streak. "You know he didn't have nothing in his life. Now at least he feels his life is good," remarked Killer, his face softening before the final monologue. "Look, we're all human beings. We like to talk to other people. No matter how much you hear about people that go in the woods to be by themselves, you still wanna associate with people. You wanna *be* somebody. The world's version of somebody and my version of somebody is two different things. But to make a long story short, Raven is a good guy, he's always been a good guy . . . You can't tell the future, bro. Live every day like you're gonna die tomorrow but learn like you're going to live forever. Who said that? I just did! Somebody else said that, too. Gandhi said that. Gandhi was a smart guy."

As we made our way to Killer's sedan, an attractive woman from Argentina stopped Raven on the sidewalk. She was with her young son. "I know you!" she exclaimed, star-struck. "You are the runner. I want to run with you."

"Come on out," said Raven, pointing to her son. "Bring him, too. What is he, about nine? Looks athletic! Youngest runner we've had is six years old. Fifth Street lifeguard stand, five thirty, hope to see you there."

FOUR

"FUGATIVE" ON THE RUN

In the beginning, Raven's running goals revolved around girls. If a pretty sunbather was up ahead, he increased his mileage. Raven, at 23, looked like Kenickie from *Grease* with buff arms, a toned stomach, and sun-bleached brown hair combed in a wave. He wore a smoldering expression on his face, which was clean-shaven except for long, wide sideburns that draped down like candlesticks. About forty years younger than the average Miami Beach resident, Robert was an attractive option to young tourists visiting their grandparents. "You could just go up to their towel and start a conversation," explained Raven. There weren't cell phones, and people played transistor radios out loud, giving Raven an easy opening line about music. "They were easily approachable. I don't know what I'd do today, where it's like you're interrupting." Following Bull-dog's lead, Raven became friends with the regular crowd at the pier and with lifeguards manning their white-box stations.

There wasn't a running culture in Miami Beach. A few old men shuffled along for a mile or two, and boxers did a couple of miles of roadwork, but casual jogging didn't exist. If you ran back in the seventies, you were either a hippie or you were racing to be like Steve Prefontaine. The sport appealed to Raven because "it was not complicated. " When he ran, he felt good. "We didn't know it was good for the heart and all that," he says. His body and jean cutoffs were the only equipment he needed. Nike's waffle-sole shoes hadn't made it to South Beach, so Raven, by necessity, was a pioneer of barefoot running.

Running gave his afternoon structure. "I'm a Libra," says Raven. "We don't like making decisions. I like knowing what I have to do." Soon, other things started falling in place. He got a job as a security guard for a condo in Miami Beach, where he could wear dark clothes and write songs in between security laps on the graveyard shift. By the end of the year, he'd saved up enough money to rent a studio in the apartment complex where his mom managed the building.

One day, Robert saw an ad in the paper from a Miami production company looking for up-and-coming singers. He showed up at the office with a cassette recording of him singing "Fugitive on the Run," which he'd written in Nashville, and the producer signed him on the spot.

At the studio, the arrangement was different from what Raven had in his head, and it took him a while to get it right. After fifty takes, a short man with thinning red hair and a huge grin walked in the room and started dancing. "He was unmistakable," says Raven. It was the actor, Mickey Rooney. When Robert finished the song, Rooney looked right at him and said, "Let me give you a piece of advice, son. You're not having fun. You gotta have fun." The song, explained Robert, was about a man on the run for a murder he didn't commit. The content required him to be serious. "But still," said Rooney, "if you're not having fun, it's never going to come out right. Come on, man. Loosen up."

Raven now considers it a terrific piece of advice. "That's true on the job or on the run," says Raven. "You do better if you have fun with it. Everyone around you will feel it if you enjoy what you do." Rooney stayed for a couple more takes, dancing silly and trying to make him laugh, before he returned upstairs to visit the secretary. After take seventy-five, the producer finally said, "You got it."

Two years had passed since his song was stolen, and Raven

thought he was going to get back everything he had lost in Nashville. In early 1973, the Great World of Sound released "Fugitive on the Run," which they mistakenly spelled "*Fugative* on the Run."

The track was only slightly more successful than its spelling. "They didn't push it," explains Raven. "It went out to little towns in Iowa, Texas, and Oklahoma or something." He got one check for fifty-two dollars, and he never heard from the Great World of Sound again. "Once again, my dreams were shattered," said Raven, gazing at the original forty-five, which is pinned to his apartment wall.

To cheer his friend up, Bulldog suggested they go and see a new Western—a nice thought, but the man who stole Robert's song happened to have a featured role. Watching his nemesis on film, Robert waited for his simmering anger to explode but instead he just sat there and enjoyed the soundtrack. "From running, I felt a change in myself," said Raven. "I was more calm and mellow, and easygoing. I could control my anger. Everything became more manageable."

ROBERT STARTED RUNNING greater distances, more often, by himself. In 1974, seven miles was getting easy but nine was too much. Like a Goldilocks of long distance running, Raven settled on the number eight. Eight miles was just right, the perfect challenge, and—though he prefers odd numbers—he liked that a sideways eight represented infinity.

When people asked him, "How can you spend that much time alone running?" Raven said he was used to being alone. If he weren't running alone, he'd probably be writing alone, sitting on the pier alone, working security alone, or at his mother's apartment not talking to the Eagle, which made him feel more alone.

His new running identity deserved a new name. "I'm not a Cowboy," he complained to Bulldog. "I don't ride horses." Bulldog studied his friend who dressed in black, a writer who stayed up all night with a little mystery to him, kind of like Poe. "Eh," said Bulldog, his face brightening. "You're more like the Raven."

Finally, Raven felt like himself.

Eight miles took about ninety minutes. Song lyrics filled the silence in his head, or he counted steps. On average it was 13,900. Raven ran in the soft sand close to the shoreline. Back then, before the Dade County beach reclamation project, there was a lot less beach. North of 15th Street, waves washed all the way up to the buildings, lapping at hotel pool decks and parking lots. At Espanola Way (between 14th and 15th Streets), a steel wall as tall as Robert stretched from the beach out to the sea and cut off access to northern sands. This wall was the first in a series of "groins" installed to prevent beach erosion and trap the sand that the tide wanted to carry south. (For those who have run with Raven, this is why we make the turn at Espanola.) Usually he looped between Government Cut and the first groin at Espanola, though once a week he ran north to 47th Street on the "obstacle course" route. Around groins, through parking lots and pool decks, Raven outran the security guards who were yelling, "No trespassing! This is private property!"

One afternoon before the run, walking along the beach by himself, Raven heard screams from the water. Three girls were waving for help, caught in a rip current. Raven took off for the waves. He had never been much of a swimmer. In the water, his body is almost vertical, legs dangling underneath like a tadpole. When he got to the first girl, the current pushed them into the steel groin. Barnacles were scraping off his back as he held her. "Grab the piling," said Raven. "Follow it back to shore." Then he swam for the second girl, who was farther out. By the time he got her in, the third girl had followed their same path and was close to shore.

They were sisters from the Bahamas, where their mother served as ambassador. "How much can we give you?" the oldest sister, age 15, asked. "Our mom will wire us money, as much as you want." But Raven refused the money, saying, "There's no price on a life."

When Raven recalled the rescue, he delivered it in the same way he would deliver any old story—no self-aggrandizement, no heroism. There was even a little regret. "I could've used the money," he acknowledged. "I ran into them on the street, and they stopped people, telling them, 'This guy saved our life.' I was kind of embarrassed."

Following the rescue, Raven added a three-tenths-mile swim to follow his eight-mile run. "In case that ever happened again," explained Raven, "I wanted to improve my swimming."

Over the next four decades, it would happen again—sixteen times.

BY THE END OF 1974, Raven was running eight miles thirteen out of fourteen days. He ran in the afternoon or evening but didn't have a set start time—and didn't need to, because nobody ran with him. Whenever he took a day off, he felt guilty. He felt like he was missing something on the beach. Running was all he could think about. "But people told me I should rest one day, so I did," he says. "It never felt right. And it was harder to come back the next day."

On January 1, 1975, it was a clear, crisp, sunny day in South Beach. Bulldog was running by Raven's side. "I made a New Year's resolution," Raven told Bulldog. "I'm going to run a whole year straight—every day, eight miles."

Bulldog laughed. "Yeah right," he said. "Come on, Johnny. What are you thinking?"

But Raven was determined. *Watch me*, he thought. After three miles, Bulldog dropped off and Raven kept going. "I had never gone through with a goal in my life except to get to Nashville, and even that, everything fell apart," recalls Raven. "Running was going to be my thing."

III
GRIT

Raven's greatest asset is his tenacity. He doesn't give up. He's like the Eveready battery. He just goes and goes and goes.
—Hurricane, age 84, 588 runs

I've seen him when it's pouring down rain so hard you can barely see, and he's running by himself. I've run twice with him in really bad thunderstorms. Lightning crashing around us, and I have a thing about lightning. I go, "Bob, I think it's getting a little hot out here," and he's like, "It'll pass, it'll pass." In 1995, his back got so bad he couldn't walk. I said, "You gotta quit, man." And he's like, "Nah, I gotta run." His gumption—I mean, that's something.
—Teen Idol, singer, songwriter, lifeguard,
and Raven Runner

I aspire for that singular dedication and focus. Today's woulda-coulda-shoulda society embraces excuses. Raven refuses, be it weather, age, or health. I mean, he is more dedicated to his run than we are to basic needs.
—Unoffendable, 51 runs

I felt invincible.
—Raven

FIVE

HOOKED

Today Raven hasn't run by himself in over a decade. When Tropical Storm Isaac came to town in the late summer of 2012, people were worried Raven might have to run alone. So that afternoon eighteen runners and two dogs showed up to battle sand and fifty-five-mile-per-hour winds. "I always say Mother Nature is on Raven's side," said Dizzy, a 54-year-old ultra-marathoner and middle school principal from Cuba, along for the eight-mile adventure. With over seventeen hundred runs, he is number two on the list. "There were three big squalls, and they all hit us when we were running north with the wind at our backs."

These days, Raven's motivation to show up comes from other runners. "One hand washes the other," he explains. "In the beginning, I was doing it for myself but now knowing that runners will be there, that motivates me to keep coming out."

For the streak's first decade, however, six runners ran with Raven. He ran alone 3,637 days out of 3,650 days. Raven was the only person expecting himself to run eight miles every day, and most people dismissed him as a loon.

Five days into 1975, Raven's grandmother died. He didn't go to the funeral because the Eagle did. Plus she was at the end of a long battle with Alzheimer's, and his grandmother hadn't recognized him for a while.

A week after her funeral, Raven opened up a can of stuffed cabbage and tomato juice for dinner. He noticed a hint of rust on the can but thought nothing of it. Two hours later, picking up his date from her hotel room, he felt like he was in the middle of a cyclone. Sweat pooled on his arms and dripped down his forehead. His stomach cramped, and the undigested cabbage pushed back up. The rusted can gave him the worst bout of food poisoning in his life.

He spent the night in his date's hotel room, going back and forth to the bathroom as she accused him of having a bad trip. "I don't do drugs," he promised. "This is from cabbage." The next morning, with all the color drained from his face, Raven stopped by his mom's apartment. "You're as sick as a dog," she said, making him a piece of toast. "You're not going to go run today, are you?"

"I'm going to try," he said, sipping on orange juice. "If I can walk, I can run."

She looked at him. "You gotta do this every day?"

Raven said yes.

"You know you don't have to."

"Yes, I do," said Raven. "Unless I'm dying." She told him not to be so dramatic. He lied and said he was feeling a little better.

After pull-ups under the chickee huts by the 3rd Street lifeguard stand, he staggered to the beach. He was light-headed for the first mile but as he inhaled fresh ocean air, the familiar rhythm shook off his nausea. Finishing mile eight, he felt relieved.

It was day fifteen.

His resolution was still intact.

Usually he ran barefoot, shirtless, and in jean cutoffs that became so caked in sweat and sand they could stand up on their own. When sand chafed off his toe skin, he put on socks, but they got holes. Many days, his socks were soaked in blood, which he rinsed off in the ocean during his three-tenths-of-a-mile swim. Bulldog gave him a pair of combat boots and old leather boxing shoes, and his mom bought him a pair of two-dollar Keds sneakers, which he wore until the blisters raised mounds on his feet and burned so much he couldn't sleep.

Not long after the food poisoning, jumping off the eight-foot wall at the DecoPlage Hotel in bare feet, he landed on a piece of plywood and a three-inch-long nail. As the nail punctured his skin, it made a popping sound, like *pshh*. Raven leaned back against the wall and lifted his leg with the plywood attached. He slowly extracted the nail from his right foot, between the ball and the arch, and cast the board aside. On his way back to 3rd Street, he tried to land on the outside of his foot. After the swim, the lump had swelled to a golf ball.

He went to his mom and asked what to do. "Was the nail rusty?" she said.

"I think it was a little rusty," he said. "But not *rusty*-rusty."

"You need to get a tetanus shot," she said. So he went to the hospital.

For the next two weeks he hobbled down the beach. His limp threw off his running stride, which hurt his left hip and knee. "It was like I was running on a ball of fire," says Raven. Soon he had shin splints. At this point, most people would have questioned the soundness of the resolution.

Raven kept going.

GETTING TIRED OF SUMMER FLINGS with tourists that breezed in and out of town, 24-year-old Raven wanted someone stable to settle down with. An older woman, Christine, with pale blue eyes and long blond hair, caught his eye. She liked to bike and swim and do yoga, eating organic long before it was trendy. She had this youthful, surfer-girl vibe about her. At 45, her body defied her age, which she showed off in a little white bikini.

When Raven tried to hit on her, she brushed him off. Then one day, the lifeguard who worked at 8th Street, Bob Romer, pointed her out to Raven and said, "I was with that woman for a night, and I think she'd be really good for you."

"She's not interested," said Raven. "I already tried." Raven assumed it was their two-decade difference in age, but Romer assured him that she was into younger men. After a couple weeks, Romer was chatting with Christine in front of the life-guard stand when Raven ran by without his usual cowboy hat. Christine said, "Hey, you look a lot better without that hat." And Raven thought maybe he did have a chance.

The next week, she invited him over for dinner. "Before I know it, she's on the floor, unbuttoning her blouse, and we were together," Raven recalled to me, rifling through a stack of old photographs. "Here she is, White Lightning," he said, hand-ing me a photo. "Tell me how old she looks."

In the photo on the old pier, Christine is wearing big sun-glasses and a green bikini with a white ring pattern. Raven is right; her stomach is flatter than mine without a dimple or wrinkle in her porcelain skin. She has her right arm around Raven, who has his bare chest out, abs tight, and cut biceps, wearing black socks and denim cutoffs. "The guy on her left is Goliath," Raven told me, referring to the bodybuilder that Dave the Wave had talked about.

In the picture, Goliath is smiling with his arms bowed out to the side. He has shoulder-length curly blond hair and is wear-ing a yellow banana hammock–Speedo. "Goliath took these big steps and lifted his legs real high, like in slow motion," continued Raven. "Everything was a pose. And Goliath would talk real mellow. He'd say, 'The sun is like my gold.' "

Raven calls Christine the Astrologer because most of her paycheck as a legal secretary went to psychics, and she knew everything about horoscopes. When they started dating, the Astrologer was having an affair with her boss, a fat man from Belgium whom she called the Heavy. To communicate with Raven if the coast was clear to come over, she left him notes in the telephone booth outside her apartment at 412 Ocean Drive, a block away from where we were sitting at Raven's apartment. "After the run, I'd go and check the phone booth," said Raven, flashing a smile. "It was pretty exciting for a young guy."

That Christmas, 1975, the Heavy went back to Belgium, and

Raven spent the holiday with the Astrologer, who cooked a big traditional organic feast of duck, millet, stuffing, and rice. "I had never eaten duck before," said Raven. Holly tinsel, blinking lights, and mistletoe blanketed the Astrologer's apartment. Her brown Maine-coon tomcat, Thomas, jingled all over the house in his Christmas bell collar. Bing Crosby blasted out of her record player. Raven was content. "The Astrologer loved Christmas," explained Raven.

As a kid, Raven never had a Christmas tree, so he was enamored by the Astrologer's zest for holidays and life in general. After Christmas, the Astrologer called things off with the Heavy, who unsuccessfully tried to woo her back with a poem entitled, "A Dark Wing Has Covered My Sun." A health nut, the Astrologer even ran a few miles with Raven. "She was all about me running and not drinking." She also encouraged his songwriting. "She had faith that I could make it," said Raven.

Raven and the Astrologer were together on-and-off for twelve years. Raven spent most nights at the Astrologer's apartment and set up an office in her bathroom. For extra cash on top of working security, Raven rented his empty studio out to a revolving door of tenants, to the point he has trouble naming all of them. "You would've liked the Astrologer, White Lightning," said Raven. "She was so intelligent and well traveled. After going out with her, I said I could never again date a woman who isn't smarter than me."

THREE WEEKS SHY of fulfilling his New Year's resolution, Raven got pneumonia. His high fever came with terrible chills, and the inflammation in his lungs made it difficult to breathe sitting down, let alone on the move. Raven was coughing and wheezing as he hammered out a set of pull-ups. Casey, an old man who hung around the pier and wore a clunky hearing aid around his neck, watched Raven in silence. "I don't get this," he finally said. "Why don't you just let the pneumonia run its course and take a day off?"

"I just can't," said Raven. "I gotta run."

On mile four, Raven was sweating and shivering and bent in half as he ran past the 1st Street lifeguard stand, where the Nay was working. A former Marine and a Vietnam vet, the Nay was the prototypical handsome lifeguard—big square jaw, dark tan, and a pith helmet to top it off. Raven considered him one of the toughest men out on the beach. The Nay leaned his head out the lifeguard box and shouted, "You're not quitting are you?"

"No, I'm not," answered Raven. The Nay gave him a nod of respect, which, Raven says, "was all I needed."

Though Raven didn't formally renew the resolution in 1976, he liked his life so much more with the run. "It made me feel like I was really doing something," he said. "Even if I didn't have any money, I was really strong. I felt invincible." Old residents were stopping Raven in the street to congratulate him. "You're doing great," said one familiar stranger. "You're a real inspiration," said another. "You've become much more focused, and you got a steady girlfriend, too. We're proud of you," said a third of dozens. It was the praise Raven had been craving his entire life.

He decided to extend the streak until one afternoon in 1976, when the Astrologer invited him to see an exhibition on the bicentennial at the downtown train station. The time was going to conflict with eight miles. Raven asked himself, "Do I really want to do the run for another year and get hooked on this crazy thing?"

He decided no.

Then an hour before meeting his friends, he got antsy. *Oh, I could just do a quick eight,* he thought. So under his pants he put on running shorts and sprinted to the beach.

MANY PEOPLE WHO HEAR about Raven will offer their non-professional medical opinion and diagnose him with OCD, obsessive-compulsive disorder. This is not news to Raven, because he was already diagnosed, by a church counselor, fifteen years earlier, but he refused medication. "It's a part of me," he says. "I don't want to take pills that make me not be myself."

Personally, if I don't exercise, I don't feel good. I consider my compulsion to move a healthy addiction, though I wanted a professional opinion. "A positive addiction," wrote psychiatrist William Glasser in his book of the same name (cited in James Fixx's classic, *The Complete Book of Running*), "increases your mental strength and is the opposite of a negative addiction, which seems to sap the strength from every part of your life except in the area of the addiction . . . Negative addicts are totally involved with their addiction, having long since given up on finding love and worth. The positive addict enjoys his addiction, but it does not dominate his life." Dr. Glasser believed that running was a positive addiction, because the exercise consistently helped people shake themselves loose from bad habits. I still think my addiction to exercise is positive, but where does Raven fall on the spectrum? Without a doubt, running dominates Raven's life, but it is through his obsession that Raven has found love and worth, which has enabled him to provide love and worth for thousands of others.

To avoid pretending that I am any kind of expert on the matter, I sat down on the couch with Dirk E. Huttenbach, MD, a child psychiatrist who also happens to be my father. Handing me a copy of a *Psychiatric Times* journal, he said, "I found this article when I was cleaning up. I think you'll find it useful. Sometimes it pays to hold on to things."

Immediately I knew he would be sensitive to Raven's condition.

"Respecting Rigidity?" was the title of the *Psychiatric Times* article that my father handed me. The author, Dr. Lewis, writes that a system, including personality, cannot progress from chaos to flexibility without a "rigid and intervening structure" in between. He gives government as an example: We rarely see a government move from anarchy straight to democracy. Anarchy is usually followed by totalitarianism, from which democ-

racy may or may not develop. The same is true for people trying to control a chaotic life: First, to rein in the chaos, they
adopt a rigid lifestyle. (After two and a half chaotic decades,
Raven sought structure through running.) But the issue, continues Dr. Lewis, is "whether the system becomes fixated at the
rigid level of organization or goes on to develop a more flexi-
ble structure." (Raven's running routine is pretty fixated.) Still,
the point Lewis gets across is that "A rigid structure, however
constrictive, is more adaptive than a chaotic one." (Through
that structure, Raven could organize the rest of his life.)

We all have people in our life who operate at different levels
of rigidity. Raven is certainly the most rigid person I know, but
in fact my father is also pretty rigid. He is a man of routines.
Every morning, he must eat the same cereal (Oatmeal Squares)
with the same brand of orange juice (Tropicana) that contains
the same amount of pulp ("lots of pulp"). He reads the newspaper. He drinks Folgers instant coffee, from the same mug. He
doesn't buy new things when the old things still work (including medicine and cheese). I think he has worn the same flannel
bathrobe my entire life, or he has bought an identical one to replace it. The only time I hear him curse is when he is trying to
use a computer, turn on the television, or load a DVD. His
1994 Honda Accord has 240,000 miles.

"Stability is attractive to a lot of people," observed Dr. Huttenbach. Furthermore, he believes, "Having certain routines
simplifies life. It may allow people to be creative elsewhere."
The stability that my parents provided in my life gave me confidence to seek out new experiences in different places.

If people are rigid, it *can* be endearing and in some ways
easier to navigate a relationship—for instance, I know what to
buy at the grocery store when Dad comes to visit. But if people
are too rigid, it can be off-putting. "Usually obsessive-compulsive habits drive people away," said Dr. Huttenbach. "It's usually
'my way or the highway,' and that's not a good way to attract
people." He paused. "But Raven has attracted a lot of people."

* * *

RAVEN'S STREAK TURNED TWO on New Year's Day, 1977. Nineteen days later, it snowed for the first time in the history of South Florida, snatching the *Miami Herald* headlines from the news of President Carter's inauguration. By the start of the run it was a balmy 46 degrees, and Raven yanked off his shirt, vowing to be bare-chested from that day forth.

That year his running uniform got new accessories. First, Bulldog gave him a black visor with RAVEN monogrammed on the front bill, replacing his spray-painted-black cowboy hat, which he had worn through the top. Then, after wearing out his combat boots and bloodying all his socks, Raven rode with the Astrologer to a store in North Miami Beach and purchased a pair of Nike's waffle shoes. "Wow, they were comfortable," says Raven. "They had so much cushioning. I felt like I could fly." He wore the bright yellow Nikes until his feet poked through the toe box and the soles flopped apart.

There was also the glove, his talisman. Heading north one day, around 38th Street, Raven found a big, black rubber glove washed up on the shore and thought, *I should put this on*. He shook out the seawater and slipped it on his left hand. When he made a fist, energy pumped through his body. "It sounds kind of crazy, but psychologically, as long as I have it on, I will never quit," says Raven. "It's the power."

Over the years, he developed a set of rules for the adoption of new gloves. For instance, he can find a glove or someone can give him one, but he cannot buy a glove. (Currently he has five gloves waiting in the wings.) He prefers left-handed gloves because he's right-handed and likes to push his hair back with his right hand. Cloth or leather gloves are acceptable, though ideally they are rubber and hug his arm up to his elbow. He wears them until they fall apart (anywhere from ten days to two years) and keeps his keys and coins he finds inside.

In the summer, sweat pools around his fingers, and one time in the late '70s, he was running by a girl who out of the blue said, "Get the fuck away from me. You're a real creep." Without thinking, Raven turned his glove upside down on the girl's head, pouring hot sweat down her face.

A few weeks later, the mean girl's boyfriend, who was a cop, approached Raven. "Hey," said her boyfriend, "you dumped sweat on my girlfriend's face." Preparing for a battle, Raven said yes but instead of taking a swing, the guy chuckled. "I wish I could've done that," he said. "She's a real bitch."

When the lifeguards heard the story, it became instant legend. Rumor was that Raven was going around the beach dumping sweat on every girl. But he insists that this has only happened once. "I know it wasn't right, but I can only take so much," Raven told me with a black glove sitting next to him on the couch. "I'm only human."

Raven's final new accessory was a poet called Coyote. Coyote was a trim, good-looking young man who loved girls with frizzy hair. He also loved baseball and boxing, wrote songs, and played the guitar and harmonica. "I liked him," says Raven. "He was always a little too friendly with my girlfriends, but I said that's okay because he liked girls with frizzy hair."

The two started writing songs together. One day, before the run, they were talking baseball at the lifeguard stand. When Raven started to jog, Coyote followed him. "Want to try the eight miles?" said Raven. He said okay.

The Astrologer couldn't believe it when she heard someone else had finished eight miles. "You should keep a list of people who make it," she said. "I'm sure you won't have that many."

SIX

RUN FREE

Many runners, wanting to impress Raven on the first run, will start rattling off their race résumé and marathon times. This is a mistake. When they finish, Raven will look them straight in the eye and say, "You shouldn't pay to run." Raven cherishes the inclusive nature of running; anyone can afford it. He hates that the sport has become commercialized, though occasionally he will endorse a running event if it benefits a charity.

Last year about 20 million runners finished one of 28,000 organized racing events that took place in the United States. The Boston Marathon alone attracted over 30,000 registered runners. When Raven started the streak in 1975, fewer than 2,000 people crossed the finish line in Boston. Bill Rodgers crossed it first, setting a new American record of 2:09:55.

Raven believes Sylvester Stallone should get credit for popularizing jogging. "Right after *Rocky* came out in 1977—that's when I noticed people started running," says Raven. "Everyone was singing 'Gonna Fly Now' and thrusting their hands in the air."

I asked Raven about James Fixx, the author of *The Complete Book of Running*, published in 1977, which has gotten credit for the modern running craze. Through running, Fixx lost sixty-one pounds and quit smoking two packs of cigarettes per day.

But he noticed the mental benefits were even better. "I was calmer and less anxious," he writes in the foreword. "I felt more in control of my life. I was less easily rattled by unexpected frustrations. I had a sense of quiet power, and if at any time I felt this power slipping away I could instantly call it back by going out and running."

This sounded like Raven (though their running theories diverge quite a bit in the chapter on Preventative Maintenance, where Fixx writes that "the chief enemy of sound training is dogmatism"). While acknowledging Fixx wrote a popular book, Raven said, "To tell you the truth, White Lightning, the first thing that comes to mind about James Fixx is that he died at fifty-two of a heart attack while running."

Every Raven Runner has a different story of how they came to run. One runner in his early 50s from Venezuela, Hype, told me, "I think the reason why a person starts to run is usually different from why he runs today." He started running when he was diagnosed with emphysema. Running replaced smoking. He has raced in several marathons and was training for his first fifty-miler. "I started running to get healthy," he said, "but once I started, I just felt bad not doing it."

Many runners speak of the sport like they owe it something—like they know what running has done for them, and they want to honor that. On the same run with Hype, I surveyed a few other runners in attendance. I asked Hitter, a fire chief, why he liked to run. "Who says I like to run?" he replied. "You run because you can't not run." (Another day, when he was running with a pulled hamstring, he said, "Yeah, you gotta be tough if you're gonna be dumb.")

Taxman told me that he ran so that he could eat ice cream. Poutine said, "I'm running to get back in shape and stay ahead of Chapter 11." Dizzy was running with Urban Myth, On Time, and the Harlem Shuffle. As a group, they agreed on three reasons to run: to be able to consume sugar, food, and beer, though they couldn't agree on the order. Yellow Rose said, "I run on my own to clear my head. I run with Raven for the community."

When Chapter 11 turned 80 years old, he invited all the Raven Runners to his birthday party. "The last three generations in my family never lived to be sixty," he told me in an email. "All died of heart failure." Today Chapter 11 is the oldest active Raven Runner. (Hurricane had to stop running a few days after his 80th birthday due to knee problems.) "I enjoy the run because of the many nice and beautiful people you meet," wrote Chapter 11. "It gives you a goal to set for getting awards and being on the list and going to the parties." In the Hall of Fame, Chapter 11 has over a thousand runs and seven hundred swims, including the record coldest swim. "People run for a lot of reasons: Health. To compete," he said. "And some people get so addicted they even love to run. But if it was not for the Raven Run, I don't think I would be alive."

Another day, I chatted with a soft-spoken, middle-aged French scientist who goes by the name Bloody Wolf. He said he uses the Raven Run to train for marathons. "The slow pace is good because it's fat-burning rather than glycemic-burning," he said. "Plus running is therapy." Bloody Wolf said that running with others creates an intimacy unlike any other interaction. "Maybe it's because every step you take, your heels pump blood to your brain, and you get more oxygen," he said. "But there's just this honesty between people. It's hard to lie and run at the same time." He had met more people on the Raven Run than in any other Miami network. "Miami is a city where you could live here for years and never know anyone," said Bloody Wolf. "But this is something you can do every day—the exact same thing—and meet different people."

In 2009, the American journalist Christopher McDougall published *Born to Run: A Hidden Tribe, Superathletes, and the Greatest Race the World Has Never Seen*. The book struck a chord with runners and non-runners alike, selling over three million copies and kicking off the barefoot running craze. "Distance running was revered because it was indispensible," writes McDougall. "It was the way we survived and thrived and spread across the planet. You ran to eat and to avoid being eaten; you ran to find a mate and impress her, and with her you ran off to start a new life together. You had to love running, or you wouldn't live to love anything else."

Today, McDougall says, running is about "getting stuff and getting it now: medals, Nike deals, a cute butt. It wasn't art; it was business, a hard-nosed quid pro quo. No wonder so many people hated running; if you thought it was only a means to an end—an investment in becoming faster, skinnier, richer—then why stick with it if you weren't getting enough quo for your quid?"

Of the characters in *Born to Run*, Raven relates most to Caballo Blanco, a former lightweight boxer who started running to mend a broken heart. He trekked to the Copper Canyons in northwest Mexico, where he sought counsel with the Tarahumara, indigenous people whose innate long-distance running ability is the main subject of the book. After years of living with and learning from them, Caballo Blanco organized a race in their homelands, in the hope that their spirit of running would breathe new life into the American culture, which he thought was corrupt and commercial. "I thought this race would be a disaster," Caballo admitted to the runners who had signed up for the event, "because I thought you'd be too sensible to come . . . But one thing about crazy people—they see things other people don't."

On the final page of *Born to Run*, Caballo gets an offer from the North Face outdoor sports company to sponsor the race. "Caballo thought it over," writes McDougall. "For about a minute. 'No thanks,' he decided. 'Running isn't about making people buy stuff. Running should be free, man.' " Raven is of the same tribe.

In his life, Raven has run one race, and he wants to make it very clear that he did not pay an entry fee. It was the first road race in South Beach—on the morning of November 26, 1978—starting at the Convention Center for an eight-mile course. The man who paid his entry fee was a local reporter called Umbrella Jack. "He figured that since I ran all the time, I'd win the race, so he wanted to do a story," explained Raven.

Raven hated every minute. He wasn't used to running in the morning and drank a cup of black coffee, which made him jumpy and nervous. Cheered on by Coyote and the Astrologer, Raven finished eight miles in fifty-five minutes at a pace of 6:52, placing 150th out of a thousand runners. In the end, Umbrella Jack wasn't impressed with Raven's finish and never wrote the article. "I was hurting—my feet, my legs, my calves," said Raven, rubbing his leg. "It wasn't worth it. It was too competitive." He vowed never to run another race again and, to get that one out of his system, he went to the beach a few hours later for eight miles, because, "You know, my thing is the sand."

EVERY YEAR IN JANUARY, around the ING Miami Marathon, Raven gets cranky. On the morning of the race, though he is no early bird, he gets up at the crack of dawn and drags a lawn chair outside his apartment to protest the event. He carries signs that he made with messages like "I don't pay to run, I pray to run," or "Run free! Run with Raven" or "Where does all this money go?" Begrudgingly, he will cheer for and slap high fives with the Raven Runners in the race. But at some point he will scold them.

It hurts his feelings that out-of-town runners will pay for plane tickets, hotels, and entry fees to race, but they will not fly into Miami for his events—which are free—like the picnic, the banquet, big milestones, or the daily event, which is eight miles. Last year, a couple days before the marathon, Raven posted on Facebook that any Raven Runner who pays to run the marathon is a traitor. (Since getting his first computer in 2013, Raven has joined Facebook.) Knowing how many Raven Runners compete in races, I worried he might alienate some people without context. I called and urged him to reconsider the status update. "Okay, White Lightning," he said. "Sorry, you know how I get around the marathon."

Raven said he didn't know how to edit the post, but he gave me his password, and I edited it while we were on the phone, removing the traitor part but leaving the "Don't Pay to Run." (He also openly advocates running the race without paying.) In the same phone call, in a moment of clarity, he told me about a new runner, Tchako, in town for the marathon. "Tchako said for him, paying to run a marathon is like paying for a therapist," Raven told me. "I get that. I guess some people need races to motivate themselves."

There is one other explanation for why Raven hates the Miami Marathon, and that is because he has a beef with one of the founders, who has run six times with Raven and is nicknamed the Promoter. He is a young guy in his 30s who grew up in Miami Beach. He is tall and attractive, fast, and wears bright colors—often, a neon green shirt that says WE RUN MIAMI. In addition to organizing the marathon, the Promoter coordinates weekly running groups that meet in various Miami neighborhoods. His runs can attract hundreds of people, which are separated into different pace groups.

When I first moved to Miami, I ran with the Promoter's group that met on Thursday nights in South Beach. There, I pushed myself to run in the seven-minute-mile pace group. A lot of the conversations revolved around training. Most everyone was polite, young, attractive, well dressed, and seemed to work as a consultant. I got faster, and I met nice people. Before every run, we would have to take a group picture to post on Facebook, tagged as the South Beach Nike Run Club. I sometimes felt like an extra in an advertisement.

In 2013, I learned from my friend Matt, who is active in the club, that the Promoter had shut down the South Beach run because he lost Nike as the sponsor. Matt became the new leader—I supported his run a couple times—until the Promoter found another sponsor and took back control. It's clear that money at least partially motivates the Promoter to do what he does in the name of running, but a lot of people benefit from his work.

Raven has never had a sponsor and can barely afford his New Balance running shoes. He has drunk Gatorade religiously for the last three decades and even painted his bathroom and kitchen walls lemon-lime, his favorite flavor. He buys and mixes the Gatorade powder himself, but Raven would rather continue buying it than ask for something or have to alter his routine. And for his eight miles, there's nothing competitive. If you show up, you're a winner in Raven's book.

His beef with the Promoter started over what most would consider a mere annoyance: according to Raven, the Promoter promised him that he could fire the gun to start the first marathon but never followed through. Strike one. Then (again, according to Raven) the Promoter promised that he would help organize a race in Raven's honor but never did.

With Raven, unless you are homeless or a recovering addict, you only get two strikes.

Raven's greatest pet peeve—in addition to people paying to run—is when people don't do what they say (God help him in Miami). So Raven has held a grudge against the Promoter and will share it with anyone willing to listen. The Promoter has a grudge against Raven, too, and when I asked him about the rivalry, he accused Raven of sending his henchmen to heckle his group while they stretched. (I'm pretty sure he was talking about a woman named Nutcracker who was acting on her own accord when she yelled at the group that they shouldn't pay to run and they should run with Raven for free. Of course Raven was delighted when he heard the news.) The Promoter wanted me to know that he doesn't charge people to run in his clubs, and if you come enough, you can get a free shirt. (I have one.)

In my observation, both men are acting like juveniles, but I will confess one occasion that made me chuckle hard, and it involves a heterosexual cross-dressing man from the Bronx called Karaoke Fred. A typical outfit for Karaoke Fred is a short sequined skirt over pink and purple spandex, a black mesh shirt, and brightly colored feather boas. He loves to sing. On Sunday mornings, he used to set up a karaoke machine next door to Raven's apartment. "God he was horrible," says Raven. "He sounded like Bob Dylan on helium. The city had to get an ordinance banning karaoke on Sunday mornings."

But Karaoke Fred was welcome to run with Raven. Even if his participation made some runners uncomfortable and even though he tried to run next to Raven every time there was media coverage, Raven wasn't going to be a gatekeeper. His run is open to everyone. Karaoke Fred racked up 149 runs. "Then one afternoon [in 2012] he got really drunk, flipped out, and threatened to kill me," says Raven. "The lifeguards wanted to arrest him, but I said he was just drunk and leave him alone."

Getting violent while on the run (or specifically threatening to kill Raven) is like the one thing that will get someone banned from the Raven Run, so Karaoke Fred became the fourth banned runner in history. (Nutcracker, mentioned above, was number five.) Since the incident, Karaoke Fred has apologized, but Raven refuses to lift the ban.

Sometime in 2014, Raven called me. "White Lightning, I just heard the best news ever," he announced. "Karaoke Fred is running with the Promoter's Thursday night running group!" This was Raven's dream scenario. "Talk about killing two birds with one stone," he continued. "Does it get any better?" Soon my friend Matt was calling me about Fred, too. "He seems, um, nice," said Matt. "Do you know anything about him?"

Today I still hang out with people from the Promoter's club, which Raven tolerates. "You know, Raven, I am friends with some normal people," I once told him apologetically. "I can pass for mainstream."

"You could fake it if you had to," Raven acknowledged. "If you had to, you could pass for normal."

SEVEN

CASTRO IS
STILL LAUGHING

The distance from the southernmost tip of Miami Beach to the inlet at Haulover—jetty to jetty—is ten miles. One day in 1979 Raven thought it'd be cool bragging rights to run the whole thing, even though the course took him through pool decks, fences, walls, and parking lots—not to mention deep, soft sand. But he put on his frog-green Adidas running shoes and headed north. One hour and forty-seven minutes later, he was sweaty in Haulover, standing next to bulldozers.

The Army Corps of Engineers had just begun the Dade County Beach Erosion and Hurricane Protection Project, also known as the Beach Nourishment Plan, beach reclamation, or just "dredging." Since 1926, when a hurricane destroyed the protective dunes, the Atlantic tides had been gobbling up most of the coastline. On top of that, hotels had built pool decks and parking lots right up to (or even over) the shoreline. In the 1960s, Dade County first proposed a plan for the Army Corps of Engineers to dredge sand in from the continental shelf to recreate the protective dunes, but the hotel owners—despite knowing this would protect them from future hurricanes and would give them desired beaches—said no, because the new beachfront would have to be open to the public.

By 1979, the rising tide had changed their minds, and so the plan was finally put into action. Barges anchored off the coast sucked up sand from the ocean floor that traveled through underwater tubes and got spit out in big mounds on the beach. Bulldozers then smoothed it over. At a cost of $68 million, fourteen million cubic yards of sand—four times the amount of construction material used in Egypt's Great Pyramids— were dredged up from offshore over a four-year period, widening the beach by the length of a football field.

Staring at the bulldozers, Raven tried to imagine the new beach. He didn't like the idea of changing nature, but dredging would eliminate the groins, and he'd have a lot more beach to run on. A few weeks later, leaping from an eight-foot-tall barrier by the DecoPlage, Raven landed wrong. Tendons in his calf exploded with an audible popping sound, and he barely hobbled home. The next day, he was dragging his leg behind him, thinking, *What the hell am I doing this for?* when a lifeguard called Ruby—name has been changed—leaned his head out of the stand. "Old people are passing you!" he shouted. "You're not even running!"

Raven, along with every other person he knew, hated Ruby. He stole coworkers' lunches and yelled at tourists if they got too close to the stand—unless they were women, in which case he produced a bottle of sunscreen to rub on them. One time, two lifeguards wearing their Beach Patrol T-shirts ran into Ruby's uncle at a tennis court. "Oh, my nephew is on the Beach Patrol," said the man. "Do you know Ruby?" His colleagues bowed their heads to avoid saying anything disrespectful. "Yeah I know," continued his uncle, "he's an asshole." (Several lifeguards that run have confirmed these stories. Hitter, now a fireman, told me that Ruby was the second-most-popular lifeguard. "Who was the most popular?" I asked. "All the rest," he said. Giggler added, "I don't like talking bad about anyone, but this is the kind of guy that even his mom couldn't like.")

As Ruby hurled insults, Raven strengthened his resolve. "Looks like your streak is done," shouted Ruby. "You done, buddy?" His stride may not have been pretty, but Raven wasn't done. He put his head down and blocked Ruby out.

Mary worried, too. "Why don't you quit, son?" she told him. "Why don't you rest a while and let it heal? Everybody rests."

But the streak was what made Raven different from everybody else. He could rest, he knew, only after he finished eight miles. The Astrologer was the only one who encouraged him to keep going. She bought a DMSO liniment cream to reduce pain and swelling, in a concentration used for horses. Applying it, the Astrologer used her training as a psychic healer and floated her hands a half-inch above his leg, channeling all her energy to make him better. "She got in a trance state—not touching me—just hovering above it," Raven says. "It helped. In a certain way, she was a saint." He never took a painkiller, not even an aspirin. The Astrologer kept saying, "It's going to get better," and three months later, one day in August, her prediction came true, though the injury left him with permanent varicose veins winding up his right leg, like vines from a banyan tree.

Raven wanted more than "something casual" with this woman who could be saintly, and one night over a romantic dinner at Picciolo's, he said, "It's been four and a half years since we got together. Do you think we should get serious?"

The 49-year-old woman looked at her 28-year-old boyfriend and said, "Eh," which hurt Raven. "Well I'm not gonna be young forever," he said. "If a girl comes onto me, I'm not going to say no."

Soon after, Raven met an exotic dancer and went back for a romp at the Sun Ray Apartments, at 728 Ocean Drive (now, Johnny Rockets). When the Astrologer found out, she didn't really care, and Raven didn't think much about the exotic dancer until 1983, when he saw *Scarface*. In the scene where Tony Montana's friend Angel gets chopped into pieces with a chainsaw in the bathtub, Raven was thinking, *That bathroom looks awfully familiar*. Then he realized: *Oh, right! That's the room where I had the one-night stand with the exotic dancer.*

* * *

THE STREAK TURNED FIVE in 1980 and five days later, on a swim, Raven bumped into a Portuguese man-o'-war. Its long blue tentacles embraced his body, tangling up his arms, chest, back, neck, and legs. Sticking to him like a cobweb, it felt like someone whipped him all over with an electrical wire. As his skin absorbed the venom, Raven became short of breath. His mind flashed back to a scene from years before, when a paramedic was zipping up two yellow body bags. "Man-o'-wars," the paramedic had told him. "Two brothers; they were allergic." Fortunately Raven wasn't allergic, and the pain subsided after an hour. Over the next thirty-five years, however, he'd endure fifty-six more run-ins with man-o'-wars.

The next day he had red welts all over. Gunny the lifeguard told him it was the worst attack he'd ever seen. Another lifeguard suggested meat tenderizer to neutralize the venom, so Raven filled an old black-and-gray film canister with the white powder. When he went swimming, he kept the canister on top of his folded clothes on the beach. One evening, he came back to find his clothes strewn about, covered in sand, and the film canister was missing. Just then a homeless man shuffled out from behind the lifeguard stand. "Hey, man," he said, brushing white powder from his upper lip. "What was that stuff in the container? It was awful salty." He had snorted Raven's meat tenderizer thinking it was cocaine. Raven was upset by the violation of privacy but figured the man had suffered enough.

This incident was the extent of Raven's participation in Miami's cocaine wars, but his city was entering the era of the Cocaine Cowboys, the Mariel Boatlift, and the McDuffie Riots. Over the next several years, residents scrambled to get out of the crossfire as Miami shattered every record in crime and homicide, earning the highest murder rate in the nation.

With all the dead bodies, Dade County ran out of storage space at the morgue, so the medical examiner rented a refrigerated van from Burger King headquarters to store the spillover, resulting in a mobile mortuary. Miami became known as Dodge City, St. Valentine's, Murder Capital. "The Beach was a war zone," says Raven. "My friends kept telling me, 'You're gonna get killed, man. The Beach is getting too dangerous.' "

But Raven never gave up on his home. "I just kept thinking it couldn't get any worse," he says. "Eventually I was right."

ON MY THIRD RUN WITH RAVEN in June 2011, we were heading south when he turned to me and said, "Today I'm going to tell you about the time a ton of chickens washed ashore." This was a typical preface to a Raven story.

Around Thanksgiving in 1980, he told me, a cargo ship was leaving the port of Miami, being tugged through Government Cut, when a container of frozen Perdue chickens tipped off the boat. As water filled the container, the chickens bubbled out and bobbed toward the beach. Before the first chicken leg touched land, news of free brined chicken had spread in Miami Beach and hundreds of people gathered at the shoreline. "So there's like thousands of frozen chickens—one ship container is about two stories high—and there's all these hungry *Marielitos*, like wolves, wanting to get the chickens." The police and the lifeguards were ordered to guard the chickens until Perdue made a decision. A few hungry residents broke through the barricade and made off with chickens while an older cop yelled, "Put them back! They belong to somebody!"

After a couple hours, Perdue called and said they were going to lose all the chicken, so the lifeguards could open up the beach. So long as people collected the chickens in an orderly fashion, they were welcome to take as many as they could carry. Raven helped himself to a crate of a dozen. Dragging his poultry treasure to the lifeguard stand at 3rd Street, he realized he could never use twelve chickens. "So I took three, and I gave nine to this crazy lady named Poodle Patty," said Raven. "She had these mangy, dirty poodles. She said she was going to cook the chicken up for the dogs." Raven ran home with three frozen chickens in a plastic bag. "They were like bricks," he said, rubbing his bicep. "My arms were sore the next day."

For the next month, Raven had to run through Perdue's aftermath as rotting chickens littered the beach. Pointing toward the coastline, Raven said to me, "All the way up to Fourteenth Street, you could see pieces of chicken on the sand—a wing, a leg. For months they were out there, and it was stinking so bad."

I was trying to picture this scene from 1980 playing out today at Government Cut, where a sidewalk promenade leads to outdoor seating at Smith & Wollensky steakhouse. I couldn't see diners taking a break from a hundred-dollar cut of filet mignon to fetch free chickens in the Atlantic. "I'm sorry—who did you say was lined up like wolves?" I asked.

"The Marielitos," he said. "This was right after the Boatlift." I'd only lived in Miami for a couple months when I heard this story, and I knew little about the Mariel Boatlift, which happened two years before I was born. Raven explained it to me like this: "In 1980, Castro basically opened up his prisons and put all his criminals on boats to South Beach. These were bad guys—murderers, rapists, thieves—and there were physically and mentally disabled people, too."

Raven's summary sounded suspect. "What was the idea behind it?" I asked. "That these people were political prisoners?"

"I guess," said Raven. "That was all done by Jimmy Carter. What a mess. Castro cleaned house. He was like, 'Great, I don't have to take care of these hundreds of thousands of people anymore.' "

"So Castro had the last laugh?"

Raven squeezed his black glove. "Castro is still laughing."

Before I could ask my next question, an older lifeguard with white hair poked his head out of the stand at 30th Street. "Hey, Raven," he shouted, "Dodgers are looking pretty good this season, huh?"

"So far!" Raven responded, waving. He turned again to me. "That's Bert," he said. "His first day on the job was February 1, 1983, at Third Street. Some Marielitos started harassing his wife, who was sitting by the stand, and Bert told them to cool it, but they started getting rough." Bert, Raven told me, ducked inside the lifeguard stand to call for backup, and the guys followed him inside. "They had these old phones with the receiver and the cord," continued Raven. "The guys took the phone and beat his face in." It took 112 stitches to sew Bert back together. "Nobody thought he was going to come back, but he did. Been here ever since. See White Lightning? Bad times."

SINCE THIS CONVERSATION, I have learned that Raven's impression of Mariel is representative of Miami Beach residents. Often the worst discrimination comes from the *exiliados*— wealthy Cuban professionals that got here first—who complain that the Marielitos stained their good reputation. Most people my age who have heard of the Mariel Boatlift know it from *Scarface*, whose main character, Tony Montana, is a Marielito. Some people think the movie is based on a true story, but everyone in Miami can agree that Al Pacino does a horrible Cuban accent.

Between April and October 1980, 125,000 refugees crowded on boats leaving the Port of Mariel in Cuba for American shores in Key West. The majority settled in Miami—with local relatives, or in tent cities pitched at the Orange Bowl Stadium or by the Miami River under I-95. While the statistics are all over the map, what is certain is that among the many thousands of good, hardworking Cuban refugees seeking freedom, Castro had tucked in undesirable or useless members of his society, including thieves, killers, rapists, and the insane. *Escoria*— scum, Castro called them—came from Cuban prisons and asylums to Key West and on to Miami Beach.

Many of Raven's memories of "the Mariel time" feed the criminal stereotype. He chased down purse snatchers and helped the lifeguards catch bad guys. "If I saw something wrong, I didn't think twice," Raven told me. "I was strong and fast and hated to see injustice." He has nicknames for the prominent criminals. There was one with bright red hair and freckles—

Howdy Doody—who, one day in 1980, snuck up behind a grandmother shopping on Washington Avenue and snatched her purse, leaving the old woman shaking on the sidewalk.

Raven took off after him, sprinting down an alleyway off 7th Street. He cornered Howdy Doody at the dead end. "I don't know if he has a gun or a knife," recalled Raven. "So I walk in slowly." Howdy Doody had the same worry about the long-haired runner with the black glove. Dropping the purse, the man ran away without taking anything. Raven picked it up and unceremoniously delivered it to the old lady, still frozen on the sidewalk. "She just said, 'Uh thank you,' " said Raven. "She didn't speak much English, and it scared her."

Another criminal tried to eke out a living fashioning cowboy hats from palm fronds and selling them to tourists. A middle-aged man with a hard face and long hair, the Hatmaker "had a nasty comment for every girl that passed," said Raven. One time, Romer the lifeguard went to lock the public bathroom at the end of his shift. Within seconds, the Hatmaker was advancing toward Romer's unattended belongings at the stand. Just before he reached the wallet, the Walrus, another lifeguard, came out of nowhere and tackled the Hatmaker. When Romer came back from the bathroom, the Walrus had the Hatmaker pinned in the sand.

Police arrested the Hatmaker but by the end of the week he was out of jail, making hats on the beach, which was also an illegal business. "You weren't supposed to sell stuff without a license, so the cops would bother him," explained Raven regretfully. "It's a shame because he made really good hats, and he probably could've survived that way."

On top of refugees from Cuba, Haitians were pouring into Miami. One day, a lifeguard was standing over a lumpy white sheet next to his stand when Raven ran by. "What's that?" Raven asked.

"Another dead Haitian," he said. "We got him by the rocks. Somebody saw him floating and called the rescue." Raven couldn't understand how all these people were drowning when they were so close to land. "They can't swim," explained the lifeguard. "They'll get rides in boats, and the captain will drop them off a hundred feet off shore. They can't make it that far. If they don't have an inner tube, they drown." Often, their makeshift boats would fall apart or capsize in the high seas.

President Carter's promise to welcome refugees with open arms didn't apply to those coming from Haiti. Though Cubans were allowed to become permanent U.S. residents after a year in the country, Haitians—if they made the six-hundred-mile journey to U.S. sand or soil alive—were held at Krome Detention Center in west Miami, next to the Everglades. When the Reagan administration took office in 1981, the United States Coast Guard had orders to rescue Cubans at sea and bring them to American shores. Haitian boats were to be interdicted and escorted back to Haiti. Though they were fleeing the brutal dictatorship of Jean-Claude "Baby Doc" Duvalier, the United States considered them economic refugees—not political, like the Cubans—and that wasn't enough to gain entry.

Pictures of Haitian corpses washing up on shore and Marielitos sleeping under highway overpasses spilled onto the front cover of *Time* magazine in November 1981, in an article entitled "Paradise Lost." One afternoon, by 4th Street, a policeman was circling around a group of twenty Haitians—men and women of all ages in a line—crouching on their heels with their heads down. The cop was yelling at them when Raven ran by. "What are you doing?" he asked the officer.

"They all washed up," said the cop. Raven studied their faces. As usual, he was rooting for the underdog. The Haitians were wide-eyed, looking scared and innocent. They spoke no English to defend themselves, and they were covered in sand. "I was thinking, *How are these people treated like criminals when we give the real criminals from Mariel papers?*" says Raven. Just before he turned to finish the run, the cop added a friendly warning: "Don't get too close. They could have diseases."

*   *   *

THE BEACH NOURISHMENT PLAN had worked its way south from Haulover by then, and pipes pumped out piles of sand fifteen feet high on South Beach, which Raven climbed over or ran around. Silt clouded the sea, changing the Atlantic from crystal blue to an opaque brown. "If you opened your mouth under water, you'd get sand between your teeth," says Raven, who was still swimming after every run. "I couldn't pull a comb through my hair, it was so caked with silt." From crime and construction, beaches were mostly deserted.

Running one afternoon, Raven passed three different men masturbating in the sand within three blocks. He reported the incidents to Bob Romer. "What do you want me to do?" asked Romer, throwing up his hands. "We can't arrest them all."

Raven looked at Romer. "But how are tourists going to come back if they see that? No girl is ever gonna come to South Beach." To get out of the crime zone, old people had been offering to Raven their condos for ten or twenty thousand dollars.

People were telling Raven to stop running and take cover, but he kept going, saving people on land and in the water. Running by the Delano Hotel around 17th Street—in the same spot where he had pulled out the girls from the Bahamas—Raven saw waving hands caught in a rip current. The lifeguards had packed up for the day, so Raven took off.

As soon as he reached the woman, he offered a disclaimer. "I will get you in, but this may take a while." She panicked and climbed on top of him, holding him under water. Raven recalls, "The lifeguards had told me some people do that, so I was careful." He swam free, but the woman soon dunked him again. Surfacing out of reach, he said calmly, "Look, if you do this, I won't be able to get you in. Don't push me down. Let me hold you." She relaxed, and Raven brought her to shore.

A few months after rescuing the woman, Raven saw a father and son caught in another rip current in the same spot. Instead of making the rescue himself, he sprinted to the stand on 21st Street, a couple blocks away, to alert a lifeguard named Tim McHale. On Raven's way back south, the father and son were getting oxygen from the rescue squad and everyone was fine. Pointing to Raven, McHale told the family, "That's the man who saved your lives. He came and got me."

After three rescues in the same block, Raven campaigned for the city to put a lifeguard stand at 17th. He even wrote an op-ed in the *Miami Herald*. "From Fourteenth to Thirty-Fifth, there was only one lifeguard stand, at Twenty-First," says Raven. "Can you imagine? That's almost two miles." He said they needed one at 17th and another around 29th. It took two more fatalities to convince the city, but now there are lifeguard stands every couple of blocks in mid-beach. At a lifeguard's suggestion, Raven tried out to be on Beach Patrol, but he failed the swim test by fifteen seconds.

EIGHTY-TWO WAS A YEAR to test the streak. At the dentist one day, Raven got thirteen cavities filled in the same appointment. "You're not going to run after this, are you?" asked the dentist. Raven said nothing. "Eh, you probably are," the dentist concluded. He was right. For eight miles, Raven's head rattled every step.

On July 1, 1982, two Doberman pinschers—one red and one black—were chasing each other around a trashcan on the beach at 1st Street. Raven ran toward the water, giving the Dobermans a wide berth, but still the black one chased him down and chomped his leg. The dog's teeth sank in, ripping open a hole in his upper left calf. "It was like someone hitting you with all their might with a baseball bat," says Raven.

The dog's owner apologized and promised to take care of medical bills. With five miles left, Raven kept going until the rescue squad, who'd heard about the attack from witnesses, showed up and cleaned the wound with peroxide. A piece of white tissue, Raven recalls, was poking out of the hole in his calf. They told him to get to a hospital for a tetanus shot, which he did—after finishing eight miles and going for a "short" swim. The doctor didn't stitch up the wound but told him to keep an eye on it. "If you start getting sick, it could be rabies," he said. When Raven called the dog's owner, the number he'd been given was disconnected.

His leg ached for weeks. Limping threw off his hip and other knee. Just as he was starting to feel better on July 20, he got the worst bout of food poisoning he'd had since 1975. "You want to die, but you can't," says Raven. "My legs felt like rubber. After the run, I just fell in the sand."

By the first of August, he was running strong again. That was the Sunday he cracked his head open on the pier piling, giving himself a concussion and requiring eighteen stitches. At the hospital, he reviewed his last month—dog bite, food poisoning, and a concussion—and thought, *Maybe now is a good time to quit*.

Then the Novocain kicked in.

That night the Astrologer followed him with a flashlight for the last five miles, before he went to his security job in his blood-soaked bandage.

The next day, Romer stuck his head out of the stand. "What's going to happen next?" he shouted. "Who's going to die first— me or you?" Raven thought it was an odd question.

On February 9, 1983, Raven was doing pull-ups when the beach patrol truck stopped in front of him. Gunny, Romer's best friend, was sitting in the passenger seat with tears running down his face. Romer had killed himself.

"That was one of the toughest runs I ever did," says Raven. "My body was shaking from shock. I just wish I could've talked to him. I wish I could've told him that I was there for him." The funeral was two days later, but it was during the run time. "It poured rain," he says. "It almost never rains in February, and I remember thinking, *God is crying for Romer*."

*   *   *

COYOTE, RAVEN'S FIRST RUNNER, disappeared sometime after Mariel, when his bike kept getting stolen and his girlfriend kept getting harassed. "When he decided to leave town, he said to me, 'I want to do a poem or story every week about one of the characters,' " Raven recalled. "I said, 'What a great idea.' Then I never heard from him again."

Though I've never met Coyote, I have heard him sing on a CD that Raven made for me, labeled RAVEN ORIGINAL SONGS, 1975–1988. Coyote plays guitar on the first track, a song titled "I May Be Leavin' (But I Sure Ain't Gone)," which, Raven says, is about the Astrologer. "I woke up from a dream that a guy in her apartment building who looked like a Cuban Nixon took her away from me," explained Raven. "The irony is that both really disliked each other."

Coyote's signature song was track 6, "Broadway Butterfly," and to my ear, he sings and plays harmonica like Bob Dylan. In the recording, the Astrologer is doing backup vocals. (Other titles include: "The Drifting Kind," "Just as Lonesome as a Train," and "Quote the Raven.")

Raven's third runner was a five-foot-six arm-wrestling aficionado from Springfield, Massachusetts, who went by the name Yul, because he resembled the bald actor, Yul Brynner. I've met Yul, now in his 60s, several times on the beach during our runs and at the Raven Run picnics. He usually carries his artwork or a cane umbrella.

His real name is Wilbur, but due to a speech impediment he says Wibbluh. His *r* is a *w* and his *th* is just *t*, and this used to make for interesting arm-wrestling challenges. "He'd walk into biker bars and say, 'You a pwetty tough guy, I can tell you pwetty big—you wanna awm wessle?' " recalled Raven. Then he went to cement walls by the old pier, trashcans, and bar counters for the competition. Yul also dabbled in amateur strength contests—who could move a giant rock or throw a brick the farthest—and organized running contests, swimming contests, and sword-throwing contests. When Yul attempted the eight miles with Raven in 1982, he wore a thick black rubber space suit; he was trying to lose weight to get into a lower weight class—that he'd created—for arm wrestling. "I thought he was going to die of heatstroke," says Raven. "But he finished, Raven Runner number three."

Yul has only one run on the books and lives in the Rebecca Towers Retirement Home with his wife, Dottie, who wears a tinfoil hat. Yul calls Raven "Jesus." Many evenings, while Yul is strolling along the beach, he intercepts Raven during his eight miles. "You suffuh so much evwy day, being out heah," says Yul. "What a buhden you have." Then Yul extends his hand for a firm shake with Raven, remarking, "What a gwip you got!"

Raven told me, "All I do is brace myself, and he puts the vice grip on me. My arthritis throbs for a day."

TWO THINGS HAPPENED IN 1984 that made Raven think South Beach had turned a corner. On Independence Day, the Beach Boys performed on the newly dredged beach, drawing crowds of 200,000 that Raven and another runner called Zero weaved through. To attract that many people, Raven thought, the city had to be getting safer. (Zero incidentally was the first runner to get banned: "One time, Zero is running close to the shoreline, and an old man named No Eyes is standing in his way, and Zero just hauls off and punches him," explained Raven. "Then he punches another guy because his dog was barking, and I said, 'That's just too weird.' He's banned.")

After the Beach Boys, Don Johnson and Philip Michael Thomas came to town wearing pastel suits and loafers without socks to film season one of *Miami Vice* as undercover detectives Sonny Crockett and Ricardo Tubbs. Since a preservationist named Barbara Capitman had gotten the neighborhood on the National Registry of Historic Places, buildings were getting facelifts. Capitman's right-hand man was Leonard Horowitz, the designer behind the pastel color palette that now makes

South Beach pop. He painted storefronts with the colors of the sun and sky and beach—teal greens, periwinkle blues, peachy pinks. Horowitz's designs matched his eclectic wardrobe; he often dressed in Hawaiian shirts, baggy pants from thrift stores, and big glasses.

Miami Vice producers loved the quirky, bright architecture—the curves and ziggurats—and even paid for some buildings to be repainted. Horowitz's friends joked that he should get credit for the set design. As Crockett and Tubbs cruised along Ocean Drive in a Daytona Spyder, sexy bikini-clad women laid on the white-sand beach while ripped men worked out; in this town, beauty has a history of covering up deeper problems. Miami was still a center of the drug trade, but *Miami Vice* made it look cool. All the fun, sex, drugs, and guns came with a pulsating musical score by Jan Hammer and Phil Collins. Gianni Versace designed the clothes.

At first local leaders resisted the show, worrying the title alone would ruin whatever was left of Miami's reputation. Instead, *Miami Vice* had the opposite effect, becoming a megahit—a weekly, fifty-minute commercial for South Beach. "When they started filming *Miami Vice*, everything changed," observes Raven. "They fixed up buildings. They brought in models. That, more than anything else, changed South Beach."

IV
FITNESS

The last three generations in my family never lived
to be sixty. If it was not for the Raven Run, I don't
think I would be alive.
—Chapter 11, age 80, over 1,000 Raven Runs

Chemo, that's something else. Ugh. It's just pure poison
to our bodies. It tries to do everything to you, and you just
fight everything it's trying to do. When I got my first dose,
I started to lie down, and I thought, God, I'm not sleepy,
what am I lying down for? That's the trick. Get up.
I went out and ran with Raven.
—Gringo, cancer survivor, over 1,641 Raven Runs

At the time I saw Raven on TV, I had stopped running
because of back problems. A doctor told me I couldn't run
anymore. I had put on weight, feeling dreadful and depressed
over my physical condition. Now here was this guy who
loves Johnny Cash and Waylon Jennings, is a huge baseball
fan, and has back problems just like me. I was so inspired. I
put on my shoes and hit the sidewalk.
—Hot Furnace, 2 Runs

The mental benefits outweigh the physical.
The physical is a bonus.
—Raven

EIGHT

NOT A RACE

The top Raven Runner of all time is a 63-year-old accountant named Taxman. From when he started running in 1994 until now, he has racked up over 1,940 eight-mile runs. I've run with Taxman at least seventy-five times, and we usually talk about our favorite food, ice cream—how much we ate the night before, new flavors, sales at Publix, or how much we're planning to eat later. Taxman is six-foot-three with white-blond hair and light eyes peering out of wire-rimmed glasses. He has a goofy, lighthearted presence. He smiles in a bashful way, like he just said something a little inappropriate. When he runs, he leans to the right but politically he is a socialist.

Taxman was the forty-seventh runner to make Raven's list, which now has more than 2,540 people. He didn't make it on the first attempt. "It was a very hot and humid day," he told me on a run twenty years later. "Raven was going fast then. After four or five miles I saw purple spots and was near fainting." Though he had to quit that time, he was persistent.

He'd heard about Raven from his then girlfriend—now wife—a talkative, well-read woman known as Lasagna Lady. Lasagna Lady had actually gone on a date with Raven before meeting Taxman, but it didn't work out. (Sitting across from me at a Raven Run banquet, she explained it this way: "We went to dinner—Raven was good looking—and he told me he didn't drink, he didn't smoke, he didn't have a car, and he didn't ever travel. Well I liked to do all those things. He said he just liked to run every day. I was like, *Hmm, this is not the man for me*.") When Taxman said he wanted to start running, she said, "Oh, you have to meet my friend, Raven."

"Running with others, particularly Raven, helped me overcome my mental limitations to running longer distances," Taxman told me. Soon he was a regular. He met fellow runners like Vulcan Pilot, an emotionless man who flew planes for American Airlines. Vulcan Pilot, a radical conservative, was on the opposite end of the political spectrum. "He used to call me Comrade Tax," said Taxman.

It's common with Raven to run next to someone who is in some way your opposite.

"Then you had Springman," continued Taxman, "who was the skinniest guy you've ever seen who piled his long stringy hair on the top of his head in a Russian bun to cover up a bald spot." Back then, Springman was a 33-year-old drummer who drove from Hialeah to the beach in his "Death Trap," a 1975 Volkswagen Bug, which he painted himself, that had over 300,000 miles. The floorboard was a stop sign. The steering wheel was a fence post. The door was tied on with rope, and the crank windows didn't roll down.

Springman was obsessed with how much people weighed. "Ask Plantain Lady about it," advised Taxman. "She'd just hold her arms out to the side and say, 'How many pounds did I put on, Springman?' because she knew he was going to tell her. Springman was hilarious."

Springman started running in 1985. He was number seven. When I met Springman in 2014, on Raven's 64th birthday run, Springman told me, "My friends all thought Raven was a drug dealer. I remember one friend goes, 'We could probably score some good dope off that guy. Go ask him for some pot.' " Instead, Springman asked Raven if he could run with him. "He was pretty much the only one out here," continued Springman, who has 735 runs with Raven. "The beaches were empty."

Nowadays, the Raven Run is like an institution. Taxman, I learned, was responsible for the Awards banquet. On a run back in 1995, he brought up the idea to Raven, "where we could all get together with wives, husbands, and significant others and get a chance to meet other runners we generally don't run with," recalled Taxman. Raven loved the idea and to this day, Taxman prints out all the certificates and a few copies of the Raven Run list. In an email, Taxman summed up his Raven Run experience this way: "Our runners come from many nationalities with varied backgrounds, careers, hobbies, and personalities. I love the many stories behind the Raven nicknames. We make an incredible family, and it's all because of one man . . . Raven."

FOR THE FIRST DECADE of the streak, Raven was still trying to get over the song in Nashville. Every day he hated that man who stole it. Additionally, he hated the chaos and crime in his city, and hated that his good-for-nothing stepfather, the Eagle, was still ordering his mother around. He hated that his real father had rejected him. Beginning in 1985, he was still running for himself, focusing on the only thing he could control—eight miles, every day.

That next decade would bring Raven fifty new runners including Springman and Taxman and more consistent company. His life started to stabilize. When people told Raven, "I wish I could do what you're doing," he'd tell them, "You can. If I can do it, you can do it." He both inspired and was inspired by the diverse people who shared the sand next to him. They expanded his horizon, and, hearing about his unusually stringent lifestyle, people reconsidered their priorities, making time for exercise and for company. In the beginning, running was his own therapy. It healed him. But in the second decade he saw he was helping other people get healthy and solve problems. He liked making connections between people. As he motivated others, they motivated him to keep up the streak.

"I went from running with one or two people making a couple friends here or there to a big flock," said Raven. "But it wasn't easy, and it didn't happen overnight."

WITH CROCKETT AND TUBBS patrolling the set, tourists and young people came back to Miami Beach. Even better, the women came back topless. One day in 1985, Raven was standing at the 3rd Street stand when he heard an old lady complain to the lifeguard. "Excuse me, I have my grandson here, and he's only four years old," she said. "Can you please do something about this topless woman swimming over there?"

The lifeguard shook his head. "I'm sorry, ma'am," he said. "We're not going to arrest them. If you don't like it, you should probably go somewhere else."

Miami Vice and breasts were improving Raven's scenery and the city's crime rates, but they weren't silver bullets. One night in early 1985, Raven and the Astrologer were leaving Mary's apartment when, from the balcony, he saw someone inside the Astrologer's car. "Call the police," said Raven, chasing the thief.

He cornered the sweaty young man in an alley and brought him back to the scene of the crime, where Mary and the Astrologer were talking to a cop named Bruce. "You got Fat Boy," Bruce told Raven. "We've been looking for him. He's robbed twenty-three old ladies, and they're all too afraid to testify. But I'll bet you're not."

A few days later, Raven answered a call from Florida State Attorney Janet Reno. "She asked me to come and give a deposition on Fat Boy," recalled Raven. "I told her as long as it wasn't during the time of my run, I'd be glad to testify." The Astrologer drove him to the courthouse—Mary came along for the ride—and Fat Boy was found guilty.

On the way home, they stopped by the Baltimore Orioles spring training camp at Miami Stadium, where Raven took a picture of Cal Ripken, going into the third year of his baseball streak. Ripken's streak would span 2,632 games over a sixteen-year period from May 30, 1982, to September 19, 1998. He holds the record for the number of consecutive games played, having surpassed Lou Gehrig's 2,130 games, completed in 1939. "When I think of a streak, I think of Cal Ripken," Raven told me. "That's a guy I'd like to meet."

IN JUNE 1985, early one morning, Raven was sitting in the guardhouse at the entrance to Sunset Island, where he controlled the security gate. With an hour left of his shift, Raven was swatting away insects when a heavy bug flew straight into his right ear. "It was like *zzzzzz*, and I could feel the legs crawling, trying to get out," recalls Raven.

He didn't know what else to do, so he stuck a pencil in his ear. The pencil extraction didn't work. The bug was lodged deep in his ear canal and every movement flicked his nerves. Trying to dial the Astrologer's number, Raven dropped the phone three times. "The pain was so intense," says Raven. "It felt like electrical shocks. I tell you, if I'd had a gun, I would've killed myself."

The Astrologer drove him to South Shore Hospital, where a doctor who looked like Frankenstein squirted medicine from a syringe into Raven's ear and slowly the bug started dying. "Then it was just like a little lump in there," says Raven. "Meanwhile they tell me they don't have an instrument to take out the dead bug."

He stumbled back to Astrologer's car, and a doctor at Jackson Memorial Hospital eventually removed the bug—a big round beetle, the size of a nickel. "The nurse in the room almost flipped over," says Raven. Raven went home with the bug in a little glass jar, which he believes is still in his apartment. The doctor knew Raven would run, but he gave specific instructions not to swim.

"Well, that afternoon it was hot as hell after the run and I went swimming," says Raven. For weeks, he would wake up on top of a soaking-wet pillow, and he didn't know why. When he was running, it felt like wind was going through his head.

Back at the hospital a month later, the doctor asked if he had gone swimming.

Raven reminded him it was the middle of summer. The last day of July, in fact, was the hottest day he had ever run. The thermometer on the bank's clock registered 103 degrees in the shade with 100 percent humidity. It felt like he was running in an oven. At the end, what choice did he have?

"So did you go swimming?" the doctor asked again. Raven said yes, and the doctor prescribed antibiotics. Eventually water stopped dripping from his ear, and the Sunset Island security office covered the medical bills, which Raven considers a happy ending.

RAVEN HADN'T SPOKEN to his real father since Father's Day in 1977, but the longer streak of silence was for two decades with the Eagle. Knowing that Raven visited his mother, I wondered how that scene played out. "Oh, we'd watch baseball games together, and she sat between us," explained Raven. "If I said to my mom that a player was good, the Eagle would be like, 'Eh, tell him he stinks.' And whenever I said anything about Johnny Cash, he'd say, 'Eh, that guy should be driving a truck.' If I opened the fridge, he'd say, 'Tell him to close the fridge—what's he trying to do, cool down the place?' He was a nasty guy."

Smoking and a sedentary lifestyle finally caught up to the Eagle, and he started having heart problems. On the day after Thanksgiving in 1984, Raven witnessed one of the Eagle's heart attacks. While Raven was eating soup at the counter, the Eagle was glued to the third quarter of a close game between Boston College and Jimmy Johnson's Miami Hurricanes. Raven noticed that the Eagle was clutching his chest and heaving forward to breathe. "Is he having a heart attack?" Raven asked his mother.

"I think so," said Mary. As she picked up the phone to call 9-1-1, the Eagle grunted. "No, wait a little."

He wanted to finish the game.

In the closing minute, Miami scored a touchdown to take the lead 45 to 41. After two drives with six seconds left at the Miami 48, the ball was snapped to Boston College quarterback Doug Flutie, who launched a Hail Mary straight to the hands of his teammate, Gerard Phelan. The Eagle fell out of his chair. "Oh, my God," he said. "Okay, call the ambulance."

When the paramedics arrived, they told Raven, "We've been responding to calls all afternoon because of that game."

As part of his recovery, the Eagle started going for swims in the ocean. While on the beach, he saw Raven running, getting attention from lifeguards and respect from senior citizens. One afternoon the Eagle marched home and remarked to Mary, "Robert actually has friends! People like him. And he's really fast."

It was too little, too late.

Nineteen days into 1987, Raven stopped by his mom's apartment to get the paper. The Eagle was in his usual perch, hunched over, sleeping in the armchair. Sometimes the Eagle would lift his head up when Robert came in, but this time he didn't. A half-hour later, Mary was banging on Raven's door. "Robert, I think he's dead," she said.

Raven followed her next door, and the Eagle was blue in his armchair, certainly dead, at 79. When the funeral home came, the undertakers were drunk. The bumbling employees covered the Eagle in a dark maroon sheet and loaded him on a gurney. As they were carrying the body downstairs, a wheel got stuck on the railing. "So I'm standing there watching," says Raven, "and they look at me—young and strong—and they say, 'Hey, man, do you wanna help us carry this guy out? We got him stuck.' I said, 'I'd be glad to.' So as I'm helping them lift it, I turned to my mom and say, 'I always knew I'd be carrying him out.' And she said, 'Oh, stop that. It's not funny.' " When Raven told me this story, I must have made a face because he added, "Don't worry, White Lightning, she wasn't that sad, and he was old."

After burying her husband, Mary called Walter Kraft. "Robert's a really good boy and you hardly know him," she told Walter. "Maybe you should come and visit."

"That's a good idea," he said. "I've made a lot of mistakes. The biggest mistake was when I left you. I should've stayed with the family. I really messed up."

Raven wouldn't find out about this conversation until two months later, when Walter had a stroke that left him paralyzed. Calling from his hospital room, Walter told Raven, "I made a big mistake, and I love you."

"When you start feeling better, you can come down and stay with me," said Raven. "I got an apartment, and the weather's nice."

Raven recalls, "I didn't say *if*. I said, *when* you get better. And I could hear him whispering, 'That'd be nice.' I'm sure he didn't really mean it, but it was kind of a relief to me."

Two weeks later, Walter Kraft moved to hospice, where he died the following night at 67 years old. The date was April 29, 1987—exactly one hundred days after the Eagle's death. A lot of Raven's friends assumed the loss of a father would break the streak. A lifeguard called Slipper offered to buy him a plane ticket to California, but he said no.

"I didn't want to miss a day," says Raven. "People said that's the wrong thing to do, that I should show respect. But I hadn't spoken to him in ten years."

Raven heard that only six people, including the minister, went to Walter's funeral. One of his father's only friends called Raven and said, "Your father was always like a fugitive, running from something."

Maybe a piece of his dad was in the run. When Raven talked to me about his father's death, he sat with his hands in his lap, looking between the floor and the window, like a little boy trying not to cry. "I felt sad," said Raven. "Not *crying* sad—the sadness was just I wish I got to know him: Why did he leave me? Why did he get married eight times? What was he looking for?"

Then he perked up and tilted his head. "Maybe it's good, White Lightning," he concluded. "Maybe if I *had* known him, I wouldn't have liked him and anyway, it could've been a lot worse. If I had grown up with a normal father, I probably wouldn't be who I am today."

NO MATTER WHAT LIFE THREW, Raven knew eight miles would set him straight. Gradually new people joined. His tenth runner was the "Testosterone Kid," an 18-year-old boxer training at the 5th Street Gym. Broke and new to town, the Testosterone Kid was sleeping in Muhammad Ali's locker at the gym, sweeping the floors to earn his keep. His first run was in July 1987.

The Kid's coach was a former boxing champion, Beau Jack, who said, "You can run with the Raven, but don't leave your fight out on the beach." In other words, eight miles was too far for roadwork. But the Testosterone Kid didn't listen to Beau Jack.

Raven was actually impressed that a boxing legend like Beau Jack even knew his name. When I didn't recognize Beau Jack's name, Raven introduced me to his story. Beau Jack's fighting experience began in the 1920s, in barbaric "battles royal"—exhibitions financed by wealthy white men who organized fights between six or ten blindfolded black men. The last to remain standing won the purse, which usually was around $2. Beau Jack's first battle royal was staged at the Augusta National Golf Club, where he eventually became a caddie and met Bobby Jones, who helped launch his boxing career. After becoming Lightweight World Champion, Beau Jack retired, ran out of money, and began shining shoes at the Fontainebleau Hotel. There, according to the Raven, Frank Sinatra recognized him and brought him to the 5th Street Gym, where he began training young boxers like Testosterone Kid. "He was nearly blind from taking so many punches to the retina, but

people would still come to him from all over to get his auto-
graph and talk about old times."

One day in 1987 around the third mile running with Raven,
the Testosterone Kid's nose started gushing blood. The Kid ca-
sually explained that, in the morning, he had been sparring
with former welterweight champion Aaron Pryor. Raven ran
the Kid to the Beach Patrol headquarters, where Lieutenant
Amwhale administered first aid. Amwhale was a four-hundred-
pound former Amway salesman who, during Christmas, dressed
up as Santa Claus and distributed tangerines to the Beach's
homeless population.

Raven jogged in place as the Amwhale tilted the Kid's head
back and plugged his nose. "I'll be ready in a minute," said
the Kid.

"No, you won't," said Amwhale. "You could hemorrhage
and die out there. Your run is done today." Raven acquiesced
and invited the Kid over to watch television later. "I knew it
was going to be a lonely night in that hot, moldy gym," says
Raven. So Testosterone Kid came for TV and "honey water,"
Raven's homemade energy drink. Later, the Kid was back and
set the first Raven Run record—twelve runs in a row.

Runner number thirteen was Barnacle, who Raven describes
like this: "The first thing he does is go straight to the refrigera-
tor. He grabs a Mountain Dew. Then he opens the cabinet and
grabs a bag of peanuts. If you have two bags, he'll open the
one that's not open and say, 'I want to make sure they are
fresh.' Then he is just there, putting his feet up on the table,
using your phone, changing the television station, wanting to
be entertained. 'What about the lifeguard in 1979? Tell me a
story.' Hour and hours, he'd be hanging out until Miracle
shows up and says, 'Barnacle, unless you want to watch, it's
time to go.' "

After Barnacle, in January 1988, came the Reverend, a Ful-
bright scholar and a professor from Baltimore. Reverend thought
highly of his own intelligence, and the maddest Raven saw him

get was after he lost a game of Trivial Pursuit to him. "He was so competitive it killed him," says Raven. "He was a professor, getting beat by a tenth-grade dropout. After every question, he'd yell, 'How did you know that? How did you know that?' And I'd say, 'Eh, I heard it on the radio.' " After Trivial Pursuit, Reverend took out Scrabble. "There I had no chance," says Raven, who still admires Reverend's intelligence.

In November 1988, a firefighter named Steve attempted the eight at an extremely quick pace. "I was going as fast as I could to keep up with him," says Raven. "Then he said, 'I'm going to pick it up.' " After running four miles, Steve quit. By the end of Raven's eight miles, his feet had swelled into bubbles, making it look like he had elephantiasis. The run with Steve gave him terrible stress fractures. For two months, the pain prevented sleep.

Today Raven's feet are mangled, swollen stubs that he refuses to have photographed. But Steve (who would complete eight miles several years later and earn the nickname Last Laugh) taught him a lesson. "I said I just want to have fun with running," says Raven. "After all, you can't beat every runner who edges past you, and you may pass the same guy later, when he's walking. It's a run, not a race."

NINE

BETTER THAN ALCOHOL

Dizzy Issie is the number two Raven Runner behind Taxman, with over 1,800 runs on the books. He was born in Cruces, Cuba, on August 27, 1958, four months before Fidel Castro and his *26 de Julio* rebel armies marched into Havana. Issie's father had been an official in Fulgencio Batista's government. Issie came to Miami from Cuba aboard the Freedom Flights in 1967 but went straight to New York, where he lived until 1999.

In 2005, Issie was recently divorced at 46 when he passed Raven and Firecracker running on the beach. "Come on," hollered Firecracker. "Join us." Raven smiled, too.

"Tomorrow," promised Issie.

The next day Dizzy was waiting for Raven at the 5th Street lifeguard stand. (Regarding his nickname, Dizzy says, "Let's just say I'm a product of the seventies. Back then, we were all a little dizzy.") His first run was right around when he accepted a new job as assistant principal at a public school just north of Miami in Opa-locka. "That place was hell," Dizzy told me on the phone in 2014. "I saw things there no one should ever have to see."

It takes him more than two hands to count the number of loaded firearms he found on campus. When a 12-year-old girl collapsed at recess, he held her in his arms as she took her last breath. Another time, Dizzy was the last person at school to see a sixth grader who was crying in his office, begging him not to send her to JAC, the Juvenile Assessment Center, for getting in a fight. He agreed and sent the girl home. That weekend, as she left a party, someone drove by and shot her in the head.

Often, at school dismissal, the carpool lines became battlegrounds for gang wars or drug trafficking. A Haitian gang called the West Side fought Latinos and African American students. "With the violence—I'm talking twenty or thirty kids going at it, and you have to break it up—your adrenaline rises, and you can't go straight home," explained Dizzy.

From June to December in 2005, Dizzy ran 136 times with Raven, earning him "Rookie of the Year." He also shed twenty pounds, which he didn't notice until five cafeteria ladies surrounded him for an intervention at lunch. "They were these older, motherly, round Cuban women," said Dizzy. "They were worried that, because I was single, I wasn't eating. They almost took me home with them to feed me. I was like, *It's okay, I'm running with Raven.*"

The Raven Run became his buffer between work and home. "There you have the clarity of sunshine, the beauty of the beach," observed Dizzy. "You meet runners from other states and countries. You hear Raven's stories. Then you go swimming. That completely relaxes my muscles. You can leave all your negativity out there. The Raven Run was better than alcohol, drugs, or psychotherapy."

Today Dizzy has a file with Raven Run memorabilia. After Rookie of the Year, Dizzy continued collecting awards—Athlete of the Year (2006), Runner of the Year (2007), Treasure Hunter (2009), Hall of Fame (2010), and Swimmer of the Year (2011). On the run, he met his best friend, Floater, who he calls his "brother from another mother." But the greatest prize of all that came from the Raven Run was a woman called Gypsy.

In August 2005, Gypsy, a professor at FIU from Spain, had come to run with her friends, Raven Run regulars Spinner and

Cholita. After six miles with Gypsy, Dizzy was smitten. (Their love story is totally Miami: At three in the morning, while they were spending their first night together, Hurricane Wilma came. Dizzy's place lost power, so Gypsy said, "Stay with me." School was canceled for the next two weeks, so one night turned into a fourteen-day honeymoon. "We got to know each other so well, it would have taken months of dating otherwise," said Dizzy. "Daniela [our daughter] wasn't conceived then, but her name really should be Wilma.") Reflecting on their relationship, Dizzy realizes, "We made our most important decisions on the Raven Run." Over eight miles, the couple decided to move in together, to get married, and to have Daniela. "I think it was the time and the structure that the run provided," said Dizzy. "For one hour and forty-five minutes, we could run together and talk about what we wanted."

In 2012, Dizzy got Event of the Year for running 50.5 miles in one day. From the finish line at the Miami Marathon, Dizzy ran home, where Gypsy had a sandwich waiting, ran to the beach, ran around the beach, met Raven at the 5th Street lifeguard stand, and ran eight more. When he finished at the lifeguard stand, he had been running for twelve hours.

Dizzy's ultra obsession started in 2008, and Dizzy says things like, "I've lost count of the number, but I've only done three 'hundreds,' " meaning hundred-mile races. "For ultras, you need to know two terms," he explained to me. "DNF is 'Did Not Finish' and DFL is 'Dead Fucking Last,' " he added. "It's way better to be DFL than DNF."

These days, because Raven is in so much pain and is running so slow, Dizzy usually takes off and runs a faster pace, which tends to piss Raven off. "Dizzy thinks because he's a middle school principal, he's normal. Then he goes out and runs a hundred miles. Yeah, okay—you're normal," Raven says sarcastically. "He's really obsessed with the ultras." He paused. "I know, White Lightning," he continued without prompting. "Like I should talk."

* * *

IN 1988, AFTER THE EAGLE AND RAVEN'S FATHER DIED, Raven was seeking more stability in his life, so he added a swim streak on top of the running streak. From March 1988 to February 1992, Raven swam three-tenths of a mile after every run, without missing one day. The extra structure gave him security to make other transitions in his life. That year—1988—he also got a new job, a new place, and a new girlfriend.

Raven and the Astrologer had been dating on and off for thirteen years, and she had become more like an older sister than a lover. Mutually, they decided to continue their friendship but cut out the romance.

Immediately Raven developed a crush on a silver-haired lady named Donna who worked out at the Police Athletic League Gym. She had pumped-up arms, deep-set green eyes, and thin lips. Raven loved the way her hips swaggered delicately from side to side when she walked—a technique she'd learned as a former runway model in New York. She had also been a farmer in West Virginia, a yogi in California, a stay-at-home mother of two in England, and a secretary at the University of Texas in Austin. She had come to South Beach to take care of her 85-year-old mother who lived in a nursing home.

Donna was 55, Raven was 37. Her voice was the biggest turn-on. "She had a real slow, sexy voice," says Raven. "I mean, wow. But she had a terrible temper. When she got mad, she sounded like Clint Eastwood."

Their first date was a screening of *Action Jackson*. Raven fell in love.

After only a couple months, walking home from dinner one night, they passed a real estate office. Rents were on their way up in South Beach, and his father had left him a small inheritance. He'd been thinking of buying his own place. "What do you think of us starting a home together?" he asked Donna.

"This relationship is nice now," said Donna. "But when I'm an old lady, you're not going to want to be with me." Raven almost started crying. "You should do it, though," continued Donna. "You should buy an apartment."

So he did. He bought the basement apartment where he lives now on Ocean Drive, in cash, from a couple who gave up on South Beach; they'd been renting the place to Marielitos who didn't pay rent, and the neighbors were drag queens and prostitutes. The low-rise was three blocks from the start of his running route. Raven thought it was perfect. "The best decision I ever made," he says.

Two blocks south of Raven's apartment, a businessman named Jack Penrod was opening a multimillion-dollar eponymous restaurant and club, Penrod's. Additionally, he was installing permanent stands on the beach to offer food, drinks, parasailing, jet-skiing, and boat rentals. Penrod wanted to make Miami Beach the spring break capital of the world. Most people in the neighborhood celebrated Penrod's opening as a sign of revitalization; the chic new establishment was just what South Shore needed.

But Raven is not most people.

As residents were kissing up to Penrod to get on his lists, Raven wanted to shut him down. A new property owner, Raven didn't like all the clubbing rabble-rousers throwing beer bottles on his lawn. Furthermore, he remembered Penrod's as the old band shell, where his grandmother and other senior citizens had paid a dime to dance on Friday nights. In a blistering op-ed to the *Miami New Times* ("Kraft Stands on Penrod," published February 22, 1989), Raven voiced his opposition. He accused Penrod of encouraging underage drinking, "so our young people can drive home from his club, heightening the possibility of killing and injuring themselves or other people," wrote Raven. Additionally, "our once-clean beach is now filthy . . . if it weren't for various can collectors, it would be a lot worse." He continued listing a litany of offenses—noise pollution, parking problems, public urination, fistfights, vandalism, vehicles on the beach. "While free enterprise is the American way," wrote Raven in his final line, "there is a limit when one is making great sums of money at others' expense, health, and well-being. This is called greed. This is what Jack Penrod stands for."

The rift between Raven and Penrod came to a head one afternoon on the beach, when Raven was running. "Hey," shouted Penrod. "Aren't you the buzzard?"

Raven looked at him, briefly considered taking the high road, and then responded, "Aren't you the Pencilrod?" (In 1998, Penrod changed the name of his club to Nikki Beach as a tribute to his daughter, Nicole, who was killed in a car accident by a drunk driver.)

After reading the op-ed, Raven's neighbor, Reverend Pearson, called to ask a favor. Penrod was trying to expand his property and build a parking lot on Ocean Drive, which would take the place of a park and children's playground. The city had already approved the park's demolition, but community leaders were up in arms. Pearson had a soft, soothing voice. "Nobody knows the beach like you," she cooed on the phone. "Do you have a poem or song that you can perform during our meeting?"

On Easter Sunday, 1989, Raven gathered with environmental activist Marjory Stoneman Douglas (whom we have to thank for the Everglades National Park), Miami Beach preservationist Barbara Capitman, and Miami Beach mayor, Alex Daoud, who is still a good friend.

Reverend Pearson introduced Raven. "Our first speaker knows the beach better than any of us," she said, "because he's been running eight miles on it every day for the last fourteen years." Raven, in his shirtless running uniform, climbed onto the stage and took the podium with a shaky hand underneath his black glove. He was "scared as hell" but focused his attention on his mom, sitting proudly in a lawn chair in the front row.

He read "When the Eagle Flies with the Raven," a poem inspired by the fraught relationship with his stepfather. "As much as I hated the Eagle," says Raven, "I knew in my gut that if someone was trying to hurt my mom or invade the shores of Miami, that we would band together to defeat a common enemy." It was a call to action for the crowd to set aside their personal differences and unite to save the park. When he finished, he announced, "Now I gotta run," and dramatically leaped from the stage, feet moving as he hit the ground. Eventually, after another protest, Penrod chose a new site for his parking lot, and Raven discovered he liked the taste of activism. Now, the playground is the Marjory Stoneman Douglas Park, on Ocean Drive between 2nd and 3rd, across from Raven's apartment.

TO THE NEW PLACE and the new girlfriend, Raven added a new job, working security for the Royale Group at a handful of art deco hotels. From an insider's vantage point, Raven witnessed the turnaround of South Beach. He started out patrolling the alleyways but soon got promoted to the lobby at the Cardoza, where he carried bags up to guestrooms and gave directions.

I met Raven's old boss at the art deco hotels on a Raven Run in 2015. He goes by the name Hoover Maneuver. "How was Raven as an employee?" I asked.

"Oh, he was excellent," said Hoover Maneuver. "Man, people were always bitching about things. But Raven did what he needed to do. He never gave me shit. So I gave him a raise. If you didn't give me shit, you were okay with me."

One of Raven's duties at the hotel was to make the wake-up calls, and Bob Kuechenberg, linebacker for the Miami Dolphins during 1972's Perfect Season, was one guest Raven woke up. A few mornings, Kuechenberg beat Raven to the wake-up call. "Raven, this is Kooch," he said. "I'm up. Don't worry about calling me." One day, Kuechenberg strapped on hand weights and joined Raven for a couple miles but never completed the eight.

Miami Beach was crawling with celebrities. Ron Wood of the Rolling Stones had opened up a live music venue called

Woody's. One night, Raven was at work in the lobby when a chauffeur dragged Wood in and dropped him in a chair. "He was high as a kite," says Raven. "He was still friendly though, smiling and waving to everyone." Wood's head of long black hair rolled back, his pointy nose pointing straight up in the air. "How does he do shows like that?" asked Raven.

"Oh, we just prop him up, and he does it," said one guy in his entourage.

Another guest at the Cavalier hotel was 25-year-old actor Matt Dillon, who asked Raven for advice on the local women. Mickey Rourke stayed at the Leslie and the Cardoza, too. One afternoon, Miami native Lauren Hutton walked up to Raven on the beach. "Hey, I always see you," she said. "What's your story? Why are you running all the time?" Raven said, "It's just what I do." She asked him to watch her stuff for a minute and then came back with a signed headshot.

Through the city's facelift, Raven kept his life the same with the run and the swim. The swim streak had its hardest test in September 1988, when Hurricane Gilbert was churning up the Atlantic. Springman had gone with him, and the two swam out past the breakers. "We were like pieces of paper in the wind," says Raven. "The ocean was a whirlpool, and we were being held under longer. We started edging toward the shore, letting the waves crash over us like a mountain of water."

V
BELONGING

A guy I was in jail with told me, "You gotta find a group to be a part of or something to get involved in." I was in a really dark place, and this run just sucks the negativity out of you. God only knows where I'd be without Raven and this run. It's the best thing that ever happened to me.
—Butcher, personal trainer with a record of
200 consecutive runs

What impressed me most was the second time I showed up at Tower 5, Raven remembered my real name, nickname, where I was from now, where I originally came from, and my birthday. It was kind of freaky. I thought maybe he just got lucky with all my info for some reason, but over the years I have seen him do the same with others that show up.
—Thunder, commuter from Los Angeles, 114 runs

I always felt like an outcast . . . now this run is like my family.
—Raven

TEN

GENTLE SOUL

One night in 2012, Raven had four free tickets to a Marlins game and invited me to come with him and Miracle. Picking up the tickets at Will Call, Raven gave the stadium employee these instructions: "If someone is looking for a ticket, please give him our extra." As we approached the gate, Raven snapped his fingers. "Damn it," he said, "I should've given our extra ticket to the homeless man we passed coming out of the parking garage."

"But then we'd have to sit next to him," I said.

"I know," he replied. "He could've sat next to me."

Raven has applied this philosophy throughout his life. He will sit next to, run with, swim with, share food with, or even live with, practically anyone. To most of society the characters are addicts, street refuse, or at least marginal people. But Raven celebrates them—drawing them in—to listen and seek wisdom. Often, he writes songs about them.

"Whiskers on the Rocks" is a tune Raven wrote about a homeless man named Eugene who'd come to South Beach with his mother from Brooklyn in 1966. When his mother died in 1985, Eugene developed a fear of germs, which is an inconvenient phobia to have as a homeless person. He loved to read and dug through trashcans in search of his favorite magazines and newspapers. He said he went to high school with Colin Powell, and they used to talk global affairs in the cafeteria.

On cardboard signs, Eugene wrote public service announcements in magic marker and tried to educate the South Beach public on issues like skin cancer, transfats, and bike paths. Most people didn't read the signs (or couldn't read his handwriting) and assumed he was begging. Once Raven asked, "What's with the sign?" Eugene replied, "It's not a sign. It's a placard." So Eugene became Placard Man.

"He wouldn't touch money or accept food," recalled Raven. "One time when we were talking—in a matter of five minutes—two people tried to give him money. He told them, 'No, I'm not homeless. I'm just roughing it,' but they stuffed dollars in his pocket."

His clothes were rags. He had a gigantic beard. His toes poked through his sneakers, which looked like clown shoes, and he wore a dirty, floppy hat. He slept on the pier and sometimes got arrested for vagrancy. Once, he asked Raven to be a character witness. "I said of course," recalled Raven. "Then Eugene goes, 'Uh, would you mind trimming your beard a little?' I couldn't believe it. I was like GQ compared to him."

Placard Man received his mail at Raven's apartment. When he came to collect it, he didn't like to touch the doorbell. Shuffling up, he tilted back his head and bellowed, "ROBERT," and Raven ran to the door before his neighbors complained. Placard Man then tucked a dollar into the black glove hanging from Raven's door. "You don't have to do that," said Raven. "You're my friend." Placard Man insisted. After a year, he started leaving two dollars. "What's this?" asked Raven.

"Inflation," said Placard Man.

Other homeless people considered Eugene a role model. He never drank or cursed. All the Raven Runners who knew Placard Man liked him a lot. They had a tradition. When they ran by, Raven shouted everybody's real name—Placard Man didn't like to use nicknames—and Placard Man repeated them. "He was familiar with most people, but if it was a different or a foreign name, it'd stump him," says Raven. After all the names,

Placard Man would announce the slogan he invented for Raven: "Robert, doing his bit to keep America fit."

On why he wrote "Whiskers on the Rocks," Raven channels Johnny Cash. "I look at the outcasts and the loners and the people who are downtrodden, and I give them some light," he said. "I want to tell stories about people that life passed by and should not be passed by. We were all babies at one point. Everybody was somebody and achieved something, whether it's good or bad. If it's good, it can inspire others. If it's bad, maybe a guy heading down that path will hear the story and say, 'If I'm not careful, I'm going to end up like him.' I love the theme of redemption. Anyway, the thing is, I don't like people to be forgotten."

Raven believes that we are all one accident away from being homeless. When he sees someone in distress, he thinks, *"That could've been me. Or that could be me tomorrow."* He's written a gospel song, "Grace of God," about it. If Raven were writing his own book, he would devote a chapter to everyone whose name he remembered. In our sessions, he named literally thousands of characters. Without one positive role model in his life, Raven looked for wisdom in dark corners and tried to extract a piece of goodness from everyone, assembling a composite of qualities to emulate.

If there wasn't goodness in someone, he told me what made the person different. Sometimes, I thought that it wasn't what I saw in Raven that drew me to his story but what he made me see in others. At the first annual picnic that I attended in March, Raven introduced me to his neighbor, an 80-year-old man named Tony Gulliver who was once a successful photographer but now lived in Section Eight Housing. At the top of his long-limbed, six-foot frame sat a shock of white hair that spilled down his sideburns and wrapped around his face and lips. When he listened, his jaw moved back and forth like a typewriter. "Tony, this is White Lightning," Raven said. "I think you two are going to like talking to each other."

I sat with Tony at that picnic table for over an hour, absorbing his stories and laughing hard. He told me, "My sister got all the brains in our family. I got the athleticism. So every time she said she was smarter than me, I'd hit her real hard." With each blink, his eyes flickered between kindness, trickster, and apology. "I'm just teasing, she doesn't lord it over me at all. She won't mention she's a lot smarter than me, and I reckon I won't mention that she can't catch a football."

Your participation in talking to Tony came through listening. If someone didn't abide by the rules, he forfeited. "Here's what I do," he told me. "If I'm talking to someone that I don't want to talk to, I just look at them real serious. I look right past them, not in the eye, but they think I'm trying to look them in the eye. Then I say, real slow, 'Can you ask me that question again?' " Tony's "again" lasted five syllables and he cocked one eye wide open. "Remember don't look at them when you say it. I've never had to ask that more than three times, and the person just walks away and thinks I'm crazy."

At one point he was trying to explain how to get somewhere, and I said, "I'm sorry, Tony, I just have a terrible sense of direction."

"Never apologize for that," he said. "It's probably your best quality, because you're always finding new places." I loved that. I've quoted Tony a number of times since then, and every time I do, I feel a little like Raven.

Raven's girlfriends all approached his—um, unique—friends with varying degrees of acceptance. The Astrologer referred to new characters as Raven's dolls. "Oh, you got a new doll?" she would say. "You're putting another doll on the shelf?" (Jovial Joe, as far as I am aware, is the only person that is literally on his shelf.) The Astrologer was reluctant at first but eventually Raven found something in everyone she could relate to. That's what Raven tries to do. He wants people to relate to each other and encourage empathy. While some characters may seem tangential, in Raven's mind they are central, because the circle is

Over his forty-one-year streak, Raven has worn out 120 pairs of running shoes,
many of which he can't bear to throw away. *(Photo by Mary Beth "Yellow Rose" Koeth)*

In 1978, Raven ran his first and only race, which happened to be eight miles in South Beach. He loves the inclusive nature of running and doesn't believe in paying to run.

Raven started dating Astrologer in 1975. "After going out with her, I could never again date a woman who isn't smarter than me," he said. They are standing on the old South Beach Pier with Goliath, a bodybuilder.

Killer (*middle*) and Bulldog (*right*) were two boxers training at Miami Beach's famed Fifth Street Gym. In 1972, they invited Raven to join for "roadwork," which inspired him to start running.

Raven, at 26, with his pet kitten.
He loves animals, especially cats.
Today he has a big-headed tabby named Joe,
whom he calls his son.

In the first year of his streak, Raven ran
in a spray-painted-black cowboy hat,
which earned him a temporary nickname
of Cowboy, or Cowboy Bob.

For three and a half decades, Raven swam three tenths of a mile in the Atlantic after every run.
He still encourages Raven Runners to swim following the eight-mile run.
(Photo by Priscilla "Miracle" Ferguson)

Raven, singing with Teen Idol, a musician and lieutenant on the Beach Patrol.

Over the years,
Raven has picked up
over $1,800 in
coins and bills from
the sand and grass.
He stores his finds in a jar.
*(Photo by Priscilla
"Miracle" Ferguson)*

Placard Man, whose love of nature and exercise influenced Raven, is a Raven Run Coach.
(Photo by Priscilla "Miracle" Ferguson)

Gringo has completed over 1,600 runs with Raven, many of them while undergoing chemotherapy.
(Photo by Mary Beth "Yellow Rose" Koeth)

Hitter, Raven, Poutine, and Sheik make the southern turn of eight miles at the new fishing pier by Government Cut. *(Photo by Mary Beth "Yellow Rose" Koeth)*

Taxman, Chapter 11, and Dizzy are all in the Raven Run Hall of Fame with over 1,000 runs each. *(Photo by Priscilla "Miracle" Ferguson)*

Raven, running toward the 5th Street Lifeguard Stand on Miami Beach, where he begins every eight-mile run. *(Photo by Priscilla "Miracle" Ferguson)*

Every afternoon before the run, Raven goes to the outdoor gym on 9th Street. There, he does three sets of twenty pull-ups and chin-ups, followed by a 45-second "hang." *(Photo by Priscilla "Miracle" Ferguson)*

Raven's workout at the 9th Street Gym also includes a set of one hundred push-ups.
(Photos by Mary Beth "Yellow Rose" Koeth and Priscilla "Miracle" Ferguson)

Raven and
his girlfriend,
a photographer
named Miracle,
have been together
for nineteen years.
*(Photos by Mary
Beth "Yellow Rose"
Koeth and Priscilla
"Miracle" Ferguson)*

Raven, running next to author White Lightning, and Dizzy, on the 110,000th mile of his streak. *(Photo by Mary Beth "Yellow Rose" Koeth)*

Raven, author White Lightning, and photographer Yellow Rose before eight steaming miles in the August sun. *(Photo by Mary Beth "Yellow Rose" Koeth)*

Raven, his mother, Mary,
and his father, Walter.
Raven was their only child.

Raven calls himself a collector, but most people who have been inside his nest use the word "hoarder."
(Photo by Mary Beth "Yellow Rose" Koeth)

When Raven's collections became a potential fire hazard, Gringo helped him clean up.
(Photo by Mary Beth "Yellow Rose" Koeth)

During Hurricane Sandy —
and many other storms —
Raven ran his usual eight miles.
*(Photos by Priscilla "Miracle"
Ferguson and Mary Beth
"Yellow Rose" Koeth)*

Raven became an ordained minister in order to marry Creve Coeur and Hollywood Flasher,
a couple who fell in love while running with him. Raven performed the ceremony during a run.
(Photos by Rudolph "Taxman" Volenec)

Miami Beach Mayor Philip Levine proclaimed February 10, 2016, "Robert 'Raven' Kraft Day." Pictured here, the Mayor and commissioners — one of whom, "Relay Ricky," is a Raven Runner — honor Raven's achievements. *(Photo by Laura Lee "White Lightning" Huttenbach)*

The Judge, a Circuit Court Judge in Miami, ran with Raven up until three days before giving birth. *(Photo by Maury "Encyclopedia" Udell)*

(Photo by Mary Beth "Yellow Rose" Koeth)

so big. He thinks the more we ostracize weirdness, the less colorful the inside. He worries that people are becoming the same, almost robotic. He longs for the time when the village idiot was mocked but also celebrated.

According to Raven, the funniest person he has ever met was a whistle blower at a train station from Essen, Germany, called Handshue. Handshue came running up to him at the lifeguard stand one day in the late eighties wearing one black glove. "I see you running, running, running—like a gorilla," shouted Handshue, rubbing his chest hair. "I am the *handschuh*, like the Raven! I will run with you!" *Handschuh* meant glove—literally a shoe for a hand—in German. Handshue would run a mile or two—up to six—but never finished eight. If a tourist held up a cracker or a potato chip to feed the birds, Handshue jumped up and plucked it out of their hands with his teeth. Then, flapping his arms with a high-pitched caw, Handshue bellowed, "Huh! I am now a seagull!"

Once, at 23rd Street on a rainy day, Handshue, carrying a wedding cake, tracked Raven down. "I have a wedding cake for Raven," said Handshue. He had found it on the beach, covered in sand. Another time, Handshue showed up to run with a leash tied around his neck. "I am a dog," he said to Raven. "You will run with me, your dog. Arf, arf." Seeing Handshue's delight, Raven couldn't say no. For several miles, Raven ran down the beach with Handshue barking on a leash.

Handshue knew the price of every hotel in South Beach, and the cheapest place he found was the Roselle Hotel, a few blocks off the ocean at 6th Street. Like many run-down places at the time, the Roselle was infested with rats, and their high-pitched squeaks were keeping Handshue up at night. One afternoon, he came to the beach hopping and prancing with a wooden rattrap clenched between his teeth. On the rattrap was a dead rat, swinging back and forth beneath his chin. "Handshue, what are you doing?" asked Raven.

Handshue transferred the trap to his ungloved hand so he could speak. "I am celebrating the death of a rat!"

Raven recalled: "So we're running down the beach, and he's got the trap in his mouth, and all the old people were going, *Oh, my God*. At the turn at the jetty, the Client [a lifeguard] pulls up in the Beach Patrol vehicle and goes, 'Raven, you gotta tell him that you can't do that.' So I turn to Handshue and say, 'Handshue, this is America. You can't be running down the beach with the rat on the trap.' "

Handshue again explained the rat had been impeding a peaceful slumber, but Raven didn't budge. "No, no, no," Raven told him. "Put it in the trashcan."

Raven thought Hitler had something to do with his insanity—Handshue was born in 1932—so Raven asked him about it. "Hitler, yes," said Handshue, pointing to himself. "Youth Corps brainwash kids." Handshue visited South Beach every summer and each year, he got a little drunker. On his last year, he fell in love with Margaret the Mermaid (who swam with Raven and a British lady called the Prune). In the middle of the night outside her place, Handshue was shouting at the top of his lungs, "Margaret! Mermaid! I love you! Hallelujah!"

The cops stopped Raven the next day. "We arrested your friend, that German guy," said the policeman. "He was walking down Ocean Drive screaming hallelujah all night."

When Raven finished telling this story, he looked me straight in the eye and said, "Every so often, Handshue was a little over the top."

So Raven doesn't always discriminate wisdom from weirdness. To Raven, something memorable is worth remembering. "But if I had to pick just one person I looked up to for life and working out," Raven told me, sitting at his apartment, "it'd be the Man of Many Rings." A former wrestler, the Man wore heavy silver rings on every finger—skulls, Indian heads, a cross, Jesus on a cross, or a Bible. Varicose veins crawled up both his legs, winding between scars from his service in World War II and Korea. The Man of Many Rings lived to work out, and he rode his bike all over town, from South Beach to Hialeah to get roasted chicken. "Being close to nature is like being close to God," he said often. His self-made gym was in the park on 3rd Street. Standing behind a big concrete bench, he lifted it slowly, holding it in place with quivering biceps. When he wasn't lifting the bench, he was sitting on it, quietly reading his Bible. Raven admired the Man of Many Rings' strength, spirituality, and bond with the environment.

When Raven started running, the Man of Many Rings nodded approvingly. "You're doing great," he said. "There's nothing like running." He couldn't run on land himself because of war wounds, but he jogged in the ocean. "He was like my father figure," said Raven. "A gentle soul, but someone you wouldn't want to mess with." I asked if the Man of Many Rings ever admonished him for drinking before the streak. Raven said no. "He wasn't like that. He'd just tell me I reminded him of his oldest son. It wasn't until later I found out his oldest son was in jail."

One day in 1987, Raven noticed a pamphlet sticking out from the pages of the Man's Bible. "What are you reading?" Raven asked. Man of Many Rings first deflected the question but wound up confessing it was a motorcycle magazine. "You're not thinking of buying a motorcycle, are you?" asked Raven. "You're sixty-two. You could get killed."

The Man of Many Rings bought a Harley and on March 12, 1988, he drove into the back of a car on North Miami Avenue, dying on impact. He had no family and no savings for the burial, so Raven collected donations from lifeguards and Beach regulars. He needed $500. When he called the county mortuary to pick up his rings—maybe they were worth something—nobody had seen any. After three weeks of fundraising, Raven was $200 short. "This man fought for our country," explained Raven, still disappointed. "He was a war hero at Iwo Jima, a Purple Heart recipient. I couldn't fail him." But the Man of Many Rings went in a pine box in a pauper's grave somewhere in Dade County.

The *Herald* published "The Raven and the Rings," an article chronicling Raven's unsuccessful plight to honor his friend. Raven is quoted: "He had a tough life and being buried in a pauper's grave, a veteran of two wars, it's not fair." Closing the article is a poem by Raven in memory of the Man of Many Rings:

> *For the lives he saved*
> *What did he get*
> *But a pauper's grave*
> *And a memory I'd not forget.*

Years later, Raven got a call from a 29-year-old man looking for someone who knew his father, Chuck Holmes. "I was good friends with your father," said Raven. "He was one of my heroes." They talked for a while, and Raven told stories of how Rings had led by example, gone to church, and was the one who encouraged Raven to work out and stay healthy. "By the way," Raven said, "how did you get my number?"

Someone from the old age home where his grandfather had lived told him that his father was friends with a guy who runs on the beach every day. "So I called lifeguard headquarters," he said. "They told me, 'Well, it has to be the Raven,' and gave me your number." He hadn't seen his father in twenty-five years. After the phone call, Raven sent him a long letter with pictures. "We really respected your father," Raven wrote.

Raven wanted a way to honor his favorite characters who couldn't run eight miles but enriched the Raven Run experience. "So we came up with the idea of coaches," said Raven. "There's pretty much six characteristics for a coach. They gotta be homeless, alcoholic, annoying, colorful, around for a long time, and feed birds. Some get all six, some only have one or two." At the first banquet in 1996, Placard Man overwhelmed the pool with votes and became the first official Raven Run Coach, but Raven has retroactively named coaches dating back to 1975. (The Astrologer and Handshue are both official coaches.)

Raven realizes that songs like "Whiskers on the Rocks" might not make him rich or famous, but he has paid tribute to Placard Man, immortalizing him in words. "It's not what people are buying these days," he told me. "But that's okay, White Lightning. Maybe when I'm dead and gone people will like it. I'm just no Taylor Swift."

ELEVEN

ANDREW

The 1992 hurricane season was so quiet that bored reporters were calling the National Hurricane Center and asking, "Where are the storms?"

In the third week of August, the Center finally had an answer: A weak storm was developing off the Atlantic Coast, but scientists predicted it would fall apart before reaching land. On August 22, that changed. Hurricane Andrew was a concentrated, fast-moving hurricane unlike the slow, sprawling giants that had come the years before. South Florida residents had two days to prepare for the third Category-Five hurricane ever to land in the Continental United States.

Miami Beach ordered an evacuation. Residents drove to newer homes of friends and family living in South Miami. City buses carried people to high school auditoriums on the mainland. The Astrologer, worried about her beloved cat, started driving north. But at a gas station, the wind blew open her car door and the cat scurried away, never to be seen again.

Raven's roommate at the time was a man who looked like Drew Carey and turned every conversation to sex. "Dr. Pleasure was probably my worst roommate of all time," reckons Raven. He weighed 250 pounds and drove a powder blue Pinto. "All you could see was his gigantic head," Raven says. At one o'clock every day, he announced, "Oh! My soap operas," changing the channel from whatever Raven was watching. He used Raven's toaster oven and never cleaned up, leaving crumbs all over the kitchen.

On August 22, Dr. Pleasure asked Raven if they should evacuate. "I'm going to stay," Raven told him. "But you should do whatever you think." He decided to ride out the storm with Raven. They drove his Pinto to the beach and filled up plastic grocery sacks with sand to stack against the living room's sliding glass door.

On the beach the next day, lifeguards were busy clearing the stands. As usual, Raven ran his eight miles, followed by a three-tenth-mile swim. "The water was a little rough, but it was nothing like the swim I took with Springman during Gilbert," noted Raven.

Baseball Man was waiting for Raven when he came out of the water. Baseball Man was chubby and baldheaded with a cigarette dangling from lips and tobacco dribble on his shirt. He cruised the beach rummaging through trashcans (his favorite find was Kentucky Fried Chicken) and searching for someone to answer his baseball trivia. When tourists didn't answer correctly, he said, "You don't know your baseball. You're not good Americans."

When Baseball Man first met Raven, Pete Rose had just been banned from baseball for gambling. "Can you believe Pete Rose is out of baseball!" shouted Baseball Man. "You know how many hits he got?"

Raven answered 4,256.

The hair of Baseball Man's bushy blond eyebrows stood up straight, all the way to his forehead, and his eyes bulged. "You know your baseball," he said. After that, Baseball Man was usually waiting for Raven at the 6th Street lifeguard stand, lying in the sand. Raven often would invite him over to watch the World Series and eat a can of Campbell's soup for dinner.

Before Hurricane Andrew, Baseball Man asked, "Do you think I could stay with you?"

Raven said of course. When Leigh the lifeguard heard that, she dug out a bar of soap from her lifeguard stand and tossed it to Baseball Man. She said, "Raven, if you're going to bring him in, make him clean up a little." Baseball Man jumped in the ocean fully clothed, soap in hand, splashing in the bubbles. When he was satisfied with the job, Baseball Man walked up to Raven, put his hand in the air, and asked him to smell his armpit. "Look, I'm clean!"

That afternoon a news station interviewed lifeguards, who told the reporter, Susan Candiotti, that she had to speak to Raven. "Are you really planning to run through the hurricane?" asked Candiotti.

"I have to," Raven said on the evening news. "But this is my thing. I don't recommend it for other people, because it's dangerous." That night Candiotti concluded her segment with: "You heard it from Raven. He's going to run *no matter what*."

On the way home, Raven checked in with Placard Man to see if he needed a place to stay. Placard Man planned to take cover at the Flamingo Park racquetball courts, so Raven headed home with Baseball Man. Back at the apartment, Dr. Pleasure wasn't pleased with Raven's hospitality toward the Beach's homeless population. Baseball Man bossed Dr. Pleasure around, telling him how to set up the sandbags, and the two bickered all night.

Around two in the morning it sounded like a freight train was about to barrel through the wall. Winds whipped around at 110 miles per hour. Every time lightning struck, Baseball Man let out a bloodcurdling scream. "It's all over!" he shouted. "It's all over." The windows rattled. The sky was painted green and purple. Baseball Man continued predicting the apocalypse, and Dr. Pleasure told him, "Cut it out."

The lights flickered twice, and the power went out for good. Raven was on the couch, holding a flashlight and pressing his ear against the transistor radio. The National Weather Service warned everyone to stay indoors. "Do not think you are in any way safe," came the announcement. "If you have not hunkered down and put the mattress over you—friends, this is the time to do it."

Twenty miles south, on the mainland, wind hit 160 miles per hour. Gusts peeled roofs off like foil from a casserole dish. Trees crushed cars like aluminum cans. On the ground floor of Mercy Hospital, a twelve-foot storm surge carried a foot and a half of water through the front doors. Fish were flopping down the hallways. In the parking lot, a fifty-foot cargo ship ran aground.

At 326 Ocean Drive, Raven prayed. Nobody slept. By seven o'clock, winds had dropped to around fifty miles per hour, gusting at seventy. Raven announced he was going to check out the damage on the beach, and Dr. Pleasure came along. Streets were blocked with felled trees. A neighbor's roof was covering Raven's bicycle. "The beach looked like a scene from *Robinson Crusoe*," recalls Raven. "Dead fish were all over, suffocated by sand in their gills. Seaweed and mangrove thorns were everywhere." Close to the shoreline, Raven made out a lumpy mass wrapped in plastic. Walking closer, he recognized the bushy beard poking out of the plastic burrito. "Placard Man!" said Raven. "How you doing?"

Placard Man had survived the night at Flamingo Park, but he didn't get a wink of sleep. Now he was trying to get some peace on the beach, but the rising tide kept waking him up and forcing him to move back every half-hour.

On the way home, they saw Susan Candiotti again. For the second day in a row, Raven made the evening news. "How'd you make out, Raven?" asked Candiotti. "Well, we made it," said Raven. "We got a little water in the house, but everything's all right." Then Candiotti turned to Dr. Pleasure. "What about you, sir? How come you didn't go to a shelter?"

"Well," said Dr. Pleasure, "Raven said it'd be all right." The camera panned to Raven and his disheveled, windblown hair, crooked glasses, looking like a wet rat.

"You had enough faith in that man?" asked Candiotti.

"Yeah, yeah," said Dr. Pleasure. "But next time I'll go to a shelter."

Baseball Man hit the road right after the storm, and Dr. Pleasure moved out soon after. "He met some woman, thank God, and he moved to her place," recalls Raven. "The address, of all things, is 6969 Collins Avenue. Oh, he loved it. He's in his glory. Then he meets this Russian woman in the elevator and married her and moved to Milton, Florida. I nicknamed her Mrs. Butterworth, I don't know why."

For seven months, Raven didn't hear anything from Baseball Man until a mission in Oregon called asking if he knew George Smith. "Yeah, I do," Raven told the woman. "He's a good friend of mine."

"Well he came in last night, had a heart attack, and gave your name as a friend. He died. We can't find any relatives." Raven said he knew George had a sister and a mother. "Well, we'll try to look," she said.

A few days later, Baseball Man's sister called Raven. "I heard you were George's friend," she said. They talked for hours. "His sister was a regular woman," says Raven. She told Raven that after recovering in AA, George got married and had a daughter, but he couldn't handle the responsibility. He started drifting. She told Raven, "I'm real happy he was your friend." She sent pictures of Baseball Man as a young man and, every year, she sent Raven a Christmas card.

When I asked Raven how many roommates he'd had over the years, he listed more than a dozen, including the Miser, Budget Man, the Bohemian, the Giggler, and Vulcan Pilot. "Vulcan Pilot was the best roommate ever," said Raven. In seven years—from 2002 to 2009—Vulcan Pilot, who has close to three hundred runs, spent a total of three nights at the apartment.

Raven was as generous with his mailbox as his living room couch. Over the years, many members of the homeless or itinerant South Beach community have used his address to get mail. To name a few, there was Placard Man, Systems Man, Big Unit, Stalker, Baseball Man, the Streak, Burke's Law, and Experiment Man.

After Hurricane Andrew, a 26-year-old runner from Madrid took Dr. Pleasure's room. Corvette Man had recently taken a leave of absence from his job as a flight attendant at Iberia Airlines to train full-time for triathlons. To cover rent, Corvette Man worked as a valet, a job that doubled as training; he sprinted from the parking lots back to the front of the hotel.

When I met Corvette Man running on Raven's 64th birthday in 2014, he was still speedy. I asked what it was like being Raven's roommate for three years. "The best years of my life," he replied. "I used to see Raven when I was a kid on vacation with my parents in South Beach. He is an athlete." If it takes one to know one, Corvette Man is qualified to make the assessment; he completed his first marathon at age 14 (he's since lost count), and he's finished many Iron Mans. Today he hopes to convince Raven to cut back on the mileage. "Pretty soon Raven won't be able to walk," he told me. Corvette Man honors Raven's run and his songwriting, but most of all he respects Raven's way of life. "The thing I learned from Raven," he said, "is to keep it simple."

MOTHER NATURE HAD GIVEN RAVEN A BREAK during Hurricane Andrew, but She was less forgiving on the morning of April 24, 1994. Shuttling between his couch and bathroom with food poisoning and diarrhea, Raven didn't know how he was going to run. *At least it can't get any worse*, he thought.

Walking out to the beach, there was a coldness in the air. The sky turned black and commenced a show of lightning. Within a mile, golf ball–size hail hammered his shoulders and face. Pulling his glasses off so they wouldn't break, he felt lumps rising on his scalp. "The surfers had their boards covering their heads. You could hear the pounding—boom, boom, boom."

Giggler was taking refuge in his lifeguard stand. "All of a

sudden, I see Raven coming toward us with blood running down his face," recalls the Giggler. "He was getting bludgeoned—like, stoned by God. I remember the captain pulled up in the truck and told me to get in, and I was like, 'Uh-uh, no way. I'm not stepping one foot out there.' "

At the next lifeguard stand, Raven ducked under an awning to take refuge. "If I had run two or three more minutes, I could've died," he told me.

"At least you had the sense to stop," I said.

"I didn't stop," he said. "I ran in place." When the hail let up, Raven took small, delicate steps to finish the eight, sliding over a layer of ice cubes. "That was a hairy one," he remarked. "But the fear at least made my food poisoning go away."

DONNA AND RAVEN FOUGHT all the time, but the make-ups were worth it. "With the Astrologer, I could get away with anything," says Raven. "With Donna, it was the opposite. She was extremely jealous." The roller-coaster romance kick-started Raven's song-writing. "I wrote more songs about her than I did about anybody in my life."

Titles inspired by his spiky, silver-haired muse include "Donna Done Me Wrong," "Give and Take," and "She was my Bonnie, and I was her Clyde." Raven teamed up with a life-guard called Teen Idol, who sang and played guitar, and the Giggler, who played the flute. On the sidewalk outside the Revere Hotel, the motley crew would play for change, which they usually gave to a homeless person at the end of the night. In all, Raven and Teen Idol have written thirty-five songs together—Raven comes up with an idea and the lyrics, and Teen Idol fills in the rest, including the melody and instrumentals. Their most requested song, "Have You Seen This Man?" is "about God, actually," Teen Idol told me, adding, "but I'm not very religious, so it could be about any man or woman." Teen Idol taught Raven how to copyright his work, and Raven holds copyright to 560 songs. "To be honest, most of our songs are doom and gloom," Teen Idol told me. "Let's see. There's 'Difficult Love,' 'Born Under a Violent Moon,' and 'Growing Old Before My Time.' " He laughed. "That one has a line: 'Grey streaks in my hair, can I even make it up the stairs?' It's pretty depressing."

Teen Idol is a lieutenant on the Beach Patrol and keeps watch from his lifeguard stand at 30th Street, which is a block away from where I lived. I became friends with him, checking in before I went swimming. When he had a break, he swam with me.

Teen Idol has five Raven runs, thirteen Raven swims, and fifteen Spring Picnic performances with Raven. "I've run twice with him in really bad thunderstorms—lightning crashing around us, and I have a thing about lightning," said Teen Idol. "I go, 'Bob, I think it's getting a little hot out here, and he's like, 'It'll pass. It'll pass.' I've seen him when it's pouring down rain so hard you can barely see, and he's running by himself."

Among the lifeguards, he said, Raven's reputation falls somewhere between psychotic and inspiring. "His gumption," said Teen Idol, "I mean, that's something." It extends to Raven's songwriting. "Art is a rough business; most of what you send out just goes in the trash. But he keeps plugging away." Since 1989, Raven has sent out his work to publishers every other day.

On what draws people from all over to run with Raven, Teen Idol believes, "It's the fortitude. When you find out the guy hasn't missed a day in forty years, you think, *How does that work?*"

CHANNEL SURFING ONE EVENING IN 1994, Raven came upon a documentary about the man who had stolen his song in Nashville in 1970. In the television program, the man confessed that for much of the early seventies, he was stoned or drunk, and those years were cloaked in fog. Raven had always thought the man had done it on purpose—to deny a young, hopeful writer his dream—but listening to him, Raven realized: *Maybe the guy just woke up the next morning with new material in his pocket and chalked it up to high inspiration.*

The hate Raven had been carrying became too heavy. "I think about what could have happened if he hadn't stolen my song," says Raven. "I could have gotten rich and famous, but maybe I could have fallen for its excesses. Maybe I would lead an unhealthy life with drugs and alcohol—no running, and no real friends. So it all worked out. That's how I try to look at it."

Of the people in his life that he respected most, he noticed a common thread. Everyone had overcome a demon. "Johnny and Waylon," says Raven, "they got sober, they found God— they beat their devil and made great music." Raven came to understand that the song thief was in an early stage of battling the devil when they met. The devil had won that round in Nashville, and Raven's lyrics were his prize. But Raven got a concession, and that was the Raven Run.

At the end of 1994, a lifeguard called the Man of a Thousand Faces organized a 20th birthday party for Raven's streak. After Raven performed with the Giggler and Teen Idol, as he was thanking his friends, a lifeguard called Pin Head shouted, "Here's to another twenty years!"

Raven, at 44, was thinking maybe it was time to settle down and have a Raven, Jr. He had chosen the streak over family, marriage, health, and jobs. What was Pin Head suggesting— that as a 65-year-old in 2015, he'd still be running?

"Twenty more years?" repeated Raven.

"Yeah," said Pin Head. "What's another twenty years?"

Raven shook his head and thought, *Man, you are crazy.*

VI
ACCOUNTABILITY

If you tell Raven you're going to be there, you
better be there, because you know he'll be there.
When you're feeling bad, you're more likely to let yourself
down than someone else. Even when I don't feel like
running eight miles, I come to the beach because I
told Raven I would, and I always feel better.

—Red Bandit, 35 years old, 178 runs

When I moved to Miami Beach, I saw Raven showing up
every day at the lifeguard stand in front of my apartment. I
was drawn by the consistency, the structure that it added to
my day as well. I could be absolutely sure of him showing up
every day at the same time, ready to take whoever wanted to
join him on a run or more like a running journey.

—Jurisprudence, Belgian attorney, 120 runs

I just want people to do what they say.

—Raven

TWELVE

SPINAL STENOSIS

Since the New Year's resolution twenty years before, Raven hadn't set a long-term goal. Every day, he resolved to run the next day. "I'm training to come back tomorrow," he says often. But in 1995, his back made tomorrow look impossible.

Trouble started when he helped Reverend, the fourteenth runner, move apartments. After carrying boxes up and down a narrow stairwell, Raven felt a dull pain settle in his lower back. A few weeks later it felt like someone was whacking him with a paddle. Each step sent shocks of pain from his glutes down his legs. Eight miles was two and a half hours of pure torture. He couldn't find a comfortable position. He tried to remember his mother's advice for when something bad happened—*just don't think about it*—but hurt was pumping through his body. At age 44, Raven swallowed his first aspirin.

By August, it felt like someone had grabbed hold of his spinal cord and was ringing it out like a dishrag. Teen Idol remembers seeing him. "He couldn't walk," Teen Idol told me. "I said, 'You gotta quit, man.' He's like, 'Nah, I gotta run.'"

On one run, after enduring ninety minutes and 5.9 miles, Raven couldn't take one more step and dropped in the sand.

I had to make sure I'd heard him correctly. *There were days when he hadn't run eight miles?*

"For me to go under, it was really bad," Raven told me, sitting in his living room in 2013. "I couldn't walk. I couldn't stand. I remember I was just shuffling. But I was out there."

He has never run fewer than ninety minutes or 5.5 miles, and he keeps track of his mileage on a calendar. When he goes even a tenth of a mile under or over eight, he marks it to keep an accurate record.

I must've looked disappointed when I learned that he hadn't in fact run eight miles every day for forty years, and Raven sensed it. "I tortured myself for more than an hour and a half," he explained, hunched over on the couch. "I was getting close—six, seven miles—but for a few months in 1995 and again for an incident in 2005, I'm sorry to say, White Lightning, there were days I was going under eight."

He was so desperate for help he went to Coral Gables on the mainland to see a surgeon. An X-ray later, Raven was diagnosed with spinal stenosis, arthritis, sciatica, scoliosis, and degenerative discs. The doctor said he needed to stop running and get surgery. "But I can't do that," said Raven.

She had nothing else to tell him. Raven got a second opinion at a doctor's office in South Beach, then a third in North Miami Beach. Every doctor had the same order: Quit running. Get surgery. The streak was killing him. But Raven couldn't survive without running.

What does a person do when the thing he loves is both killing him and keeping him alive?

Corvette Man took him to a natural healer who worked in Aventura. Once a week, Corvette Man drove Raven to get acupuncture and ultrasound. In between appointments, when he was moving and when he was still, everything hurt. He thought the streak was over.

But one day he had an idea, and it came from a lifeguard named Eggplant Man. From his stand at 6th Street, Eggplant Man was holding a calculator and a notebook when he saw Raven running his way. "Hey, Raven," shouted Eggplant Man, "You know you've run like seventy-four hundred days in

a row?" Raven didn't know that. "If you keep going," continued Eggplant Man, "you might get to ten thousand."

That sounded pretty cool.

After the run, Raven sat down with a pencil and paper. If he
kept pace, he calculated that he'd hit 10,000 days—80,000
miles—in seven years, sometime in May 2002.

Raven took stock of what he was creating. Sixty people had
completed eight miles with him, but on most days, he still ran
alone. He had run through Mariel, the Cocaine Cowboys, a
blighted neighborhood, and beach dredging. In the tumult, Raven
took solace in the consistency of his daily run. Anything was sur-
mountable.

He didn't want to quit. In fact the streak was just getting
good: Taxman wanted to organize the Awards dinner. Raven
was even getting media coverage: *Seven-Thirty*, a local television program that became *Deco Drive*, did a short story. The
show attracted more attention than the newspaper articles. For
the first time in his life, Raven felt like he was contributing
something to society. He had found his niche.

On the last Monday in January 1996 at Puerto Sagua, a Cuban
restaurant in South Beach, Raven hosted the inaugural Raven
Run banquet. There were seven award categories: Top Runner
(Sailor), Top Swimmer (Algae Man), Top Athlete (Vulcan
Pilot), Rookie of the Year (Question Man), Most Improved
(Taxman), Comeback of the Year (Budget Man), and Event of
the Year (Copy Kid, for being the youngest Raven Runner at
age ten).

There were no time categories. "That's when people push
themselves and get hurt," Raven told me. "The Raven Run is
not a race. It's about finishing." The fast accomplish the same
as the slow. "The only times I'm interested in are good times
and fun times."

The most prestigious final honor was induction into the Hall
of Fame. As a template, Raven used the BBWAA's (Baseball
Writers' Association of America) rules. To be eligible, a run-

ner has to be on Raven's official list for at least five years. The top five runners according to completed runs appear on a ballot. Election is through votes, though ballots are not secret. (Raven counts them and can recognize handwriting and tells nominees and other voters alike who is in the lead and why.) In 1996, Vulcan Pilot was the first inductee into the Raven Run Hall of Fame.

With chronic pain, a person needs a long-term goal because, day-to-day, the tomorrows don't seem worth it. At the banquet, he made his first long-term running goal since the original resolution of 1975: He would run 10,000 days in a row—about six more years—until May 18, 2002. "I may have held on to things a little too long in my life," said Raven. "But I am not a quitter."

A few weeks after the first banquet, the acupuncture started working, and Raven's back pain went away for a little while. But the taste of chronic pain made him sensitive to the fact that, sometimes, people just can't run eight miles. "I said that if I couldn't do eight, I can't make everyone else do it," said Raven.

So began the tradition of a "partial." To get on the list at first, runners must finish eight. After that, you're allowed to do between three and five miles, which Raven will combine and tally up so that he still keeps track according to eight-mile segments. There is a stigma—encouraged by Raven—against those who run partials. When I hurt my back playing beach volleyball, I started doing partials and felt like I had to apologize. "Don't worry, White Lightning," Raven told me. "A partial is better than nothing."

I ATTENDED MY FIRST RAVEN RUN BANQUET in January 2012 and sat across from the Giggler at Puerto Sagua Restaurant. The Giggler is someone that I've never consciously smiled around, but his positive aura just makes my lips curl upward. For dinner, he ordered a peach cobbler and a mango milkshake. "I have a sweet tooth, too," I told him. "What's your favorite dessert?"

"I'd say Mrs. Motts's German chocolate cake."

"Oh, I've never heard of that," I said.

"Mrs. Motts was my next-door neighbor in Detroit." The Giggler, who wore a plastic recorder around his neck like a necklace, had brought a portable sound machine and a microphone for Raven. We didn't have a private room or a formal program. At some point Raven just stood up and started giving out awards while non-affiliated patrons tried to maintain dinner conversations and wondered what the heck was going on.

The Giggler had started working on Beach Patrol in 1982 and described his introduction to Raven like this: "Another lifeguard told me, 'You gotta meet Raven. He's an incredible athlete and the nicest guy. You'll see him. You can set your watch by the Raven.' So my shift started at eight thirty, and I'm waiting, waiting—noon, one, two, three—no Raven. Then around four, he starts coming up, just like today, black shorts, glove, and nobody's with him, just running in circles talking to me." It took the Giggler a decade to attempt the eight miles, but he made the list in 1992—number 30—and now runs with Raven at least once a year and always swims.

I have been to every banquet since 2012 and usually they are very nice events. In 2013, I received the Fitness award, and I invited my mother to come. She'd already met Raven and several other runners—whom she liked a lot—and kind of knew what to expect. Unfortunately, that was the year that Raven insisted on inducting Firecracker into the Hall of Shame.

Firecracker has over a thousand runs with Raven and is in the Hall of Fame, but their relationship soured around the time when Firecracker went to prison. (Chapter 11 told me later that he'd actually given her a ride to jail.) In 2013, Firecracker had just gotten out before the banquet. Jail time seemed enough of a shame to most of us. But Raven said, "Well it's by vote, and a few people voted for her."

When he presented Firecracker with the Hall of Shame certificate, she hooted and hollered, and my mother just looked at me like, *What kind of running group is this?*

A lot of runners don't like the Hall of Shame, but the Raven Run is no democracy. On the write-in ballot for Hall of Shame, I always scribble it out with a note to Raven that I don't support this practice.

It started in the late nineties as a joke with a flaky runner called Colonel. Raven believes that the Hall of Shame should encourage people to become more trustworthy and reliable. "Oh, White Lightning, it's easy to get out of the Hall of Shame," he says. "You just have to do what you say."

THIRTEEN

You're the Miracle

Priscilla Ferguson, Raven's girlfriend for the last twenty years, can talk for hours about fishing and hunting. Once, when we were running together, I asked about her first date with Raven. "My only strategy was to set the hook deep," she said.

"From a fisherman, that means something," I said.

"Oh, yeah, I'm the type of person who will spend all night sharpening every hook in the tackle box before going fishing." She went on to describe, in detail, how to sharpen fishhooks, emphasizing it's not the tip of the hook that matters but the side. Equally important was tying a good knot. "That's why I stopped smoking pot," she said. "When I was high, I couldn't remember how to tie the knots, and my line kept breaking." Now marijuana is no part of her life, and she can tie a Bimini Twist with her eyes closed. "It's beautiful to tie a Bimini Twist," she said. "It's like a dance."

She riffed for thirty minutes, and I listened closely; I'd thought it was a metaphor for their relationship, but when she warned me that decaying fish skeletons excrete an alkaline component that dissolves boat propellers, I realized that she was just talking about fishing. "From five years old, I could easily tell the difference between the wake of a stingray, a bone fish, or a blue fish," she told me. "My father taught me to pay attention to details. I'm not saying I wouldn't have become a photographer without that, but from him I learned how to see things."

On her childhood, she says her parents reigned with a "cascading tirade of logic." To illustrate, she gave this example: One time, she took a cookie from the cookie jar. "Did you take the cookie from the cookie jar?" her mother asked. Priscilla answered, "I was hungry." Her mother said, "That's not the question I asked. Answer the question I asked. It's a yes or no answer, Pris. Did you or did you not take the cookie from the cookie jar?"

"There was absolutely no wiggle room," recalled Miracle. "That was from the age of eighteen months. It's part of the reason I'm so damaged."

Another relationship that did damage was her first marriage. She and her husband lived in a small house on a five-acre farm surrounded by eighteen uninhabited acres. Sometimes, when her husband drank too much, he would lock Priscilla in the bathroom. Once, after a day of captivity, she ran the hot water and steamed the bathroom like a sauna. After shedding a couple pounds of water weight, she greased herself up with soap and slid her way out the tiny window above the shower.

Another time, she and her husband had just come back from a sailing trip to the Bahamas. While she was making a dinner of stuffed pork chops and collard greens, her husband was drinking bourbon. As soon as the food hit the table, he shoveled in a fork of steaming greens, which burned his tongue and mouth. Furious, he grabbed her ponytail and dangled her face in front of him, then threw a glass of bourbon into her open eyes. She could only hear the clicking of his lighter. Once, twice, three times—when he realized the lighter was out of fluid, and he couldn't set his wife on fire.

The next day she got a fax machine and a lawyer and six weeks later, she was divorced. Shortly after, while hunting, her ex-husband fired his shotgun from a blind in a tree. The kickback sent him tumbling eighteen feet to the ground, from which he was picked up a quadriplegic.

Now Miracle carries a baseball bat in her car. But she cannot shake a fear of entrapment. Her nightmare is a cramped, dark space that reminds her of that bathroom.

Raven lives in a ground-floor apartment and keeps his blinds drawn. Objects of his hoarding spill out of every corner and pile up on the ground and under tables, like we're one sneeze away from an avalanche. When Miracle feels trapped, her instinct is to flee. Raven's greatest fear is of abandonment. When Miracle flees, Raven is in his most vulnerable, terrified state that he will forever be alone. "We have these two terrible conflicts of entrapment and abandonment," Raven says. "It takes a lot of trust."

It has also taken counseling. Miracle says her reaction is nothing personal. "It's just after thirty hours with Raven and his—uh—rigid schedule, I start thinking, *It would be nice to be at my house now, with my dogs.* So I leave." She returns to her home, an hour away in Palmetto Bay, where Raven has never spent the night.

THEIR RELATIONSHIP BEGAN in snapshots. In 1994, Miracle, who is seven years younger than Raven, was spending a lot of time on the beach documenting characters and nature with her camera. She saw Raven running all the time, but knew him "as nothing more than an annoying silhouette" in the background of her pictures. His presence "commanded so much attention" and would throw off the weight of her photo. One day, late in the afternoon, Miracle was standing by the rocks at the jetty, camera loaded with black-and-white film around her neck, admiring a rainbow that stretched across the purple sky. Raven walked up—he had a massive crush on this new blond surfer-girl—and said, "There's a nice rainbow, you should get a picture of that."

His comment upset Miracle. "It's what any normal person would say," she admits. "But I really chewed him out. I told him, 'How can I improve on something like that?' " Scared of her temper, Raven backed away and admired from a distance.

Around Christmas, Raven was at a neighbor's party with Donna when Miracle showed up with her boyfriend Charles, a pale, bald intellectual artist. "Miracle's holding court, talking about fishing, using bad words—you know how she talks," says Raven. "I thought, *That's a cool chick*." At the party, Miracle was attracted to Raven, particularly his strong upper body, but she didn't talk to him. "I'm not the cheating kind," she says. She liked that Raven was dating an older woman because "I knew he wasn't a phony. He was with Donna for who she was, not how she looked."

The next year, after breaking up with Donna, Raven saw Miracle on the beach. "Hey, are you still seeing that guy Charles?" he asked. "He's a little strange."

"Oh, he's an artist," she said. "They're like that. But no, we're not seeing each other anymore." Raven handed her his business card, which listed his profession—songwriter—and his number—531-RAVE. He asked her out, and she said maybe, tucking his business card in her shoe.

The next run-in, she was sitting at 3rd Street on a picnic blanket. He sat down next to her. "I can't remember exactly what he said or if he tried to kiss me, but I told him, 'Why don't you try flirting?' I specifically remembered using that word, flirt. I wanted to be teased a bit." Before she dismissed him, he handed her a copy of the official running list. Then he got up and started running. A few seconds later, when he was only about thirty yards away, she realized she had forgotten to tell him something, so she got up and started chasing him. "You think it's only thirty yards, it should be easy to catch someone," she says. "But no, in the soft sand, it was impossible. I couldn't do it. That's when I first came to understand how difficult the run was."

For months after that encounter, unbeknownst to Raven, she studied the list. She found the culture fascinating. She decided, "I will have that man." On what initially drew her to Raven, she said, "It was a carnal thing." She hadn't run a step in twenty-three years since snapping her back in a waterskiing accident, but toward the end of 1996, she started training.

On November 23, Raven was running with Corvette Man when Miracle appeared. "Come on, run with us," said Raven. So she did. "Of course they tricked me into doing the whole eight miles," she says. But at the end, she threw her hands up in the air and proclaimed, "It's a miracle."

"You're the Miracle," said Raven. They went on their first date after the swim, to dinner at Puerto Sagua, where she did set the hook deep. The next month, on a cold and dark night after the run, Raven heard a voice beckoning him from the ocean. It was Miracle, waiting for him to swim. Raven thought, *That's the girl for me.*

WHEN MIRACLE AND RAVEN are getting along, they act like teenagers with displays of affection that can turn heads even in South Beach. "When she's good, she's the best," says Raven. But sometimes Miracle will be out of touch for weeks. She loses her phone, or turns it off, and Raven can't talk to her. It drives him crazy to have no control. Yet it is his need for control that drives her away in the first place.

"He's got this thing about hair, okay?" she said one day, as the three of us were sitting and talking in Raven's living room. "He'll never let me touch his hair in the back, in all these years."

"Oh, come on," said Raven.

"It's true!" she said. "*Oh, come on*—it's absolutely true!"

"I comb it," said Raven. "I don't want her to mess it up. She likes to mess it up."

"It can never be messed up," she said. "You have to have the roll. Every time you swim, the last thing you do before you get out of the water is to do the roll."

"Then the wind comes," said Raven. "Like today, it's going to be all messed up. I like to comb my hair when I go out."

"But why would it matter at one o'clock in the morning—we're both in bed—if it gets messed up or not?"

"I want to go to sleep looking right, in case I die or something."

"You have no leg to stand on there," said Miracle. "You just have to have it your way. You can never forget about yourself enough to let your hair go. In any situation where it's possible to control it, it is one hundred percent controlled."

I was watching their dialogue like a Ping-Pong game. Perhaps with all the time apart, they have reflected on their relationship to the extent that they can speak about it almost as if neither is a participant. "Everything has to be precisely in the same place," continued Miracle. "If we move something, he'll know."

"Like if I need scissors, they should be right here," said Raven, leaning forward and reaching under a pile of letters to extract scissors. "The stapler is always right there," he said, pointing toward the answering machine, buried under newspaper clippings.

"But every night on the bed, he has the radio, the CD player, a couple CDs, and some reading material, and sometimes the newspaper, on my side, and I can't go to bed until he moves it. Now of course I can get in bed and just do this," she said, pushing her arms out front, "but he'll freak out."

"One time you knocked the radio on the floor."

"One time," repeated Miracle. "Something got knocked on the floor—did anything bad happen? It was no big deal. If I broke the radio, I would replace it. How many times can I tell him that? Logic cannot suffice in this situation. Anything falling is a big deal, papers falling—but you see how precarious everything is. Gravity is my personal enemy. If I haven't been here for a week, things tend to migrate, 'cause it only needs to accommodate the width of his hips. He's Mr. Swivel Hips."

"I'm just sliding right through," he said with his hand bending and swimming along like a fish.

"I asked him not long ago, 'Has it ever occurred to you that it might take a lot of patience to deal with you?' He said no. How much patience do I need to deal with that?"

"Sometimes I'm clueless," said Raven.

"Yeah, thank you—I needed that," said Miracle. "Fucking A."

When Miracle is ready to leave, she is out the door (even if it is without her keys). Raven, on the other hand, checks things so many times an ordinal number doesn't exist. It's not double-checking or triple-checking. It's checking things twenty-something times. "I move real slow," said Raven. "I talk slow."

"We run at different speeds," added Miracle. "It's a gift and a challenge. Perceptual doors will open. I'll see things I never would've seen because I'm moving at Raven's speed. But God." At the end of every run, Raven puts five items in a plastic black grocery bag: two socks, a headband, his glove, and Raven Run promotional postcards. "Everything's very precisely done," said Raven. "I check the lock about twenty-one times at least. If I start talking to somebody, she's like, 'I'm getting out of here, I gotta go, I'm cold.' "

In our conversation, Miracle would launch into monologues—mostly profound, occasionally incomprehensible—and Raven would listen silently and then say something at the end like, "That's good, White Lightning, you're getting a little Miracle talk." Miracle has the most extensive vocabulary of anyone I know in South Beach, though she relies heavily on the F-word. In class at FIU, she tells her students, "The beginning of wisdom is the proper naming of things." Outside of Raven time, she runs in an intellectual crowd. "I'm not near as smart as her," says Raven. "She tells me, 'Don't pronounce it that way, Raven—it's supposedly, not supposebly.' "

Miracle was nodding. "There are many times I'd like to talk with you about ideas, but you're not interested at all."

"I sometimes don't know things, and I shut myself off," said Raven.

When she requires intellectual fulfillment, she seeks other outlets. "Why have the expectation that you're going to get all the things you need from one person?" she said. She doesn't bring Raven to art openings because he is uncomfortable. Plus, she hates how her associates speak about him. "They make these dismissive judgments about Raven, on account of his haircut. Or love of Johnny Cash," she said. She feels the need to defend him, even when Raven isn't offended.

In Miracle's reckoning, the meanest thing a woman has ever said to her about Raven was contained in a three-word question: "How's the 'The'?" Recalling the incident, she raised her voice and narrowed her eyes as she repeated the question, *How's the The?* "It was breathtakingly mean," she said. Raven had no reaction. She explained, "It meant, 'Who is this crazy arrogant motherfucker who refers to himself with an article in front of his name?' " As she retold the incident, Miracle wiped a tear from her eye.

Raven remained unmoved. "A lot of people think it's The Raven, but it's just Raven," he said.

These days Miracle tires easily of the company of artists. She finds their elitism and self-importance tedious. She'd rather just talk about the run with Raven. "Artists can just be so nasty and cutting and close-minded, which is precisely the opposite of what they fancy themselves to be," said Miracle. "In their world the worst sin you can commit is to not be on the cutting edge . . . and you can't be on the cutting edge if you have too much respect for the past."

"Well, I am stuck in the past," said Raven.

"But you know that's who you are. You have completely owned it," said Miracle. "I'm not convinced having your ass sliding on the cutting edge is the best place to be." Before going off on the problem with art today, she announced, "I'm not going to go off about the problem with art today," then continued. "The problem is it lacks heart. It's absurd, and they take it so seriously. They don't find any irony in how they worship the prices. A guy sold a stuffed shark for twelve million dollars and of course you were totally uncool if you even mention he didn't catch it or stuff it himself. That's not the point. They're just such hypocrites. With that kind of milieu, how are they ever going to recognize somebody that's as authentic and true as Raven?

"They think they're doing a superb post-modern analysis of the hegemony of style, and its effects on the praxis of culture and reification of daily practice of inauthentic individuals— you know, some other bullshit. So yeah, I really want to defend Raven against elitists who coldly excise their own hearts so they can't recognize the heartlessness in their own work, and they project that on the guy whose got the biggest heart of anybody I have ever known. How dare they think they're so fucking important they can make a judgment about Raven like that? How dare they?! And I've lost so much interest in the art world because of shit like that. I'm just so over it." Wiping another tear from her eye, she concluded, "Fuck them," and asked me for another question.

RAVEN IS OBSESSED with anniversaries and birthdays and dates in general, yet Miracle considers a date "something off in the near future or distant future   who gives a shit?"

"She didn't know my birthday for the first five years we were together," said Raven.

"I knew," she said. "I would be planning for his birthday on a Thursday for two weeks and then three days before—this is typical—I show up Tuesday [and think], *Oh, fuck, it's Thursday*. Then between Tuesday and Thursday, I'll forget the birthday altogether. I've done that shit all my life." She turned to Raven. "You think I don't care, but I actually get so anxious about it that I overcompensate and show up to stuff early."

One of their biggest fights started over a plate: Miracle served

Raven dinner on a white plate, but Raven eats on black plates. "I went crazy," Raven told me before a run the day after it had happened. (Though I don't ask, Raven volunteers stories when things are bad.)

"Raven," I said in a tone to scold a child.

"I know," he said, putting his head down. "It's the pain. I just can't think about anything else." After this, the two didn't talk for months.

I have tried to understand the relationship of Raven and Miracle, but I don't think someone from the outside can ever understand the chemistry between two people who conduct most of their lives when you are not around. (Furthermore, when Miracle told me their relationship sprung from carnal desire, I did not ask for specifics.) Raven forces himself to give Miracle a life outside his regimen. And Miracle understands that he is who is he, in every situation. When that gets to be too much, she checks out.

There is rarely hope for reform. There's no trying to make the other person into something he or she is not. Their relationship is a beautiful, if not impossible, acceptance of incompatibility, for which they both put forth a great effort to enrich each other's lives in the ways they can, when they are together.

FOURTEEN

THE BIG WAVE

The third decade of the streak brought Raven 308 new runners—a big jump from the first decade (6) and the second decade (53). The stories from this era are unbelievable. For instance, on the way home from a run, Raven thought he recognized a runner called Answer Man. "Hey," said Raven, realizing at the last moment that in fact it wasn't Answer Man. "Sorry, you look just like a guy called Answer Man."

"Really?" said the stranger. "He must be a good-looking guy if he looks like me."

Chuckling, Raven said, "That's actually something Answer Man would say."

The following afternoon, Raven passed the same guy again. "It's the Answer Man lookalike," announced Raven.

"Do I really look like this guy?" he asked. Raven said yes. "Who's his best friend on the run?" It was Taxman. "When does Taxman run?" asked the impostor.

"He's supposed to come tomorrow," said Raven.

"Then so am I."

The next day it was raining when the impostor showed up. Taxman came fifteen minutes late. Without Raven saying anything, Taxman turned to the new runner. "Answer Man, what are you doing here?" he asked. "I didn't know you were coming to run."

"I can run with Raven any time I want," he responded.

"How's your girlfriend?" asked Taxman.

"She's fine."

"And work?"

"Everything's good." At this point, when Raven started giggling, Taxman got suspicious. "There's something different about you. Didn't you have a mustache or something?"

"I'm not him," said the impostor.

Taxman's mouth hung open. He turned to Raven. "What year was Answer Man born?"

"1945," said Raven.

"I was born in 1945," said the impostor.

"He's from New Jersey," said Taxman.

"So am I."

"There's something you don't know, Raven," said Taxman. "Answer Man was adopted."

And the guy said, "So was I."

Not long after, when Raven introduced Answer Man and the Impostor, they were like long, lost brothers who hung out all the time. They went on vacation to each other's summer homes in New Jersey. "Last I heard, they were feuding a little, as brothers do," says Raven. "But I think they're making up." Raven Runners offered to pay for a DNA test, but the men refused. Raven has a picture of the two together. The only difference is that Impostor has blue eyes, and Answer Man has brown. "But same height, same voice, same hair, same mannerisms," says Raven. "Crazy, huh?"

SPANKY WAS A HALF-COLOMBIAN, HALF-GERMAN who'd grown up in Miami Beach, where he was known as Marathon George—a self-appointed nickname—that came from running several marathons. In the seventies, he was tall, skinny, and fast. He disappeared in the eighties and when Raven saw him in 1996, he was 40 and weighed 250 pounds. "Yeah I got fat," Spanky told Raven. "I was in California."

"You're an athlete, man," said Raven. "You should be running with us."

So Spanky started training and in November 1996 made all eight, becoming the ninety-first runner. Spanky had a personal vendetta against yuppies and hated that South Beach—in particular, the establishment of the News Café—was attracting so many. Often, Spanky used the eight miles with Raven to vent about yuppies. Running with Raven, he dropped fifty pounds and landed a job as a greeter at Williamson Cadillac on Bal Harbour. "He wanted to be a Cadillac salesman," explained Raven.

One day in February 1997, Spanky came to run straight from work dressed in a suit and tie and polished shoes and announced to Raven that he was conducting a one-man, anti-yuppie rally. That afternoon, he ran eight in his suit carrying a gin and tonic martini in hand, squealing, "Hey now! Oh, my! Look at me, I'm a yuppie runner!" By mile six, he'd finished the drink, hardly spilling a drop.

On the same run, a guy from New York called Cargo Man was attempting his first eight miles. When I ran with Cargo Man in 2012, he told me, "I thought I couldn't do eight if my life depended on it, but I looked at Spanky and thought, *If this guy can do the run, I can do it*. So I just stayed in his shadow and got my nickname." Cargo Man was runner 102, and since then he's gotten in some thirty runs as a commuter. (When I met him, Cargo Man was in town for Art Basel to set up the "Untitled" tent on the Beach, and he arranged for Raven to get exhibit credentials. At six o'clock, as the city's movers and shakers sipped martinis and discussed art, Raven busted through the front door with three runners in tow, including Cargo Man. They wove through the tent, then out the back door, leaving attendees to wonder, *Was that a live installation?*)

While some running groups might shy away from antics like Spanky's Yuppie Run, in 1997, it won "Event of the Year."

* * *

GRINGO'S FIRST RUN was also in 1997. Until 2015, when Taxman overtook him, Gringo was the top Raven Runner with over 1,600 runs and 650 swims. I've probably run with Gringo fifty times, and he is one of my favorites. He was born the same year as my father, in 1938, and has the kindest eyes. Gringo senses your best quality and brings it out. After five minutes of conversation with anyone, I think he could give the eulogy at that person's funeral. (When I mentioned this to Raven, he said, "Oh, I know at least one person Gringo hated, and that's Headlock Dreadlock Harold. But there's a very good reason for it.")

In 1997 before a run, Gringo was standing by the 5th Street stand. He was 59 with striking blue eyes and an all-American look that Raven thought resembled Tommy Smothers. Gringo had seen Raven hanging out with Placard Man. "I've tried to give him food," said Gringo, "but he won't take it. Is he okay?"

"Oh, Placard Man? He's fine," said Raven. "He's scared of germs. Anyway, you should run with us."

So he followed. The nickname came from when Gringo was a kid, playing ice hockey with some rough kids from Point Place in Toledo, Ohio. He didn't want them to know his name or the affluent neighborhood he came from, so one boy named him Gringo. Before Miami, Gringo had been a land baron in Spain until he lost everything in a pyramid scheme. Penniless, he moved his wife and kids to western Colorado, where he'd gone to college, but his family hated it, so they tried Miami Beach. "I was never a beach person," Gringo told me. He'd spent his life around mountains, a terrain that makes it easy for a person to identify goals. Any time he needed a challenge, he just looked up. "When you climb mountains, it can be extremely hot and every foot forward is a struggle, but you got the peak at the end. You make great sacrifices for the journey," said Gringo.

In the flat sands of Miami Beach, he saw no destination until he met Raven. "Here he is climbing a peak every day, getting those eight miles in, doing such a stressful activity on a flat beach. After every run, we'd get back to the barnyard and Raven would raise his arms—we made it! It was a thrill. We'd climbed a peak." Then they swam, which Gringo used to fear. "I'd tell him, 'There's just so much liquid out there, Raven. I'm not used to all that liquid.' " But with Raven by his side, in 1998, Gringo became the second Raven Runner to get one hundred runs and one hundred swims. (Miracle was first.) "So I wasn't let down," concluded Gringo. "He fulfilled a real personal and emotional need that I have for mountains, and it was a lot of fun."

From the early days, Gringo paints this scene: "Raven used to move along that beach, and it was like he owned it. Nice Day Phil [a retired bodybuilder] would be riding his bicycle, setting our pace, and reciting Shakespeare. Then Raven would let loose with that voice of his, and we'd start singing. Then he'd holler out to someone that was going through a [waste] basket. Then a lifeguard was hollering at Raven about some baseball game. There began a feeling of envelopment—that Raven is owning this place, that the ocean isn't winning, that it's just out there on the edge. The big wave on that beach is Raven. He's moving out or moving down, he's going north or going south. He took his runners with him—that brotherhood that he kept so united, because back then everybody ran together."

A QUINTESSENTIAL RAVEN RUN MOMENT for Gringo came on a sunny day in March 1998. A law professor named Tim was running his second mile with Raven when he got the urge to jump over a trashcan. Like John Adams who said, "Every problem is an opportunity in disguise," steeplechasers like Tim see an obstacle in the path as extra conditioning. Trashcans should be overcome, not avoided.

Raven, around mile four, told Tim, "You know if you were

to hurdle every garbage can left on this beach, you'd probably get Event of the Year." Then he added, "But nobody's ever gotten it on their first run with me." This was all Tim needed to hear.

"It was a challenge," recalled Tim in 2014, as he recounted it to me. "Raven didn't mean it as a challenge, but I took it as a challenge." (In my observation, however, Raven always means it as a challenge.) So he started hurdling the metal trashcans. In the three-thousand-meter steeplechase that Tim used to compete in, there were forty barriers and seven or eight water pits to jump over. The beach trashcans, Tim figures, "were probably two or three inches shorter than the steeplechase barriers, but a much wider distance across the top." The garbage cans presented a greater challenge "because I didn't just have to go up three feet but also carry my body two feet across. If I didn't clear [the trashcan], my trailing knee would bang against the metal top, which happened more than once."

South of 20th Street, every block has a few cans. In the northern, less-crowded beaches, the trashcans are sparser but the sand is softer. Gringo, along for the run, sprinted ahead for crowd control, warning beachgoers in both Spanish and English. "I was telling people in Spanish to step back, that a gentleman was about to jump over the trashcan," said Gringo, retelling the event in a separate conversation. "They looked at me like, '*Como*? I'm just trying to throw my trash away.' "

Catfood Lady, a coach who was always chasing down plastic bags, was the closest call for interference. "You had to, like, throw her in the trashcan to get her out of the way," Raven reminded Gringo.

"I really couldn't have done it without him," said Tim of Gringo, who also leveled the tops of the garbage cans, pushing down any overflow. The way back got tougher. "The cans come one right after the other, in soft sand—that's where it really becomes a ball buster," observed Tim. His knees were blue from grazing the metal tops, but encouragement from other runners kept his spirits high. Raven kept count, and at 6th Street, Tim cleared trashcan number 281, earning the name, the "Hurdler."

The next day, in a lecture hall at the University of Miami, Hurdler had trouble writing on the board. "There was so much pain in my neck, my arms," he said. Still sore a few weeks after the event, he was watching television when a Nike commercial came on, and its message spoke to him: *Pain lasts several minutes, but glory is forever*.

But the glory didn't end there.

A year later, teaching in Albuquerque, homesick for Miami and rehabbing a broken fibula, Hurdler received his Event of the Year certificate in the mail from Raven. Holding the certificate, he decided: *I'm going to hurdle every garbage can on the beach and get Event of the Year two years in a row*. That winter, training in the foothills of New Mexico at an elevation of five thousand feet, Hurdler got ready for spring break.

On cold, difficult days, Hurdler asked why he was killing himself to jump over hundreds of trashcans on a Raven Run. Even today he can't fully articulate his motivations, but it reminded him of high school, when he was captain of the cross-country team. "You train so hard—[and] for what?" he asked. "To go to a starting line with your teammates," he answered. You push through pain on the race and when you finish, "There's a certain type of glory." In Albuquerque, he was "wanting to make a comeback and not just accept that I had a broken leg, and I'm getting older, and my best years are behind —me." He paused, then asked, "Does that make any sense?"

On a sunny afternoon in March—his last day of spring break in Miami—Hurdler showed up at the 5th Street lifeguard stand, surprising Gringo and Raven. By the fifth trashcan, Raven predicted he was going for all eight miles, and Gringo knew the drill. "That was my most challenging run," says Gringo. "I had to be ahead of him, and he could run pretty fast. I was so afraid he was going to make a mistake because he could've had a terrible fall, oh, my gosh." Cargo Man happened to be in town again and couldn't believe his luck to witness another Event of the Year.

After 571 trashcans, Hurdler was approaching the final one when Gringo announced, "Okay, my job is done. You're all alone for the last basket there. Go ahead." There, in front of 5th Street, the Hurdler glided over the last trashcan of the eight miles. "Oh, it was phenomenal," says Gringo. "So exciting—one of the classical events on the run."

Raven considers Hurdler's feat the greatest athletic accomplishment ever performed on the run, and Hurdler says it was the toughest athletic thing he has ever done. The next day, heading back to New Mexico, Hurdler "was such an old man shuffling through that airport. I was in pain for months." Today, when his students come to his office hours, they see Hurdler's Event of the Year certificate hanging on the wall. "Of course they have no clue what *hurdled eight miles of garbage cans* [means]—*what the hell*?" And Hurdler just nods and says, "Yes, that's your law professor."

ACTUALLY THERE WAS A TIE for Event of the Year in 1999. On October 15, Hurricane Irene was supposed to come at seven o'clock at night, but she arrived early—right when Raven, Miracle, Gringo, and Springman were walking toward where the 5th Street lifeguard stand usually stood, but in preparation for the storm, the Beach Patrol had moved the stands inland. While Irene wasn't Miami's strongest hurricane—Andrew and Wilma beat her—she was the only one to strike at the start of the Raven Run.

Wind whipped around at seventy miles per hour. "At that speed, the sand feels like needles when it hits you," says Raven. "Like someone is scraping off your skin." The flock headed toward the shoreline, where the sand pecked less at their flesh.

Gringo recalls, "I felt I was the only one smart enough to be completely covered." Everyone was wearing at least long pants and a windbreaker, except Raven, who was shirtless in black shorts. "I looked down and thought I was going to see blood all over my legs," says Raven. "It was extremely painful."

Turning at the pier, the wind picked up to eighty-six miles per hour. "With that, you can't see five feet ahead of you. You can't open your eyes," says Raven. "You just feel your way." Meanwhile Gringo was running like a child—arms stretched out like an airplane, looping in the wind. "Oh, it was tremendous fun," says Gringo. "We lost Spring because you couldn't see anything, it's just gray. But when we got to the pier, he was sitting on that table where you clean fish, with the faucet open, running water all over himself saying, 'Oh, the water feels so good!' "

After eight, they walked to the public shower on 4th Street, trying to spray off the sand caked to their bodies. "Raven was literally in a sand shell," says Gringo. "I'm not exaggerating. His whole body was in a hard sand shell."

As Raven was laying on the cement underneath the tap, Gringo said, "How about a swim?" Before Raven could answer, Miracle said, "Don't start with him, because if you challenge him, he's going to do it."

Gringo capitulated. "Okay, no swim."

Raven says he found sand tucked into every crevice of his body: "It stuck to me for two weeks."

FIFTEEN

OFF THEIR BUTTS

Well into the late nineties, most new recruits were by word of mouth or curious observers. The *Miami Herald* and local news had done a few stories, but Raven didn't appear in the national spotlight until August 1997, when *Runner's World* profiled him in the Human Race column. "As punctual as the sunrise and as sure as the tides, Robert Kraft runs on Miami's South Beach," the article begins. "In twenty-two years, his routine may be the only thing that hasn't changed on this strip of beach."

Raven says that's when he noticed the first big spike in numbers. One person who read the article was a reporter named George A. Hancock, who was putting together a list of American streak runners. It turned out Raven wasn't alone in his everyday running habit. In fact, at the time, his streak of 8,000-plus days didn't even make the top ten. The longest-running streak—more than 10,500 days—belonged to a man named Mark Covert, who started in 1968, seven years before Raven. Eventually the list turned into the United States Running Streak Association (USRSA), of which Raven is a charter member. USRSA bylaws define a streak as "running at least one continuous mile within each calendar day under one's own body power (without the utilization of any type of health or mechanical aid other than prosthetic devices)." All running surfaces—

roads, tracks, and treadmills—meet the criteria, though swimming pools do not.

Raven is currently ranked number eight. A writer from California named Jon Sutherland owns the longest streak registered on the USRSA, which started in May 1969. Sutherland took over the number one spot from Mark Covert, his running buddy from college, after Covert "pulled a Cal Ripken," according to the USRSA president Mark Washburne, and voluntarily ended the run.

"I've run every day, but I've done it in various states and countries," Washburne, whose streak is going on twenty-seven years, told me on the phone from his home in New Jersey. "The fact that Raven runs the same course every day—that really separates him from the list. I don't know anybody else who's done that." In 2011, when HBO *Real Sports* producers called Washburne looking for someone to feature in a segment on obsessive runners, he suggested Raven.

As of 2015, there were 523 runners with registered streaks and 374 runners on the retired streak list. "Professionally, it's a diverse group," continued Washburne. "There's a lot of teachers and track coaches, obviously. I even saw a truck driver in there. You gotta wonder how he does it. And there's a lot of doctors."

"Have any of the doctors written about the consequences of a running streak?" I asked.

"Well any article you read about running will say you need to take a day off, but the truth is nobody's ever really done a scientific study on streak running." He hopes, one day, someone will. It annoys him when reporters refer to streak runners as obsessed. "We like to say we're dedicated. We prefer a positive spin. I mean, he's doing something healthy, like brushing your teeth every day."

The year before, Washburne had run in fifty-six races. One was the Boston Marathon, his ninth time. "This year I'm not doing as many," he said. I asked why. "I started dating someone, and she's a runner, but she thinks I'm a little crazy with all the races." At the end of our conversation, he said he hoped to make a Raven Run soon. "I need to get one of those nicknames."

Raven enjoys the camaraderie of the association, and he thinks it helps to motivate people. "Streak running is becoming really popular," says Raven. "It's a good thing. It gets people off their butts to do something every day. It pushes people. It gives them a reason not to take a day off."

On New Year's Eve in 2014, I met Stephen DeBoer, a dietician from Minnesota whose forty-four-year streak (started 6/7/71) ranks number three on the list. He was in town to run with Raven and deliver an award on behalf of the USRSA. De-Boer—shirtless and wearing high white socks and short black shorts—ran next to me for several miles. He bobbed his head when he ran, like a pecking chicken, but his graceful, steady gait looked like he was on top of an elliptical machine. DeBoer echoed Washburne's pet peeve. He hates that everyone writes off streak runners as being OCD, though he admits he is OCD himself. "The way I look at it is everyone's got passions, and I think running is a pretty good one," he told me. He credits the streak with providing stability in his life. "The highs are still high, but the lows seem more manageable," he said. Consistent running, he believes, lowers the rate of depression and provides as many emotional benefits as physical.

I asked him the first question that most people ask Raven: "What was your hardest day?"

He had two. When he broke his ankle stepping into a gopher hole on a trail run in Minnesota, the doctor put a walking boot on his leg and told him he could bear weight according to pain tolerance. He tolerated pain running at least a mile every day for six weeks. "It was slow," he conceded. "But I did it." He thinks running helped his recovery. A kidney stone caused his second hardest day, but, after surgery, the pain disappeared quickly. "What did your doctor say when you told him you were going to run that afternoon?" I asked.

"I didn't tell him," he said.

Unlike Raven, DeBoer travels and keeps his streak alive in a variety of locations. He also competes in marathons. "It's funny, though," he said. "I still get a little sore after I run a marathon, so the following day, I only run one mile."

After eight miles with Raven, DeBoer became "Tundra Star."

The next day—January 1, 2015—DeBoer presented Raven with the 2015 Runner of the Year award on behalf of the USRSA, and Raven's streak turned forty. The award ceremony was at the 5th Street lifeguard stand. Before DeBoer made his speech, he shook Raven's hand. "Hey, you showed up," he joked.

When we started the eight miles, I said, "Raven, I want you to know yesterday was a record for both of us." I had run eight miles with him two days in a row, making it my all-time longest streak of running eight miles every day.

"Wow," he said. "You doing eight today?" I wasn't. "You hear that, Tundra Star?" said Raven, turning to DeBoer on his right. "Our streaks are safe."

"You never know," said DeBoer. "She may wake up tomorrow and have to run and then—it just happens."

VII
CAMARADERIE

You tap into a pool of great people, all professions, all ages, all cultures, all fitness levels, all sizes and shapes . . . It gets you energized, opens up your mind, and gets me thinking about my own life. You enjoy the "here and now."

—Transporter, from Germany, 11 runs

Miami is a city where you could live here for years and never know anyone. But this is something you can do every day— the exact same thing—and meet different people.

—Bloody Wolf, a French scientist and marathon runner

Raven is unequivocally, universally welcoming, providing companionship and camaraderie while on a run in an absolutely beautiful location. What could be better?

—Chocolate Chip, 723 runs

I run with Raven for the—how do you say it in English—camaraderia?

—Dos Equis, a boat builder from the Dominican Republic

Knowing I'm not alone, that there's people here that want to be with me, that motivates me. If I had to come out and run by myself, I don't know if I could.

—Raven

SIXTEEN

True Story Lory

Raven has given identities to more than 2,500 people and as may already be evident, nicknames are a big part of the Raven Run. Usually on the first run, when he is confident you will make eight, Raven conducts a little interview. He asks about past nicknames, hometown, work, diet, hobbies, passions, and obsessions. By virtue of knowing that you will walk away from the experience with a new name, people tend to reveal more of themselves on the run. They want to get a favorable pseudonym, which they wear every time they show up. You have to be careful what you say on the first run, because any pleasing word to Raven could become your identity.

One time, my friend Randy, who is a swim coach, happened to talk about crabbing, and he remarked turkey necks made good bait. "Turkey Neck," repeated Raven. "That'd be a good nickname." After our protests, Raven finally agreed to call him "Kickboard."

Nicknames are ubiquitous and as a result many of us never learn each other's real names. Sometimes this can make for awkward interactions outside the beach context. Raven, whose preferred means of communication is still the U.S. Postal Service, sends me letters addressed to White Lightning. (The postman has yet to report me as a drug dealer. Letters, for the record, are handwritten in legible cursive, and he sends at least one letter to someone every other day. He always closes with, "Run Free." Sometimes he writes, "Love, Raven." They come from the heart. They make me smile and say, "Aw, Raven!")

One time, a group of us wanted to visit Tony Gulliver, Raven's old neighbor I met at the picnic. He'd recently moved to assisted living in Hialeah, and I called the social worker to get visitation hours. "Who can I tell him is coming to visit?" asked the social worker.

I hesitated. If I said Laura Lee, Tony wouldn't know me, and she might think he had dementia. So I had to say, "White Lightning, Yellow Rose, and Raven."

One reason that I love the nickname tradition is because you are guaranteed a story when you ask the origins. For instance, on a run in June 2013, I met Trusty, a cop from Garfield, New Jersey, who got his name when he told Raven, "I work with trusties in jail." We were heading north to 47th Street when I asked, "You got any good cop stories?"

"I'll have to think about that," he said. About a mile later, he said he had a couple.

Once, at the police station, a guy walked up to Trusty's desk and threw down a brown paper package, setting off a flurry of white powder. The man was livid, and Trusty took cover under his desk. "I want this man arrested," the guy shouted. "He was supposed to sell me a kilo, and he sold me a half-kg." Trusty poked his head out from under the desk. "Is this cocaine?" he asked. The man said yes. "So you bought a kilo of cocaine from your dealer, but he gave you a half-kg." Again the man said yes, and Trusty had to arrest him. (When I retold this story to the Giggler, he predictably laughed, then observed, "It just goes to show you everyone wants justice.")

I asked, "What's the craziest excuse you've heard to get out of a ticket?"

"Oh, the usual," said Trusty. "My grandmother just died. I have to go to the bathroom. I have cupcakes in the oven."

"Cupcakes in the oven?" I repeated. "That's a good one. Did it work?"

"Oh, yeah, I never write tickets. I feel bad. We all make mistakes. I give them a warning." The next story had to do with a naked criminal who jumped into a river from a bridge, and Trusty went in after him, leaving the keys to the cop car in the ignition. "I was new to the job," he added. "You're not supposed to leave the car." The naked man turned out to be an excellent swimmer and a good runner, and he wound up beating Trusty back to land and stealing his cop car.

When Trusty finished the tale, I dropped off to go home. Right after I left, Trusty turned to Raven and said, "Oh, I got a better story than that." (I heard this from Raven on the next run.) One afternoon, Trusty had to report to an apartment where an old Italian lady had just died. After pronouncing the woman dead, Trusty was waiting at the apartment for the woman's grandchildren. On the stove was a big, beautiful bowl of pasta and meat sauce. Trusty was "hungry as heck" and really wanted to try the pasta, but he resisted. After an hour, he opened the fridge to get a glass of water. As more time passed, he kept eyeing the pasta. Finally, to tide himself over, he grabbed a handful of peanuts from the bowl sitting on the counter.

When the family arrived, they were in remarkably good spirits. One grandchild saw the peanuts. "Granny sure did love her sweets," he said. "We never knew why, but she would buy bags of peanut M&M's, suck off the chocolate, and then spit out the peanuts in the bowl. And there they are."

SOME NAMES ARE SELF-EXPLANATORY. Sleeper is a narcoleptic who has fallen asleep while on the run and swim. "Did you ever see the Stork?" Raven once asked me. I said no. "He looked just like a stork—six-five, a hundred and sixty-five pounds, beak nose, always wearing biker shorts. One time, when we made the turn at the jetty, Shaquille O'Neal was standing there with his kids, and the Stork goes, 'Shaq! How you doing?' And Shaq looks at the Stork and says, 'How you doing, big man?' After that the Stork told everybody, 'Shaq called me big man.' "

A man with pitch-black hair and one gray streak down the

middle walked up to Raven and said, "My name is Mehi. I am from Transylvania. I am a bloodsucker. I am a physicist." He sounded exactly like Count Dracula and had a bite mark on his neck. He was wearing a shirt with a big red heart and instructions to "Give Blood." To nobody's surprise, Mehi became the Blood Sucker.

"This one girl running with us was like four-nine," began Raven. "Her hair was so blond that you could see her scalp. She had small features—tiny teeth that protruded a little. When she told me that her classmates used to call her Hamster, I said, 'I can see why.' And then she said, 'Yeah I know, my last name is Hamley.' " She was called the Hamster.

When I asked why the good-looking triathlete was called 31 Kilo, he responded, "I'm in the military, and 31K is my MOS"—Military Occupational Specialization—"I train dogs." I asked how he got into that, and he said, "I got lucky." Today he mostly trains airport dogs to detect bombs and drugs, but on the side he works for "three-letter government agencies."

Most days, he dons the bite suit, which he says is "fun." Raising his left arm, he pointed to a puncture wound in his bicep that blended into his tattoo. "That bite went right through the suit," he said, smiling. "She was a German shepherd, a *real* good dog." He has trained dogs in English, Dutch, Portuguese, German, and several other languages. I asked what I should do if I'm attacked by a police dog, and he said, "Don't get attacked by a police dog."

Floater, Dizzy's best friend, escaped from Cuba in 1992 and paddled to American shores in a two-man kayak with a man named Nany. "We get about a mile offshore," Floater told me on a run in 2012, "And he asks me, 'Do you think we're going to tip over?' I told him I didn't know, that it probably depended on the weather. Then he goes, 'Right, because I lied. I can't swim.' " Today Floater and his wife, Chicken Fricassee, teach middle school and run races to raise awareness for childhood obesity. Recently, Floater ran from Naples to Miami. "My last eight miles in Miami," said Floater, whose feat earned the Event of the Year, "I ran with the Raven."

Fiddlesticks got his name because he told Raven, "You know I've got a streak of my own." When Raven asked what it was, he danced around the issue for five minutes until Raven tired of the conversation and stopped asking about it. Then the man said, "I haven't cursed since I was a child. The closest I've come is fiddlesticks." I wasn't on that run but when Raven reported the conversation, he added, "I tell you, White Lightning, after eight miles with him, I started to think, *Maybe I am normal.*"

Warden is a prison warden who, in 2002, ran with Raven 305 times—six out of seven days per week—a Raven Run record. Occasionally, Warden met inmates who had run with Raven, and he'd facilitate communications between the men. But Warden's claim to fame is as Treasure Hunter. Along the run that one year, Warden scooped up forty-eight watches, including a Rolex, from the sand. "I've never seen anything like it," says Raven. "One time, he was behind a concessionaire truck, and the wheel was spinning in the sand, and a Rolex flew right into his leg!"

Story Lory, who is 55, got her name because, on the fifth mile of her first eight-mile run, as they were getting a sip of water at the water fountain, she said in her Italian accent, "You know I am the most famous woman in Italy." Raven studied her face, then exchanged a suspicious look with "Mad Cow," a thirty-something marine biologist from London whose real name is Henry Potter.

"What do you mean you're the most famous woman in Italy?" asked Raven.

Lory rattled off her résumé. "I was a model and an actress on television shows and movies. I was a Miss Universe contestant. I won *Survivor: Italy*. I dated George Harrison and Eric Clapton." At Eric Clapton, Mad Cow sighed deeply, as if in pain. "Oh, that God-awful song," he moaned in his British accent about "Tears in Heaven."

"Yeah," Lory responded. "That was about my son." Clapton had written the song after his four-year-old son, Conor, fell to his death out of a window on the fifty-third floor of a New York skyscraper.

"To be honest, I didn't believe her," Raven recalls.

Mad Cow said, "Sorry, what did you say your name was again?"

Lory Del Santo.

That night Mad Cow called. "Raven I looked it up, and everything is true," he said. "That was her son. I can't believe I called it a God-awful song." Raven hung up the phone and called his friend Freebird, a lifeguard from Italy. "Have you heard of a woman called Lory Del Santo?" asked Raven.

"Of course, Raven," said Freebird in his Italian accent. "She is the most famous woman in Italy. Growing up, you might've had a poster of Raquel Welch on your wall, but I had Lory Del Santo."

Story Lory was the real deal, and Raven immediately changed her name to True Story Lory. A few days later, she was back to run eight miles, and Raven told her how very sorry he was to learn more about her son's death. "She wasn't mad at Mad Cow," says Raven, "but he really had put his foot in his mouth."

When I met True Story Lory in August 2014, she was running with "Magnet," her 21-year-old boyfriend, who is younger than her children. "See, White Lightning?" said Raven. "I don't make this stuff up."

SLEAZEBUSTER IS A RETIRED Northwestern law professor who earned his name after explaining in detail on the run how he liked to take down sleazy divorce lawyers. This impressed Firecracker, who was running beside him. "You're like a sleaze buster," she observed, and Raven immediately approved. "The problem," Sleazebuster told me, "is that runners have shortened it just to Sleaze, so I'll be walking around South Beach, on vacation with family or work colleagues, and people will be shouting, 'Hey, Sleaze! How's it going?' And my friends are like, *Why are they calling you sleaze?*"

I asked Raven if anyone has ever asked to change their nickname. "The Cadaver did," he answered. Cadaver was a long-distance swimmer from Cuba who completed his first eight miles on his 59th birthday in 1994. The man's dark hair matched the circles under his eyes, which looked as if they had been carved into his face with a scalpel. On hot days, he collapsed in the sand like a corpse.

The Cadaver ran with a fanny pack to carry a homemade concoction of peach juice and coffee. He carried a big radio and blasted boleros, Cuban love ballads. When it rained, he sometimes wore a shower cap. The Cadaver was okay with his nickname until one day Bigfoot the lifeguard hollered, "Look alive, Cadaver!"

Cadaver was offended. "I don't like this," he told Raven. "I am not a cadaver. I am alive." Raven gave in, and the Cadaver became the Instructor, after he got certified as a Red Cross swimming instructor.

A year later, Cadaver collapsed in the sand. "He was lying in a gully like he was dead," says Raven. Two old ladies came up to Raven and asked, "Is that man all right? He's not moving." At that moment, the Instructor's arm shot up again, and Raven walked over and picked him off the ground. "He's okay," Raven told the ladies. "He just came back from the dead." After that, Raven changed his name back to Cadaver. The next time the lifeguards teased him, he stopped running.

Today Raven misses the Cadaver terribly. I asked Raven, "Can't you just change his name so he'll come back?"

Raven winced. "You really have to see him, White Lightning. He looks just like a cadaver."

SEVENTEEN

CHUCK NORRIS AND
JESUS CHRIST

On May 18, 2002, Raven was on the front page of the *Miami Herald* for his 10,000th day in a row—80,000 streak miles. On the run was Tom Fiedler, the editor of the *Miami Herald*, who earned the nickname Daily Planet—the fictional newspaper from *Superman*. "They took a picture of me shaking Marble Man's hand," says Raven. "He was a really weird-looking guy— a one-time runner—but still it was a great, memorable day."

Thirty people ran with Raven to commemorate the mile-stone, and nineteen people swam. "That was the all-time record for swimmers," says Raven. Graphics Man—Pimm Fox—a Bloomberg News anchor on the show *Taking Stock*, flew down from New York for his sixth run with Raven. Springman, Miracle, Poet, Gringo, Sailor, Bookworm, the Giggler, and Pokerpace were there, too. The *Herald* story enticed a lot of new recruits and as soon as Raven had checked off goal one, he made goal two: a hundred thousand streak miles.

THAT SUMMER, it felt like someone was lashing his arches with a bullwhip; a callous on the sole of his foot was so tender he couldn't step on it. Rolling onto the outside of his foot changed his stride, which hurt his hip and back. On August 15, 2002, after the run, his knee was killing him when a tourist came up to him and said, "There's people that just fell off a Jet Ski at Sixth Street. They're in trouble."

Raven looked to the water and saw an empty Jet Ski floating, doing circles as it bumped up against the Gulf Stream. A family of three was shouting for help. Raven threw his wallet, glasses, and glove on the lifeguard stand and took off for the waves. The parents were Latin, in their 20s, and the son was 2. Another person helped get the son and father, who was a better swimmer, and they made it to shore. When Raven got to the mother, a helicopter was flying above him. "I see the cops, I see the rescue squad, the beach is filled with hundreds of people, there's a Coast Guard boat a little farther out," Raven told me. "But nobody's in the water. I don't know why. Maybe they figured I had it under control."

Raven offered his usual disclaimer, "I'm going to get you in. It's just going to take a while." Tugging the woman behind, he fought the current for fifteen minutes. When they could stand in the water, the woman hugged Raven as hard as she could, repeating "Thank you" over and over. Then she ran to her husband and toddler. "They were going crazy in Spanish," said Raven.

A large policeman had watched the whole scene and recognized Raven. "I thought all you did was run," he said.

"No," said Raven. "I can swim a little."

A FEW MONTHS LATER, his ankle was so swollen it couldn't bend. He had to drag his foot when he ran. On one run in January 2003, eight miles took him three hours and six minutes. "When Sailor, our slowest runner, flew by me, I thought, *The streak's over*," recalls Raven.

That night Mike "Flatfoot" Flatley, a runner and a podiatrist, called. "I heard from Reverend that you had a bad day," said Flatfoot. "Come to my office tomorrow, and I'll look at your ankle. Plus your orthotics came in." Raven had been Flatfoot's celebrity endorsement for an ad for the *Miami New Times* and to return the favor and take pressure off the calluses, Flatfoot had taken a mold of Raven's mangled feet for orthotic inserts.

Warden drove Raven to the doctor's office, where Flatfoot wrapped Raven's foot with a medicated bandage. It was a bad sprain. "Now don't be stupid," said Flatfoot. "Take it easy and let it heal. Don't run the full eight. And don't swim."

Raven promised he wouldn't swim, which actually was a relief, because the Atlantic was clogged with jellyfish. Wearing orthotics that afternoon, Raven shaved one hour and twenty minutes off his time and proudly shared the feat with Flatfoot. "You were going too fast," said Flatfoot on the phone.

"Well it didn't hurt as much," said Raven. The next day, Flatfoot came to run with Raven to slow him down. Then he rewrapped the ankle. After a couple of weeks running with the orthotics, the pain went away. "I was running faster than I had gone in years," recalls Raven. "I felt like I was seventeen again."

As RAVEN'S RUNNING FAMILY GREW, he started losing his only real family left. In 2005, Mary had a heart attack at age 88. After three days in the hospital, she was transferred to a nursing home. "That was a dirty, dirty word," says Raven. "She made it a point never to put her mother in a home, and she told me never to put her in a nursing home. She wanted independence." At the nursing home, Mary stopped eating and accused the nurses of being mean. Though Raven had no experience as a caretaker, he took his mother home to her apartment.

Beginning in May 2005, Raven visited his mother twice a day, before and after the run. He bought her groceries, cooked her dinner, and watched television with her for hours at night. "I never knew how I was going to find her," says Raven. On ten different occasions, Raven had to pick his mother up off the floor. Still, Mary insisted that a nursing home was a death sentence.

"At least God gave me a window where my back was better," says Raven, "and I could lift her." On her eleventh fall in December 2006, Mary broke her hip and went to the hospital for three months. Every hospital visit broke Raven's heart, and every eight miles put it back together.

A new runner from Seattle became a great support. Jim was a 58-year-old pilot who flew for Alaskan Airlines. With blue eyes and a little mustache, he looked like any plain Irish American guy, but on Halloween he liked to dress up as an Arabian prince and go by the name Abdul, which was the identity he requested from Raven.

When Abdul came to town, he ran from his hotel on 65th Street to meet Raven—that's 5.2 miles—and then ran eight with Raven, swam, and jogged back home. He was a tough athlete—a graduate of the United States Naval Academy in Annapolis who had finished seventy-eight marathons and a couple of Iron Mans. A lot of runners respected Abdul. "I adored that man," says Gringo. "Not only was he humanly healthy, he was creative—earthly creative and spiritually creative at the same time. He really had a balance."

Raven admired Abdul, too, and opened up to him about how difficult it was to take care of his mother. Abdul could empathize; his mother, who had been a piano teacher, was also sick. The two swapped caretaker stories, offering mutual encouragement. To know someone else was going through the same thing and was taking it in stride made Raven feel less alone.

In March 2007, Mary was discharged from the hospital and needed more assistance than two visits per day. Raven set up home help for her, but the nurses refused to take a house key, and Mary couldn't open the door to let them in. "I thought I could do anything for my mother," says Raven, "but I just couldn't change her diaper." He thought he had no choice but to put her in a home. "Then God sent an angel," says Raven. "That was Poutine."

POUTINE IS CANADIAN, named after her favorite national dish of French fries smothered in gravy and cheese curds. She holds many Raven Run records: Most swims in a year (202), most runs in a year for a female (232), most consecutive runs and swims (143), and she is in the Hall of Fame. For a living, she walks dogs and pet-sits.

She met Raven in January 2007, when she was on vacation in Miami, petting a cat on the sidewalk outside the Lord Balfour Hotel. From her legs, Raven could tell she was an athlete, and he invited her to run. "I'm not really fast," she said.

"Oh, we got this guy Hurricane, he's almost eighty," said Raven. "If you want to run slow, you can run with him." That afternoon she walked-ran with Hurricane but got tired of the slow pace after four miles. "She thought she was just stuck with Hurricane," says Raven, who convinced her to try again the next day, when she became fast friends with Adbul's wife, Fatima.

That night, Poutine came to the annual banquet and was sitting next to Fatima as Abdul led the runners in a prayer before dinner and later accepted the Rookie of the Year award. "Abdul was very spiritual," says Raven. "Always Jesus-talking, and he lived it."

That year, Gringo and Firecracker tied for Favorite Runner. Most Improved went to Chocolate Chip. Chapter 11 got Comeback of the Year. Treasure Hunter went to Reverend. For juggling three balls for eight miles, Spinner got Event of the Year. "He dropped them a couple times," says Raven. "But he is an excellent juggler." Bookworm was inducted into the Hall of Fame. Taking it all in, Poutine promised, "I'll be back."

She happened to move to South Beach on the day Raven was going to put his mother in a nursing home. When she mentioned she was looking for part-time work, Raven asked if she would like to meet Mary. The two hit it off, and Raven hired her immediately. In May, Poutine and another runner, Cooker, asked Mary if she wanted to run with Raven.

They borrowed a beach wheelchair from the lifeguards and pushed Mary in the sand from 5th Street to Government Cut, then up the boardwalk to 47th Street. Mary was rolling parallel to her running son, waving and laughing the whole time. After eight, Raven asked, "Did you like that, Mom?"

"Yes," said Mary. "Let's do it again."

She requested the name "Boardwalk Mary," from her years as a teenager selling ice cream on the Atlantic City Boardwalk, or she also liked "Pretzel Mary," because her cabinets were stocked with pretzels. But even for his mother, Raven wouldn't bend the rules, and Mary never made the official list.

Her dementia set in not long after the boardwalk run. At first, Raven got angry when Mary couldn't remember things. Once, she thought his name was Jack. Another day, she called him Robert, but when he asked, "And who am I?" his mother answered, "I think you're a friend."

"And what about your son?" asked Raven.

"He's no good," she said. "I haven't seen him in years. But you're a nice man. You feed me every day."

Raven took it personally. "How can she not know who I am?" he asked Miracle, who had lost her mother to Alzheimer's.

"You're not going to win this battle," she said. "You just gotta let it go."

As HIS MOTHER WAS FORGETTING HIM, the city of Miami Beach was planning an event to recognize Raven. On October 17, 2007—Raven's 57th birthday—at City Hall in Miami Beach, Mayor David Dermer proclaimed it Robert Raven Kraft Day as he read:

> *Robert Raven Kraft, longtime Miami Beach resident, local legend, and avid runner has been running on the soft sands of Miami beach for the past twenty-nine years without missing a single day's run or a single Miami Beach sunset in that quarter century-plus stretch . . . Over 344 people have completed the "Raven Run" and all of them—whether one-time runners or regulars—are better for the time that they spend with Robert Raven*

*Kraft. The "Raven Run" continues to grow and is a
bona fide Miami Beach Institution, with a devoted
following that includes members of the Miami Beach
Ocean Patrol . . . We are grateful to him for sharing his
simple, peaceful, and healthy lifestyle with so many over
the years and look forward to the miles of sand that
lie ahead.*

"For years, I always thought I was a nobody, a nothing,"
says Raven. "Talk about not an overnight success. But when
the mayor said those nice words, I was humbled. I thought, *I'm
finally getting some positive feedback for what I've done,
through sweat, blood, and tears.*"

Soon ESPN followed with more recognition. In December,
they published an online story on the culture of streak running,
and Raven was the poster child. "Kraft is a member of a rare
and obsessed breed, a streak runner," wrote reporter Joshua
Hammann, who called Raven "the Forrest Gump of South
Beach."

He also called people who ran with him "a mixed bag of
Raven-wannabes who will follow him anywhere, like baby
ducklings trailing behind their mama." (While I might agree
there are quacks, followers are uncommon—except Eva "Fol-
lower," a 53-year-old woman from Warsaw, who usually runs
ahead of the group kicking a tennis ball or dribbling a soccer
ball. She has more than a hundred runs.)

For Raven's thirty-three years and 95,000 miles on the streak,
"the only tangible reward . . . is the number eleven spot on the
United States Running Streak Association's active list," noted
Hammann. Raven told him he was chasing a goal of 100,000
miles—on track for March 2009—and after that he might end
the streak. This news caught Miracle off guard. In the article,
she is quoted: "I'm surprised he's actually able to discuss ending it rationally. I just don't think he'll ever be able to stop."

As the Raven Run recruits poured in from the story, Raven

heard that journalist Chris Connelly wanted to feature him on the program, *Outside the Lines*. For his hundred thousandth mile, ESPN would be sending a camera crew.

ONE AFTERNOON, Abdul the pilot was sitting on a wall by the beach entrance at 5th Street with a shaved head and a full beard. "Are you allowed to fly with that beard?" asked Raven.

Lowering his chin to his chest, Abdul pointed to a new scar that wrapped around the base of his scalp. "I got a brain tumor," he said—a malignant glioma, the same as Ted Kennedy, who'd just been diagnosed in May 2008. "I'm on medical leave," Abdul told Raven as they walked to the beach.

It was a short vacation for Abdul, but he squeezed in several runs with Raven. When he got back to Seattle, he started radiation. To get to the treatment center, Abdul ran six miles each way. Raven was his pen pal throughout. Abdul sent pictures of his running trail at home, around the lakes, through the forest. Raven kept him updated on Run gossip, as well as Mary and Gringo, who was going through chemotherapy.

"Chemo, that's something else," Gringo recalled to me. "Ugh, it's just pure poison to our bodies. It tries to do everything to you, and you just fight everything it's trying to do. When I got my first dose, I started to lie down, and I thought, *God, I'm not sleepy, what am I lying down for?* That's the trick. *Get up.* I went out and ran with Raven, and I thought, *I'm gonna take my shoes off, just for the discipline of feeling my feet going over the rocks.*"

In 2008, both Gringo and Abdul completed eight-mile runs with Raven while fighting cancer. "I'm saying this not for me but for everyone that goes through this chemotherapy," says Gringo. "Don't cede to it. Never. Don't cede to it. As sick as you can be, you can get up."

When Abdul came to the banquet in 2009, his words were scrambled as he accepted the Fitness award. Though few could understand him, all Raven Runners respected him. Abdul's last run with Raven was on March 28, 2009—the day before the hundred thousandth mile. When they finished, Abdul grabbed Raven's hand and said, "You made it."

A CROWD WAS WAITING FOR HIM at the 5th Street lifeguard stand on March 29, 2009. There was a police escort, an ESPN film crew, *Miami Herald* reporters, local news, and hundreds of Raven Runners. "It was a thrill," says Raven. "If I had to pick two moments in my life, I'd say that day and meeting Johnny Cash."

The adrenaline made Raven run faster than usual, and he finished eight miles in eighty-five minutes. "But I had this thing where I couldn't run less than ninety minutes," says Raven, "so I ran in place for five minutes. The news crews were there, and they were looking at me like, *This guy really is crazy.*"

Before going home, Raven announced, "Depending on how I feel, I may not come back tomorrow."

That night Raven did some thinking. He thought, *I'm fighting a lot of injuries. I'm not making money. I'm not getting a family. Maybe I should do something else. Or retire and travel.* "But it just so happened the next day, I was on a high, I felt good and what else do I know how to do but run? I didn't want to disappoint anybody. I was there."

The episode aired two months later in May to an audience of 97 million. "People were calling me day and night," says Raven happily. "Kids would call and say I was their inspiration, that they wanted to run with me. Or people would say that running had saved them. One guy in California was calling me all the time, saying that I keep him going. Women were calling, saying, 'I just had a baby, and I'm going to start running because of you.' I would write letters to people. There were tons of comments online. Tortuga printed them out for me. I really got a kick out of reading what people thought of me."

I asked if he still had the comments. "I'm a hoarder," he answered. "You know I have them. But really most of the comments were positive. No one said that I was a total nut. People said it's crazy but it's great. People asked what was with all the chest hair. Some said that I looked like an old hippie, or a hybrid of Chuck Norris and Jesus Christ."

Fortune didn't come with fame, and Raven is okay with that. "The idea is to get people healthy," he says. "If people see it and say, 'If that guy can do it, I can do it,' and they start running, it's a good thing."

HELPING OTHER PEOPLE took his mind off his own problems. Many days, Raven came home to a full answering machine with panicked messages from his mother. "Everything was an emergency," says Raven. Mary literally wore out her telephone keypad from dialing, and Raven had to take away her Rolodex when friends complained she called too much.

One day, after listening to desperate messages from his mother, Raven ran to her apartment and found her crying. She held up her beloved teddy bear, Adam, and shrieked, "He's not eating! He's not eating. He's going to die." Adam's face was covered in banana. Prying the stuffed animal from his mother's hands, Raven patted Adam's stomach. "It's okay, Mom," he said gently. "I fed him earlier." Then she couldn't remember Adam's name and got more and more distressed. "His name is Bagdad," she said, pausing. "No, it's Sinclair. Or is it Billy? Oh, I know—it's Adam!" Raven smiled and said, "That's right, Mom. It's Adam."

The compulsive calling eventually stopped when Mary forgot about the phone. She also lost vocabulary. The air conditioner became a wind-blower, and when she couldn't remember the word "peel," she asked Raven to "break" the banana. "When they're slipping into Alzheimer's, they fight it, and they can get mean," says Raven. "Even her voice—she always sounded young, but the disease turns you into a different person. It was hard."

Sometimes Mary believed she was in a train station in

Philadelphia or Arizona. "It was strange," says Raven, "because she had never been to Arizona. So I would show her pictures and tell her, 'Look, here are your things. You're home.' And that would comfort her a little. She'd say, 'Oh, I'm home.' "

Bedbound, Mary couldn't do anything for herself. "I compare her to a baby," says Raven, "but the thing is, with a baby, there's a lot of satisfaction; you're seeing growth and progress, they're walking and talking and learning. But this is the other way around. Everything is going down. I really hate to say it— I feel so guilty—but I just wanted my life back. I thought, *God, is this woman ever going to die?*"

A neighbor from El Salvador named Berta helped to take care of Mary, but despite the sponge baths and position changes, Mary developed bedsores. That is when, in May 2010, Raven called the paramedics. A woman from Adult Protective Services, a branch of the Department of Elder Affairs, showed up, too. Cornering Raven, she demanded, "What did you do to her? Tell me what you did." Raven recalls, "Here I am, my mother is dying, and this woman is threatening to take me to jail."

At the hospital, Mary was a vegetable. Raven didn't know what to do. "My mother always said, 'Where there's life, there's hope,' " recalls Raven. But looking at her, he saw no life. "If I ever get like that, give me something. Get me out. I'd want to die."

When Mary stopped eating, the nurses asked about a feeding tube, which Raven declined. Mary was transferred to hospice, where they managed her pain with morphine. "She was smiling," says Raven. "The last thing she said was, 'I feel fine.' "

Just before midnight on May 17, 2010—a year to the day after ESPN aired his hundred thousandth mile—Mary closed her eyes and died in her sleep. "It was like her time ran out," says Raven.

The next day he was running with Philly Rock, whose father had died of Alzheimer's. "It's funny," Raven observed, "as soon as she died, I imagined her as young again. She was like thirty-five, we're going down to the beach, or she was taking me to school, holding my hand. It was a nice feeling. I don't remember her as old." Philly Rock said the same thing had happened to him when his father died.

A few weeks later, people from the Raven Run community gathered in front of the 5th Street lifeguard stand to celebrate Mary's life. Tortuga, Electrolyte, Barnacle, Karaoke Fred, and the Giggler were all there. In his eulogy, Raven said Mary had been a great mom. "She believed in me so much that if I ever killed somebody, she would've said, 'Aw, he didn't mean it.' Or, 'Maybe the guy deserved it.' " Poutine started crying. Creve Coeur and his wife, Hollywood Flasher, were filming.

As the building manager for a thirty-two-unit apartment, Mary "dealt with people from all walks of life—from Holocaust survivors with tattoo numbers on their arms, old Florida people, rednecks, Latinos, and people from every country you can imagine," continued Raven. During the Mariel Boatlift, she rented an apartment to three transvestites. "She always talked their language. She knew how to get along with everybody."

Raven said she was a character herself. She tried to lead by example and live the right way. "Although she wasn't perfect, which none of us are, hopefully she's with God in heaven." When he finished, he invited people to say a few words.

Firecracker read a poem. Miracle remarked, "I've never seen anybody take care of a mother like he did, and he became more of a man through that."

"There's not a day that goes by that I don't think of my mother," Raven told me. "I'm very sentimental; just about every little thing brings up memories." There is both sadness and fear in his voice. "And I can't help but think, *What if I end up like that?*" he asks. "*Who's gonna take care of me?*"

VIII
LEGEND

I run with Raven to be a part of history.
—Encyclopedia, 205 runs

There's this need for the kind of myth that people used to have and we don't have anymore. Nobody believes in the Man of Steel, and people want something they can believe in. No matter where you are in the world, you know there's this superhuman guy doing something that's impossible to imagine.
—Miracle, 302 runs, 775 swims

He's a legend! Once people hear about this mysterious man running on the beach every single day since 1975—and that you're allowed to and invited to join him—well you just can't help yourself. You want to know more. You want to be part of history being made. And on top of it, you get a nickname!
—KittyCat, commuter from NYC, 17 runs

So much is mental, really. All I gotta do is think about these legs moving, and somehow they move.
—Raven

EIGHTEEN

EQUAL IN
RUNNING CLOTHES

Raven is my number one suggestion for things to do in Miami Beach. When people come to visit, I tell them to bring their running shoes. "There's no way in hell I'm running eight miles," said my brother Eric, who is a psychiatrist, when he arrived from Massachusetts with his friend Kerry, an osteopathic physician, in March 2014.

"No problem," I said, "I just want you to meet Raven."

"Great," said Eric. "I'll run a mile or two with him."

This is usually how it happens. Someone is curious about Raven's story and gets convinced to try one or two miles with him. Eric is 40 years old, about six-foot-one with an athletic build, but he's never been a distance runner. He is a smart guy—a member of Mensa with a medical degree and a Juris Doctorate. He is shy at first. Knowing me like he does, he expected his little sister to find a pocket of athletic oddballs in South Florida with whom to associate. But he didn't expect to show up to the Raven Run and meet another member of Mensa, named Close Call, who is from Finland. He also didn't expect to meet Sleazebuster, the Northwestern law professor. Eric also met Dos Equis, a boat builder from the Dominican Republic who looks like and has lived like the Most Interesting Man in the World.

His friend, Kerry, was familiar with the Hash House Harriers, a running group that calls themselves, "a drinking club with a running problem," and also uses nicknames. She was ready to like Raven and his runners from the get-go.

After a mile or two at our slow pace, Eric was in deep conversation with Close Call. Then another mile passed, and another mile, as Eric made his way around talking to different friendly people. At six miles, Raven turned to me. "I think your brother is going to make all eight," he said. "We need a nickname." At that moment, Eric and Kerry were talking about a trip to Hawaii, where they hiked around volcanoes. Close Call said, "Have you ever seen lightning produced in a volcanic plume? It's called Volcano Lightning." Raven loves nicknames within families to be related, so two miles later, finishing at the 5th Street lifeguard stand, Eric became Volcano Lightning, brother to White Lightning. Kerry became Morning Dew, because she is a morning person and her middle name is Dew. They couldn't believe they'd run eight miles.

For the next three days, Eric couldn't walk properly, but I was proud of him, and he was proud of himself. When I asked his professional opinion on Raven, he said, "Look, he's found something that works for him, and a lot of people have benefited from it and made connections." (In another conversation, my father had said the same thing. "I think running has been a good thing for Raven," said Dr. Huttenbach. "It's good to have a sense of mastery over something. He has found a group of people who honor what he's doing. He's found respect and companionship. Some people find that through marriage, a profession, or church. But Raven's found meaning through running.")

Meanwhile Kerry was worried about Raven's physical condition, elaborating on complications that he could face in the future. "He could get stress fractures, his arthritis could impinge the nerves so much that he loses motor function in his legs," she said. Basically, Raven was running toward a wheelchair. She asked, "He does know that he will still be Raven even if he's not running, right?"

WHEN YOU ASK A RAVEN RUNNER how they met Raven, the responses run the gamut. "It was the afternoon of December 31, 2013," recalled Lutefisk, a 56-year-old journalist from Norway, in an email to me. "I was running on the beach southward heading for the pier—alone. Toward me comes a group of twenty cheerful people. I pass them, but the laughter and fun atmosphere catches me. I turn around and catch up with them. I ask one runner what it's all about. And soon Raven invites me to run with them. And it is just great!" His nickname comes from his country's traditional dish, which is dried cod soaked in lye until the fish becomes like a gel. (Originally he liked the name but now he's campaigning to change it because his roll call is, "The smelliest fish in Norway!")

During Lutefisk's first short holiday in Miami Beach, he completed seven eight-mile runs. Since then, "I have come back from Norway three times to run with this legend of a man. I have made good friends thanks to Raven. It feels good to be around nice people. It is social, it is healthy, and it is always exciting to see who shows up. To me, being Norwegian, it is sort of like having a family in an exciting place like Miami Beach. I no longer feel like a tourist, but a part of the community."

Thunder is a man from New Haven living in California who was in town for a business trip in 2007. "I was lucky enough to call a Miami running store while I was there and ask if there were any running clubs," Thunder explained. "They said to run with Raven. I came across his old website and saw photos of people with nicknames like 'Angry Man,' a list of runners named 'One Run Wonders,' and I said to myself, 'I have to check this out.' " After his first eight miles, he got the nickname from his favorite basketball player Darryl Dawkins, aka

Chocolate Thunder. "I think what impressed me most was the second time I came to Miami Beach and showed up at tower five, Raven remembered my real name, nickname, where I was from now, where I originally came from, and birthday," he recalled. "It was kind of freaky. I thought maybe he just got lucky with all my info for some reason, but over the years I have seen him do the same with others that show up." I've run with Thunder several times, and those miles have consistently come with the worst weather, which we joke that it's because Thunder and White Lightning are together.

When I asked Thunder what it was about Raven that drew people from all over the world to run eight miles with him, he responded: "I really do not know for certain, though I do believe most, if not all, runners are insane. And I think Raven takes insane as far as you can take it (I mean that it in a good way). Maybe some strange 'insanity attraction' that makes us show up. I say insane because why the heck do we spend all that time running and, in many cases, beating our bodies up? For some reason, I keep doing it. There's a little celebrity status meeting and running with Raven and saying you did, maybe a bucket list item for some, maybe something different from all the tourist things to do while in Miami Beach. And granted it would be a lot harder for people to come run with the Raven if he was living in some strange place like Montezuma, Iowa (yes, I've been and ain't nothing going on). Miami Beach is an ideal location for Raven and for visitors to come together. It's a great beach to run on. Now if you ask me what was my most memorable Raven Run moment . . . I'd have to think about that one for a while. There's more than a few."

On Raven's 64th birthday run—October 17, 2014—I was next to Butcher, a man whose twelve-pack abs defy his 50 years. Two years before, fresh out of prison for drug trafficking, Butcher was seeking a regimen to get his life back on track when, at the pull-up bars, Raven invited him to run. "A guy I was in jail with told me, 'You gotta find a group to be a part of or something to get involved in,' " recalled Butcher. "Because, you know, there's no transition from prison to the free world." After working up to the eight miles, Butcher set out to run with Raven every day for a hundred days, but instead kept the streak going for two hundred, setting a new Raven Run record. "It's not only Raven but all the positive people you meet out here. I was in a really dark place with anger management issues, and the run just sucks the negativity out of you." These days Butcher is a calm but demanding personal trainer whose clients include fellow Raven Runners. "God only knows where I'd be without Raven and this run. It's the best thing that's ever happened to me."

A LOT OF PEOPLE ARE SURPRISED by how much they like Raven and how much they relate to Raven Runners. Shoe Guy first ran with Raven on March 29, 2009—the day that Raven hit 100,000 streak miles. "While I had seen Raven on the run, I had not known his story," Shoe Guy recalled to me in an email. "What I learned from other runners about Raven that day was so impressive that I had a hard time reconciling that as a runner, I had not known his story."

So he came back.

A lot.

"Over seven years and [almost] seven hundred runs, I've seen that like the Pied Piper, Raven draws a varied lot," Shoe Guy observed. "Unlike the Pied Piper, very few are rats and many bring their own interesting stories from all around America and all over the world. And, many great friendships have resulted from uncommon people meeting and following this one-of-a-kind world-beater." Through Raven, he met one of his best friends, a financier from Rhode Island called Salt Shaker. Shoe is also a terrific recruiter, having brought many friends and family members to run, including his hometown friend from Wisconsin who completed eight on two replaced knees, earning him the nickname, Replacement, and the 2011 Event of the Year.

I was running with Raven and Shoe Guy once in October 2012 when Raven said, "I got a quick story for you, White Lightning. It involves you, Shoe."

"Oh?" said Shoe.

"It's about one of our records," said Raven. "The coldest swim." Shoe Guy smiled, immediately recognizing the story. "Well, the first part of the story was on January 8, 2010," began Raven. "We finish the run, and the air temperature is forty-five degrees—the coldest day so far for a swim—so Shoe Guy goes in the water and breaks the record."

"Congratulations," I said.

"Yeah," said Shoe Guy with a smirk. "It was a short-lived record."

Raven continued. "Well, I get home and tell Miracle that Shoe Guy broke the record, and she said, 'I want that record— will you go back to the beach with me and make it official?' She's probably the only one I'd do it for, but I went back and strolled along the shoreline until she finished. When she left the water, the air temperature was 44 degrees, so she broke Shoe Guy's record like an hour after he got it. "

"Can I interject something?" asked Shoe Guy. "About Dictator?"

"Yeah, I'm getting to that," said Raven. "Shoe Guy's friend, Dictator, said that since Miracle was wearing a wetsuit that day, it shouldn't count. Anyway, the next day, it turned out to be even colder, and Chapter 11, in his seventies, tried to get the record from Miracle, but Miracle showed up, too. To make sure Dictator didn't have anything to say about the wetsuit, she stripped down and went in the water naked. Then Chapter 11 mumbles, 'Err, mm, I'm going to take my clothes off, too.' All I remember is Miracle's round, white butt running into the water and then Chapter 11's old, flat butt a few steps behind, trying to catch up."

"All for a Raven Run record," I said. Shoe Guy and Raven looked at me like I just wasn't getting it.

"Yeah," they both answered.

That was the story as told on the run. The next day, I sat down with Miracle and Raven for an interview. "I heard that Dictator challenged your coldest swim record because you wore a wet-suit," I said.

"What? I don't remember Dictator saying that," she said. "I really struggled the first day to finish the swim because the zip-per on my wetsuit was broken, and it filled up with water." She took a deep breath. "Then the next day, I'm at home in South Dade, happily reading on my couch when I looked outside, and it was raining. I opened the door—it was about five thirty—and I could feel the temperature dropping. I went, 'Oh, shit, it's going to be just as cold tonight.'" Miracle looked at me for a response, so I nodded.

"Well, I knew that son of a bitch, Chapter 11, was already at the beach, and all he had to do was walk out of his apartment, so I just jumped in the car and raced over here. I didn't even stop to check the Weather Channel—nothing. I drove as fast as I could in the fucking rain. I ran at least one red light and parked illegally on Fifth somewhere and ran to the stand. I got here just in time 'cause there's Chapter getting ready to go.

"By this time, I've already gotten the information from Raven that it's thirty-whatever degrees [36 degrees], and I'm going to have to do it again," said Miracle. "That's when I realized, 'I'm still toasty warm 'cause I drove twenty-seven miles with the heater on full blast and if I take the time to put on a suit, I'll be really cold.' So I just said, 'Fuck it. Gentlemen, avert your eyes. I'm going in.' I was naked in six seconds. I hit the water flying, and knocked it out. Oh, man, it was so fucking cold and raw. So that's it. It's not much of a story."

"Not much of a story?" said Raven. "It's a classic!"

"No," Miracle corrected him. "I just—I couldn't have endured that awful, fucking, first-record-breaking swim to lose it the very next day on a freaky cold front situation. I couldn't let that happen. I mean, come on."

"So you did it all for a Raven Run record?" I asked Miracle.

She shot me a similar look to the one that I had received from Shoe Guy and Raven. "Yeah," she said. "All for a fucking record."

CREVE COEUR IS A FEDERAL MARSHAL and bodybuilder in his 40s from Creve Coeur, Missouri, who I met on a run in June 2011. He has a shaved head and silver eyes and looks like he could lift me over his head with one hand. Creve first heard of Raven when "a homeless guy and Raven Run coach, Eugene, said that I should run with him," Creve recalled to me later in an email. "I had crossed paths with Raven while running on South Beach about a dozen times over 2005, but thought he was a bit too different than my clean-cut self and a tad unapproachable. So I had only just nodded or waved to him." When his then friend—now wife—Isabel seconded Eugene's recommendation to run with Raven, he finally agreed. "Isabel said Raven was really interesting and shared my devotion to fitness and running," wrote Creve. "Little did I know Raven was exponentially more devoted than myself to running."

Creve and Isabel completed their first eight-mile run in September 2005. Isabel, a photographer from California, became Hollywood Flasher. In Creve's words: "I admired Raven's eternal determination and discipline. I enjoyed Raven's evening leisurely distance pace and learning all his South Beach stories . . . thousands of miles' worth over the years. I have never belonged to a group before so it was fun to start friendships through running and constantly meet new runners. I was also slowly becoming more attached to my future wife through all the runs. I tried to remain distant from her (wanting to remain a bachelor till I was 50), but she really started growing on me with her devotion to keeping up with me on the run. The more miles we ran the closer we became. Finally, at the start of a Raven Run one day, I proposed to her."

When Flasher said yes, Creve turned to Raven and said, "I'd like you to marry us."

Raven said, "I wish I could, Creve, but I'm not ordained."

Creve said, "Oh, we can take care of all that online." So Raven was ordained under the official title, Right Reverend Robert Running Raven.

On December 5, 2009—Creve's 40th birthday—at four o'clock, guests gathered at the 5th Street lifeguard stand to witness the first-ever wedding ceremony on the Raven Run. Hollywood Flasher wore a short, strapless white gown with running shoes and a garter belt. The groom ran shirtless with a bow tie and passed out extra bow ties to his male attendants. Runners Seaside Sparrow, Poutine, Firecracker, and Tortuga held cue cards with Raven's lines written in magic marker. Film crews from Channel Six attended the ceremony as well, and the story made national news and NPR. (The run was the second ceremony of the day. "I did one ceremony for them in the morning at the pier—you know, in case some of their guests couldn't run the whole eight miles," explained Raven.) The occasion won the Raven Run Event of the Year, though Flasher and Creve hold a couple records. They both ran on the hottest day (102 degrees), and Flasher holds the record for most miles ever run by a female in a day—forty-one miles, including eight with Raven—while wearing a thong. She is in the Hall of Fame.

Now Flasher and Creve live on a farm in Redlands, Florida, and have two kids. Though they don't get to run with Raven often, Creve credits the run for the couple's happy ending. "The run is what's kept us together," he said. What at first put him off from meeting Raven now Creve finds most admirable. "Raven is unique in a world of domesticated clones and people who struggle to fit in everywhere," Creve wrote to me. He has seen Raven encourage many runners and non-runners alike to complete eight miles and keep coming back. "Personally I've always been a self-motivator, but from my experience most people need a motivating friend or trainer to get them to work out or go jogging," he said. "Knowing that every day at the same time Raven is running is comforting for people to get off their rear and go out and run with him. I have to admit there were times I was going to skip my run because of a thunderstorm or cold weather and the only reason I ended up going was because I knew Raven would be there."

FIVE YEARS AFTER CREVE AND FLASHER'S MARRIAGE, Raven officiated his second wedding between Raven Runners, Extra and Molder. Extra met Raven when she'd just moved to Miami and was going through a rough time, out of work and uncertain about love. "I used to go running on the beach at odd times of day," she said. "As I made it over the dune one day, Lobotomy handed me a flyer for the Raven Run. I was very happy because I'd been feeling so lonely and isolated, and Oscar [Molder] wasn't a runner, so these solo runs were becoming monotonous." The following afternoon at five thirty, she came to the 5th Street lifeguard stand. "I'll never forget running with Gringo, listening to his life story, then looking out across the water at a cruise ship on the edge of a lavender horizon; flaming orange, reflecting the last rays of the October sunset." Soon Extra, who is a painter, accepted an artist residency in Vermont. "I told Oscar I wasn't coming back," she explained to me in an email. "Well, he knew I had been running with Raven, and decided to go check it out for himself (which was shocking because he never liked running). I couldn't believe he actually ran the full eight and got a name . . . it made me re-evaluate him and his dedication to our relationship. I knew he did it to feel closer to me while I was away." When she came back to South Beach, Molder, a professor of sculpture at FIU, proposed.

In a stationary ceremony in January 2013, Extra wore a short taffeta mocha dress and sparkly high heels. Molder wore a gray suit with a blue Oxford and a yellow striped tie. The Reverend wore a fringed black leather jacket, black denim jeans, and a homemade black shoelace belt. His clergy card was in his left pocket.

I know this because Raven invited me to attend the wedding at the rock wall jetty by Government Cut. "I even wore my boots," said Raven, clicking his heels against the pavement.

"I love the fray," said Extra, pointing to his shoulder. Raven smiled and raised his arms so the leather tassels jiggled in the wind. "We wanted an intimate ceremony and someone who knew us," explained Extra. "Not just a stranger with authority. We thought Raven would be perfect. He's someone we know and love and trust." Her fiancé added, "He's a friend. We wanted a friend to marry us."

As we approached the shoreline, passersby shouted congratulations. The very sweet ceremony lasted five minutes. At the end, Raven turned away from the couple and looked at us. Then he remembered the closing line. "Now, you may kiss the bride," even though the blissful newlyweds were already locked at the lips. After they signed the marriage certificate, I asked Raven if he had advice for the newlyweds. "Compromise," he answered without hesitation. "And the woman is always right."

CHOCOLATE CHIP IS A DENTIST who eats chocolate four or five times a day. Though he'd been running in Miami since 1967, he first heard of Raven in the early 1990s. "I heard something about a weird-looking man who lived on Miami Beach and was rumored to run eight miles every single day . . . on the *sand* . . . in the heat of the *late afternoon* . . . dressed in *black*," Chocolate Chip wrote to me. "As someone who had been running in our hot and humid climate for several decades, and was quite familiar with how challenging that could be, I dismissed the information about that guy as pure hyperbole. However, every so often over the next ten years, I would hear the same hard-to-believe story about the Miami Beach Running Man. Then, in 2001, when I heard that his name was the Raven, I resolved to see this for myself."

On a steamy August afternoon, Chocolate Chip showed up at the 5th Street lifeguard stand. "Even though I had never run on the soft sand before, I figured I'd be able to stay with him until he pooped out," he recalled, pointing out that he had sixteen marathons under his belt. "When I was about fifty yards from the lifeguard stand, I spotted a well-muscled, hairy-chested man in black running shorts. My first thought was that he looked like a cross between a pirate and an Oakland Raider season-ticket holder. I was intimidated by his appearance and didn't want to approach him. My second thought was to hang back, give him a two-hundred-yard head start and tail him, noting just how long he could go before he stopped. So I did! I lasted two and a half miles. He left me eating his dust (er, sand). I walked off the beach with my tail between my legs. My skepticism and disbelief turned to respect."

He came back months later, when it was cooler. "This time I completed the run," he said. "In the process I met a very nice man and learned a great deal." Since then, he has run 723 times with Raven—all complete, eight-mile runs without one partial on the books. He began the tradition of a "half-way joke," where, beginning at the four-mile mark, he delivered a funny story that usually took up at least a mile. He explains, "I thought it would be a good idea to tell a lengthy joke at the midpoint of the run so as to make the second half seem shorter than the first half." It worked.

(Raven told me his all-time favorite from Chocolate Chip, which went like this: A surfer finds a genie in the bottle, and the genie pops up and says, "I'll grant you any wish in the whole world." The surfer says, "I'd love to have a bridge from California to Hawaii so I won't ever have to fly to go surfing."

The genie says, "Man, you're really asking for a lot. Really. What else can I do for you? Give me something else." So the man says, "I'd really love to know what makes women tick, to understand them and know what satisfies them and makes them happy." The genie thinks for a minute and says, "How many lanes you want in that bridge?")

In 2009, Chocolate Chip was inducted in the Hall of Fame. On Raven, he says, "He's a genuinely nice guy that has a unique lifestyle. He lives simply, but is extremely interesting on many different levels. He is unequivocally, universally welcoming, providing companionship and camaraderie while on a run in an absolutely beautiful location. What could be better?"

TRANSPORTER IS FROM GERMANY and was invited by the man himself to run. "I remember I was playing in the sand with my one-year-old daughter wearing a Marines shirt, which apparently triggered Raven to greet me 'military style' while running past me. I later found out who he is and pledged to come back to run with him." He kept his promise and completed his first eight in 2009. "Nobody will ever understand how much this run means to me," he wrote in an email. In bullet points, he listed four reasons why he runs with Raven: "Because I enjoy Raven's stories and being a part of history, I meet wonderful people along the way, I get inspired to try new things in life, and I have become a better person since running with him."

In another email, he expounded on his motivations that he believes he shares with many runners: "The 'semi-regulars' (my segment) repeatedly join, because they feel connected to the free spirit of the run, to Raven, to the other runners, to the 'Raven community.' Runners not only learn from Raven, but also from the other runners' stories, about all sorts of things in life. You tap into a pool of great people, all professions, all ages, all cultures, all fitness levels, all sizes and shapes . . . It gets you energized, opens up your mind, thinking about my own life, you enjoy the 'here and now'—I personally experienced that it helps me to become more innovative and creative. Through Raven so many people started a new episode in their life, at least started to work on 'projects' they would not have thought of without the run. In one sentence: The Raven Run is magic."

By doing the same exact thing every day, Raven inspires Transporter and many others to do something new.

JURISPRUDENCE, a beautiful and bubbly blond lawyer in her 30s, met Raven in November 2010. She had just moved from her hometown of Brussels and was living in an apartment with a balcony that overlooked South Beach at 5th Street. "I saw Raven showing up every day at the lifeguard stand in front of my apartment," she told me. "I was drawn by the consistency, the structure that it added to my day as well. I could be absolutely sure of him showing up every day at the same time, ready to take whomever wanted to join him on a run, or more like on a running journey." An athlete herself (the former national karate champion of Belgium), Jurisprudence became a regular. "I got the family feeling. I loved the diverse interesting group of people you get to run and talk with. Everyone is equal in running clothes. We all shared a passion for sports and a true caring for each other and for Raven."

HOT FURNACE CAME WITH HIS FATHER-IN-LAW from Alexandria, Louisiana, to run with Raven in August 2013. In his words, "I first learned of Raven when I saw him on *Real Sports with Bryant Gumbel* [that aired in October 2011]. I was fascinated with this man who'd not let anything stop him from running. Running had been a big part of my life. In a way, it was my best friend. I first began running as a very obese youth determined to lose weight and fit in. I lost a hundred and fifteen pounds at the age of fourteen, and used running for the next twenty years to keep it off. Running changed my life. I'd hate to even think about what my life would have been like had I not taken that weight off and continued as that fat awkward kid that I was. At the time I saw Raven on TV, I had stopped because of back problems. A few years earlier, after being diagnosed with one bulging and one ruptured disc, a doctor told me I couldn't run anymore. I had put on weight, feeling dreadful and depressed over my physical condition. Now here was this guy who loves Johnny Cash and Waylon Jennings, is a huge baseball fan, and has back problems just like me. I was so inspired, I put on my shoes and hit the sidewalk! It hurt, but I shuffled out three miles. I set a goal to run three miles every day for a month. Three months later I was still going, except many days doing five miles. The pain was almost gone, and my speed wasn't what it had been in my younger years, but not bad.

"One day, while on vacation, I was running atop a cruise ship in the middle of the Gulf of Mexico. The view was so spectacular that I just kept running. When I stopped, I had run seven miles. It was at that moment I realized, *I can work up to eight and go run with Raven!* I booked a flight and hotel the moment I got home. Even talked my father-in-law into training and going with me. I wanted to be able to talk with and thank this man who'd brought me out of the funk I'd been in. I didn't want to struggle or 'God forbid' not earn my nickname, so I trained hard during the hottest times of day. When the day came, I was forty-five pounds lighter and running eight with ease. The run was great. Raven and the other runners really made me feel welcome. I earned my nickname on that first run August 26, 2013. Raven gave me the name partly because of my job, and partly because I collapsed immediately after the run from the Miami heat and humidity (which I was not accustomed to). But I ate well, rehydrated, and returned the following day and completed the run again (without passing out afterward)." Since then, he suffered a knee injury. "No eight-mile runs for me currently, but Raven keeps inspiring me to keep trying. We converse through Facebook from time to time about music, baseball, and of course running. Thanks to him,

I'm on a three-week streak of three miles a day (on my tread-mill). Slow but steady!"

CANUCK IS A DARK-HAIRED, DARK-EYED, middle-aged, bespec-tacled attorney who, since 2003, has run over two hundred times with Raven while commuting from his home in Toronto. When he listens, his chin pokes out, and it has the effect of al-ways making you feel like you're saying something important.

Canuck had seen Raven running during their respective evening jogs but was scared to approach him, because he thought Raven was "a bit of a freak of a guy," recalled Canuck in an email. Then one morning at breakfast at the News Café, Canuck struck up a conversation with the waiter, who was a triathlete. "We chatted about where to train, and I told him I ran on the beach. He asked me if I ran with 'that guy.' 'Which guy?' I asked. He told me about a guy with long hair who al-ways wore black who ran the beach every afternoon. He said that they called him 'the Falcon.' "

That afternoon, as usual, "that guy" came running toward Canuck. "As we passed each other I asked him if he was the Falcon. Looking somewhat confused, he answered, 'No, but I am the Raven.' "

Raven invited him to run. "These were pre-Internet days, and I didn't know the story," continued Canuck. "I showed up the next day to run with him and learned he had been running eight miles daily (same time, same place for over twenty-five years . . . as it was back then), keeping a list of all those who had done 'a complete,' with memorized details of their Raven-given names, their real given names, birthdays, place of birth, and number of complete Raven Runs (and swims). Quite frankly I am still not sure what's more impressive, the forty-one-plus years' streak or his memorization of all of 'the list' details."

Canuck, like many of us, came to meet a legendary character

and wound up finding a friend and connecting to fellow runners. "While running is the excuse, it is the people who have made this run into the special thing that it is," wrote Canuck. "That starts with Raven and extends outward into what is now over twenty-five hundred individual stories, many of which have become intertwined."

NINETEEN

WEAVER

It was six o'clock when I listened to Raven's voicemail. "I got your message about you not being able to run today, White Lightning," began Raven in a breathy, desperate voice. "That's all right. I'm still having these chest pains real bad. It's hard to breathe. I think I'll have to go to the emergency room tonight after the run. In case anything happens to me, Miracle knows where my writings are. I told her to give them to you. Anyways, good luck finishing your work. See you soon—I hope."

Who schedules an emergency room visit?

I laced up my running shoes and grabbed my keys. Hitting the beach at 14th Street, I ran south toward the pier. Fourteen blocks later, I hadn't seen anyone. Picking up speed, I headed north, scanning the beach for Raven's familiar gait. His message replayed in my head, "In case anything happens to me, Miracle knows where my writings are." The 15th Street lifeguard stand dropped behind me. Still no Raven. I passed Lincoln, 20th, and that's when I saw a small pack of runners.

"She's not moonshine," crowed the Raven, "she's Whiiittteee Lightning!" I asked how he felt. "Better now. I just can't breathe. Miracle's taking me to the hospital."

A bony homeless man rummaged around in a trashcan on our left, and Raven called out his greetings. "Pigpen!" Pigpen, a coach, dropped a Coke can and managed a nod before returning his attention to the garbage.

"They'll need to run a lot of tests," continued Raven, "hook me up to the machines and stuff." Walter Kraft had died of a stroke at 67, and Raven figured he ran the same risk.

"What's going to happen if they won't let you leave tomorrow?" I asked.

"I'm bringing my shoes," he said, smiling. "If it gets to five o'clock, I'll start running in the hallways. What can they do?"

Five hours later—just after midnight—Raven, Philly Rock, and Taxman met at the lifeguard stand to run one mile, so that if Raven needed surgery, the streak would be safe for an extra twenty-four hours. Documenting the midnight run with her camera, Yellow Rose was there, too. "It was a pretty somber mood," she said. "Raven made a little speech that this could be his last run, and we believed it. Everyone was scared."

At five in the morning, Miracle drove Raven to the hospital for an angiogram. As nurses shaved a patch of Raven's chest hair, Yellow Rose—there again with her camera—asked how he felt. "Oh, it'll grow back," he said.

The procedure took a few hours with Raven under full anesthesia. When he woke up, the doctor said, "I've got great news. Your chest is totally clear. It looks great."

As soon as the IVs came out, Raven slipped on his running shoes and watched the clock. When it got to be five thirty and he hadn't been discharged, Raven took to the hallways like he said he would and started running. "There wasn't a lot of foot traffic," recalled Yellow Rose. "But every time someone passed, they looked at Raven like he was crazy." By counting his steps, Raven kept track of the distance. By the time he got the discharge papers, he'd racked up two miles in the hallway. "When the elevator doors opened, Raven shot out running to the parking lot," continued Yellow Rose. "It was one of the funniest things I've ever seen."

Miracle dropped him off at 5th Street, where he ran the last five with Chapter 11.

Relieved the problem wasn't with his heart, Raven still worried that he couldn't breathe well. "It was the mold in his apartment," Gringo told me. "Yeah, he had a lot of mold. You've seen his place, right?" I said yes. "It used to be a lot worse." Gringo felt like he himself was living on borrowed time, which he owed to Raven. Through all of his health problems, Gringo's one goal had been to keep running with Raven. The men had covered more than twelve thousand miles together. Gringo wanted his friend healthy.

Armed with a mask, gloves, and clothes he threw away, Gringo showed up to clean. "We had four categories," explained Gringo. "Baseball, the run, songs, and the history of South Beach. We were putting all these clippings into shoeboxes and crates." As they sifted, Gringo got a lesson in history and psychology. "In Raven's world, every single item has an importance," says Gringo. "It helped me understand how worldly items can become a part of our real selves. If the worldly item is smashed, there is pain inside the person. And this is Raven's world. Oh, my God, he's got everything."

Gringo calls the apartment Raven's "nucleus," and he says Raven's phone was like a hotline. "He had people calling him from all over," says Gringo. "They would say, 'You know I was reading about you, and I thought maybe you could help me. I've just got to stop drinking. I'm an alcoholic. I don't know what to do.' And it'd be very typical of Raven to say, 'Okay, you call me once a week, and we're just going to talk. We are going to talk.' "

To Gringo, one particular anecdote sums up Raven. "At my apartment, we had *cucarachas* [cockroaches] on top of the freezer door. Then one day they started disappearing, and I discovered this little spider. She was eating those cucaracha babies . . . So I was just falling totally in love with this animal. She was so noble. I didn't have the heart to destroy her. I couldn't do it. Then she got under a glass shelf and laid a lot of eggs. The drama started. I'm almost filled with tears—that animal was so noble and so great—I can't believe that we killed her and her eggs, and she's gone forever."

Gringo had grown attached to a spider that nobody else valued. When the spider died, it crushed him. "All I could think of was Raven and his world [that] must be terrible for him," reckons Gringo, "of people dying, storefronts that don't exist anymore. So much that was a part of Raven is gone completely. In his house, he's observed as being this terrible word—hoarder. But those items are part of him. They're like my spider there."

For weeks Gringo cleaned pro bono. "He wouldn't accept a dime," says Raven. Gringo would've liked to continue the work, but "it was a huge time consumer," says Gringo, adding, "I lived with a woman who was so perturbed; she didn't want the mold coming in here, and I had mold on my clothes." He doesn't know how Raven survives. "He's just a strong person, that's all. In my opinion there should be a professional group of people that go in and ransack the whole place and clean it up if he wants to keep his health up."

Raven doesn't like to let strangers in to that world. When people ask to see his home, he generally refuses. To Gringo, in this intersection of Raven's worlds, we see a generous but conflicted person. "This is a person that really believes in what he does," says Gringo. "He's a real giver of himself yet he's a very private person. I think that's extraordinary."

With Gringo's help, Raven started breathing better. "It also helped a lot to keep the apartment cooler," says Raven, half-relieved, half-stressed over high electricity bills.

Gringo, like a lot of longtime Raven Runners, is nostalgic for the old group and the old beach. "There used to be a real unification with the lifeguards, too," says Gringo. "They were an intrinsic part of Raven's run. We meant something to them. These lifeguards now, they don't even speak. It's a strange situation. Times change. But the old characters were wonderful."

Gringo doesn't run with Raven anymore. He runs in the mornings. "I can't be on that run with him because of his pain," he says. With the breathing, Gringo could help, but with the back pain, there's no fix. Gringo doesn't want to be complicit in making it worse and, more than that, it hurts him to see Raven hunched over. "I can't take it. I told him I feel terrible—I adore Raven—but I'm too sensitive. Inside I'm crying all over."

MIRACLE USED TO CALL THE RUN Raven's "mistress," though now she is completely supportive of the exercise. "It's been a long process of understanding that every day meant every day, no exceptions—until when?" Miracle told me sitting with Raven in his living room. She used to dream of the day when Raven would stop the streak. They could travel together. "Oh, change!" she said sarcastically. "So many new horizons will open up, blablabla. But knowing him as I do, would he want to continue a life even where he had reasonably good health but wasn't running?"

She accepts they're not getting younger, and she speaks of mortality so stripped of sentimentality that it makes you forget you're talking about someone dying. "When you're in your sixties, you can't help but think it's probably going to be a question of one, two, or three—one decade, two decades, or three decades at the outmost for my life. It's not an endless horizon any longer. Of course that never was true, but we operate much of our lives under some kind of delusion of endless horizons. Time changes its role. Now I just want him to be able to run as many times as he can. He wouldn't be who he is without the run, so why would I want this to stop?"

His previous girlfriend never attained, or accepted, that wisdom. "Donna would always say, 'What are you doing? You're nuts.' She didn't understand." Turning to Miracle, he continued. "But you were always supportive. More so now than ever. She knows I need to run, and it keeps me going."

"It's your reason to live," she said. "Who would want to live in this much pain without something really good in your life?" Her eyes moved to me. "The pain is just sickening, to see someone going through it and not be able to fix it for them."

Raven was nodding. "I feel the same with you."

Miracle was 16 when she snapped her back in a waterskiing accident, so chronic pain is one thing they have in common. "Up to a certain level pain is entirely manageable," said Miracle. "Once it gets above that level, whatever it is for you—it's a completely different monster. I've been in unbearable pain for years now—well, I survived it, so somehow I bore it, but that terrible, terrible pain steals everything." One torturous aspect of anyone's pain, she believes, is how it eludes description. "Language fails pain," she said, shaking her head, "that's one of the torments. Once you run out of metaphors—it's like steel spikes, cold fire, blablabla—there's not much you can say to make someone understand the intensity." Hospitals don't help. "Our health industry has this visual analog scale of pain that you're supposed to give a number between one and ten," she continued, "but everyone who knows anything about experiencing pain knows what a crap system that is for communicating."

Many nights, Raven watches Miracle cry herself to sleep, and in the morning Miracle watches Raven get out of bed—a drawn-out process where putting his pants on is torture. He kneels to brush his teeth. "You know each movement is costing him so much," said Miracle.

Raven hates that he wears his pain on his face. "When new runners get to the lifeguard stand, they're scared to come up to me. They think I'm unfriendly, but I just hurt. I get relief out there," he said, nodding in the direction of the Atlantic. "When the endorphins kick in around mile three, the pain goes away. But I know it's not as pretty as it used to be. I used to run real nice. Now I'm all hunched over. I hate it. Sometimes I can fake it for a little while, but the pain draws me down." He doesn't think he could be with someone that doesn't understand the experience of chronic pain. "Our bond is the pain," he said. "I call our relationship the painful love."

Miracle doesn't like that. "I don't think that's right," she said. "Okay, relationships are painful. But love isn't painful. The love is great. It's better now than ever. It's like love in spite of the pain. That's what I would call it. And maybe sometimes because of the pain. But I would never call it painful love."

I couldn't tell if Raven understood her distinction, and Miracle sat still in silence, then smiled. "But in some ways, it's getting so much better. More people are learning about him. He's enjoyed that. There's renewed hope of people hearing his music. All this good stuff is happening. Yet there's doubt and pain and fear, every day, about an ending. When will it end? How will it end? How much more can he endure?"

"I could get a hit song," Raven told me on a run. "That'd be a great ending to my story. I could go back to Nashville for the Country Music Awards. I've been working fifty years trying to be an overnight success. What do you think, White Lightning?"

I asked him how long he wanted me to wait to publish the book.

Then he proposed an alternative ending, which his friend Killer had written in a short story years ago. "I could be running during another hurricane, and a lifeguard stand could just tip over on me." He'd be killed on the spot mid-stride. (Miracle was familiar with this idea. "Yeah, the lifeguard stand killing him," she said. "That's his fantasy.") I told Raven I'd figure out an ending for the book, but in truth all books about living people end on a question mark.

EVERY DAY THAT I LIVED in Miami Beach, I knew where I could find a friend. Probably multiple friends. Through Raven, I've met doctors and lawyers, homeless people and millionaires, judges and prisoners. I've learned a people's history of the city that I'd found so foreign. I met two best friends, Yellow Rose, the photographer from Dallas, and Juris Prudence, the attorney from Belgium. We were all born within two months of each other and act like sisters. If I'm running on Miami Beach, I'm pretty much guaranteed to see people I know from

the Raven Run community. I shout out to them by name—
Gringo! Taxman! Hitter! Butcher! Sleazebuster! Hurricane!
Poutine! Teen Idol! Shoe! And they respond with equal enthu-
siasm, fist bumps, and cheers of "Hey, looking strong, White
Lightning!"

I run into people like All-American and Deep Dish (who,
after losing forty pounds, started going by the name Thin
Crust) when I'm out on dates on Lincoln Road. Once, I ran into
Giggler at Publix when I was sick. "You might not want to hug
me," I told him. "I have the flu." Giggler laughed and said,
"Eh, I'll take my chances." He wrapped me in his arms. "If
that's how you look when you have the flu," he said, letting me
go, "more people should consider getting it."

At banquets and parties, I sit next to people like Hurricane,
who ran with Raven two days after his 80th birthday. (He
couldn't run *on* his 80th birthday because he went skydiving
that day.) Once, he came to a dinner with his best friend, Marvin, who told me, "Our morning routine is we wake up and
read the paper. If our names aren't in the obituary, we get out
of bed and have breakfast." Hurricane always told me stories
about the *old* Miami Beach, in the fifties and sixties with Frank
Sinatra and Milton Berle, and his trips to the casinos in Havana. He remembers when the Fontainebleau opened in 1954,
the same year he graduated from the University of Miami.
"You couldn't get in to the Fontainebleau lobby without a
dress shirt, jacket and tie," he told me, pausing. "Well you also
needed pants."

Where else in Miami Beach could I be seated next to Hurricane and Marvin?

Society today is giving us fewer spaces to talk to people that
are different from us. You can hold a world in your hand through
your smartphone, so there's little pressure to engage with someone next to you. Why do so many people have interesting conversations on planes? Because that is one of the few venues left

where we are in a contained space with strangers without access to all the friends we already have.

Over eight miles, Raven wants different people to connect, and he has extremely high expectations for me, and for everyone, to *be* different. He's protective of my inner quirk. He brings it out. He stokes it. It's like he sees an ember inside, and he hones in on it, cupping his hands over his mouth to blow until it catches flame and burns bright for other people to see. That's how people connect on the Raven Run—to that ember within, more than the package outside. And it feels *good* when people connect to the ember.

When I left Miami in December 2015, I was sad to leave my friends and the ocean, but only one thing made me cry. Running a partial, before I peeled off to run north, home to my apartment on 29th Street and Collins Avenue, Raven said to the group, "White Lightning's gonna be leaving us for a bit, but she'll be back soon, don't worry." Raven extended his fist for a bump, and I met his hand with mine. "She's not moonshine," he said, beginning my roll call, "She's White Lightning!"

It was a gusty night, so I could blame my tears on the wind, but they started falling before I said good-bye. "Keep in touch, White Lightning," he told me. "You've got my number."

"305-532-RAVE," I said.

"531," he corrected me, repeating mine by heart. "I'm going to miss you, White Lightning," he said. "We're all going to miss you."

Raven's gift to me has been the community more than the exercise. "He is a master weaver of tapestries of diverse people," said Miracle, "not only culturally or ethnically, but his gift is in finding chemistry between people," and often these people would find no other venue to run next to each other. Raven's legacy, she believes, is the interconnection of those who have run in and out of his life. "He is like Braque, creating a four-dimensional Cubist painting—each person a cube, over time and space."

Since Raven was a child, when he had to spend those nights alone, hugging his pillow like a friend, waiting for his mom to return from the graveyard shift, Raven has spent his life battling a fear of abandonment. Now, if he is more than twenty minutes late to the run, someone—if not many people—will notice and come looking for him. "I've found the place where I shine," said Raven. "Everybody has a place where they shine."

Recently, Raven went out to eat with Shoe Guy, and the restaurant owner approached the table to greet them. He had been in Raven's tenth-grade class at Beach High, and Raven recalled he was a popular kid on the school yearbook staff. "Do you remember what I got for our class superlative?" asked Raven.

"I think it was Most Likely to Commit a Murder," said the man.

"I thought it was Most Likely to End up in Prison," said Raven.

"No, it was for murder," he said. "But now that I know you—nah."

The man didn't offer an apology, but Raven didn't need one.

Raven, now, knows who he is. But he is humble about what he's done. When I asked him what he considered to be his greatest asset, he struggled. He said, "I'm just a two-trick pony. I run and I write songs. Other than that, I can't do anything." Then he clarified, "I'm not even that good of a runner anymore. I'm just consistent." Finally, to conclude the question that clearly made him uncomfortable he said, "Well, White Lightning, I'm nice to people I like."

When it comes down to it, Raven wants the spotlight on characters like Placard Man or the Man of Many Rings more than himself. I think often he is surprised to be holding a microphone, and he wants to use it to give voice to people that society is forgetting about. In writing this book, I have gotten to know the man better than perhaps I would've liked, because when you learn everything about a person, the flaws can unpolish the assets. But more than anything, Raven is a person

I'm grateful to call a friend. If he says he will do something, I know I can count on him. How many people in your life can you say that about?

When he stops running, Miami Beach will feel different. Nobody is going to pick up his reins, because they're way too heavy. Maybe we'll get together on his birthday or on New Year's, but it won't be the same. "Raven's spirit will still be running in the sand long after he stops the streak," remarked the Giggler over eight miles one day, adding, "but his spirit was running here before he started because what Raven does can't be of the body."

The book ends where it started, with a question of who is Raven? Who is this man that runs eight miles every day, no matter what, and takes a world of individuals with him?

Raven is a rare bird that I hope you'll find at the 5th Street lifeguard stand in Miami Beach at 5:30 p.m., any day, every day. No weather hotline, no confirmation number. If he can make it out the door, he'll be there. He hopes you will be, too.

RAVEN RUNNERS LIST

(Hall of Fame Runners denoted with ***)

NICKNAME	RUNS	HOMETOWN
1975–1984		
Coyote	2	New York, NY
Phoenix	2	Minnesota
Spider Man	3	Puerto Rico
Yul	1	Springfield, MA
Natural Man	3	New York, NY
Zero	6	New Jersey
1985–1994		
Springman***	735	Miami, FL
Parrot	1	New York, NY
Firelady	1	Miami, FL
Testosterone Kid	22	Tallahassee, FL
KO Killer	20	Washington, DC
Barnacle	168	Cuba
Reverend***	705	Baltimore, MD
Solo Man	3	South Africa
Termite	79	Miami Beach, FL
Linguist	22	Canada
Lennon Glasses	1	Virginia
Vulcan Pilot***	285	Tucson, AZ
Pale Runner	3	New York, NY
Budget Man	12	Anderson, IN
Gentle	1	Tallahassee, FL
Graphics Man	5	San Francisco, CA
Barefoot	5	Finland
Baseball Player	1	Cuba
Walk Man	3	Los Angeles, CA
Crabby Fries	1	Miami, FL
Warden***	667	Honduras
Giggler	27	Detroit, MI
Renaissance Man	20	Chicago, IL
Papa	9	Cuba
Corvette Man***	221	Spain
Stalker	10	New York, NY
Pounder	1	UK
Iberia Man	3	Spain
Scarf Man	21	Chicago, IL
River	1	Miami Beach, FL
Ring Man	?	Dominican Republic
Butt Man	2	Florida
Photographer	1	France
Fireman	1	Chicago, IL
Potato Man	23	France
Gator Woman	1	Luxembourg
Sailor***	966	Atlantic City, NJ
Keyhole	1	Cartersville, GA
Taxman***	1959	New York, NY
Copilot	1	Denver, CO
Roadrunner	4	Rex, GA
Algae Man	59	West Covina, CA
Brazilian Drummer	1	Brazil
Cadaver	86	Cuba
Copy Man***	344	Mexico
Treasurer	11	West Palm Beach, FL
Garment Man	1	India
Alien	1	Belgium
Sprinter	22	Dominican Republic
Advisor	18	Miami, FL
Speed Skater	5	Chicago, IL
Latin Cowboy	3	Chile
1995–2004		
Christmas	4	Miami Beach, FL
Johnny 99	1	Alabama
Researcher	7	Puerto Rico
Question Man	39	Queens, NY
Violinist	2	Westchester, NY
Many Miles	8	Nicaragua
Fast	5	Daytona Beach, FL
Investigator	21	Miami, FL
Coach	11	Boston, MA
Journalist	9	St. Louis, MO
Duplicate	6	Santa Monica, CA
Copy Kid	13	Miami, FL

Name	Number	Location
Generation X	1	Switzerland
Backward Doc	1	Des Plains, IL
Endless Summer	4	Miami Beach, FL
Flame	4	Stowe, VT
Pin Head	2	Miami, FL
Lady Law	8	Miami Beach, FL
Secret	26	Miami, FL
Rainbow Rok	3	Brooklyn, NY
Lt. Wolfman***	233	Fort Lauderdale, FL
Tango to Go	13	Argentina
Cosmic Surfer	7	Brazil
Samurai Devil	7	Mexico
Marble Man	1	Colombia
Peaceful	7	Denver, CO
Paradox	3	Canada
Colonel	125	Belle Harbor, NY
Longboarder	18	Pacific Palisades, CA
Jungle Therapist	6	Venezuela
Dragon	1	Brazil
Burke's Law	327	Chicago, IL
Miracle***	302	Miami, FL
Spanky	56	Colombia
Entrepreneur	8	Venezuela
Rice Puddin'	5	Peru
Diamond	29	Miami Beach, FL
Volcano Runner	7	Hilo, HI
Gentleman	1	St. Thomas, VI
Sportscaster	1	Ventnor, NJ
Mother Hen	1	Chicago, IL
King of the Clevelander	1	Ardmore, PA
Cargo Man	37	JFK, NY
Smiling	10	Germany
Champ	2	Puerto Rico
Mountain Lady	1	Switzerland
Gringo***	1641	Toledo, OH
Clone	1	Los Angeles, CA
Stingray	4	Richmond, VA
Teen Idol	5	South Miami, FL
Lightning Baltz	3	Chicago, IL
Bulldog	1	Howard Beach, NY
Xena	16	Charleston, SC
Sprocket Man	2	Providence, RI
Baseball Ambassador	6	Newark, NJ
Eggplant Man	6	Miami, FL
Answer Man	4	Denville, NJ
Second Wind	3	Sweden
El Niño	6	Spain
Big Unit	32	Ohio
Hurdler	8	Merrick, NY
Chubby Chaser	3	Edinburgh
Nestle Quik	1	Manhattan, NY
12-Pack	40	Albuquerque, NM
Terminator	13	Louisville, KY
Dr. Deco	126	Miami, FL
Headlock Dreadlock	1	Boston, MA
Deliverance	11	Argentina
Abstract	1	Switzerland
Bureaucrat	17	Liberty, NY
Kick Boxer	11	Colombia
Soul Man	126	UK
Watercolor	6	Spartanburg, SC
Lady LeDuc	3	Canada
Fruit Cup	2	Brazil
Outlaw Crow	1	Houston, TX
Water Bottle Man	11	Cuba
Schwooper	2	Colombia, SC
Lumberjack	1	Kodiak, AK
Defender	5	Los Angeles, CA
Shiatsu Lady	2	France
Chapter 11***	1089	Miami, FL
Flat Foot	32	Oshkosh, WI
Steno Girl	10	Miami, FL
No Limit	1	Laurel, MD
Body Dude	85	El Salvador
Trauma Queen	14	Fredericksburg, VA
Novocain	6	Colombia
Smokestack	3	Miami, FL
Southpaw	3	Columbus, OH
Plantain Lady	259	Ecuador
Sleeper	216	Germany
Human Compass	6	Miami, FL
Teddy Bear	6	Bulgaria
Santería	1	Santa Rosa, CA
Incentive Runner	1	Fredericksburg, VA
Beacon	53	UK
Digital Xerox	1	Mexico
El Bigote	45	Cuba
Rising Sun	18	Japan
Rumpelstiltskin	15	Germany
Michelangelo	1	Argentina
Venus Di Milo	1	Argentina
Movie Star	1	Argentina
Boomerang	7	Australia
Kiwi	2	New Zealand
Nitro	2	Korea
Fashion Man	1	Spain
Mr. Enthusiasm	4	Chicago, IL
La Niña	1	Spain
Formula 1	1	Italy
Ghost Runner	1	Lanai, HI
Silent Runner	1	Fort Collins, CO
Semper Fi	1	Wilmington, DE
Jillie Bean	1	Miami, FL
Stryper	155	Elverson, PA
Net Surfer	1	Colombia
Mr. MG	25	Mathews, NC
Sweet 7-22	12	Mexico
Angry Man***	961	Naples, NY
Computer Guy	225	Ada, MN
Billboard Man	26	Saint Paul, MN
Shark	6	Richmond, VA
Boardwalk	3	Atlantic City, NJ
Pre-Mop	2	Mathews, NC
Count	67	Italy
Grunt	30	Cuba
Bookworm***	346	Rochester, NY
Administrator	5	Pembroke Pines, FL
Pucker	2	Canada
Prancer	12	Spain
Bonecrusher	2	Miami, FL
Vegan	1	Norwich, VT
Hoss	2	Pacific Palisades, CA

Name	Number	Location	Name	Number	Location
Auditor	2	Argentina	Meat Man	4	Kendall, FL
Methodical	1	Miami, FL	Angel Wings	2	Venezuela
Cruise Mama	1	Miami, FL	Love Machine	1	Cuba
Proud	8	Naples, NY	Frost	2	Argentina
Tangerine Dream	7	France	Evil Twin	76	Miami Beach, FL
Delta Dolly	3	Newport, RI	Brave Heart	14	Los Angeles, CA
Historian	1	Newport, RI	Salsa	4	Dominican Republic
Sinus Man	5	Redding, PA	Malicious	2	Miami Beach, FL
Fair Weather	1	Buffalo, NY	Ibis	2	Lumberton, NC
Appalachian Trailer	7	Owings Mills, MD	Wonder Stroke	1	Colorado Springs, CO
Hard Burner	4	Newport, RI	Tombstone	58	Winter Park, FL
Terrified One	1	Pittsburgh, PA	Hi-Tech	50	Cocoa Beach, FL
Buckeye	1	Saint Paul, MN	Patent Pending	39	Miami Beach, FL
Crazy Legs	36	Venezuela	Mortgage Man	38	Venezuela
Cessna Flyer	4	Norway	Ozark***	875	Mexico, MO
Tex	6	Austin, TX	Butterfly	15	Philippines
Flyin' Dutchman	6	Charlotte, NC	Fettuccini	9	Silver Spring, MD
Majik City	2	Miami, FL	Queen of Hearts	6	Sarasota, FL
Low-Key	34	Miami, FL	Objection	6	Madison, NJ
Cool Smoothie	18	Chicago, IL	Cable Man	5	Cuba
Slippery Eel	2	New York, NY	Truant Officer	53	Red Hook, NY
Poet	82	Kansas City, MO	Sugar Daddy	8	Easton, MD
Inca Man	3	Peru	Jelly Girl	1	Chicago, IL
Gladiator	3	Austria	Canuck	206	Canada
Recruiter	3	Jacksonville, FL	Blood Sucker	171	Romania
Dialectician	1	Los Angeles, CA	Dounder	5	Erie, PA
Rose	27	Argentina	Fun Loving	1	Philadelphia, PA
Spartana	10	Detroit, MI	Hyper	1	Charlottesville, VA
Hornet	7	Hinsdale, IL	Husker	1	Omaha, NE
Streak	5	Miami, FL	Blade Runner	1	Austin, TX
Sax Man	5	Argentina	Blue Jay	13	Mansfield, OH
Scrap Metal	3	Argentina	Unicorn	10	UK
Brain Surgeon	3	Mauritania	Candy Crunch	2	Marlboro, NJ
Drea	2	Daytona Beach, FL	Gucci Girl	2	Chicago, IL
Moon Dog	2	Homestead, FL	Sparkler	13	Miami, FL
Ultra Man	7	Yorktown, VA	Mouse	1	Cuba
Dirt Rider	1	Fredericksburg, VA	Longhorn	149	Dallas, TX
Booker	1	Washington, DC	Petroleum Man	111	Brazil
Commerce Man	3	Tallahassee, FL	Latex Man	59	San Diego/Albany, CA
Locus	1	Sweden	Purple Paws	11	Baton Rouge, LA
Shamrock	2	Elverson, PA	Rain Girl	1	King of Prussia, PA
Squeegee	1	Miami, FL	Amazon	1	Brazil
Parrot Head Pilot	1	Saint Paul, MN	Legal Limbo	37	Bulgaria
Procrastinator	7	Coconut Grove, FL	NonConformist	5	Miami, FL
Wolf Queen	2	Sweden	Insomniac	1	Miami, FL
Electrolyte	272	Chicago, IL	Hurricane***	588	Miami Beach, FL
Consultant	3	Mexico	Hop Scotch	12	Washington, DC
Chocolate Chip***	723	Miami, FL	Ghetto Gourmet	7	Berkeley, CA
Poker Pace	5	Pompano, FL	Cement Man	4	Miami, FL
Bare Buns	2	Canada	Torpedo	1	Sitka, AK
Qu	2	Miami, FL	Creole Princess	7	Haiti
Dr. Czech Up	2	Czech Republic	Tank	1	Elverson, PA
Daily Planet	1	Cape Cod, MA	Mellow Yellow	1	Manhattan, NY
Firecracker***	1092	San Diego, CA	Flipper	7	Halleck, MN
Scooby-Doo	53	Columbus, OH	Pulmonary Man	7	Philippines
Unruly	27	Philadelphia, PA	Mediator	3	Brooklyn, NY
Swat Man	20	North Miami, FL	Family Man	2	Pembroke Pines, FL
Blue Fish	17	Riverhead, NY	Young Hawk	2	Fredericksburg, VA
Captain	12	Palm City, FL	Fossil	1	Gaithersburg, MD
Tiger Lily	8	Nicaragua	Sleazebuster***	613	Chicago, IL
Reborn	1	Atlanta, GA	Lusty	57	Islesboro, ME

Gas Man	11	Alexandria, VA	Razorback	41	Springdale, AR
Cardinal	5	Newport, RI	Raynbeau	29	Acton, MA
Metropolis	2	New York, NY	Big Trouble	6	Burlington, IA
Ivory Tickler	1	Croatia	Magnum	2	Marquette, MI
Square Foot	124	Fort Lauderdale, FL	Ski	1	Steam Boat Springs, CO
Iron Curtain	20	Binghamton, NY	Emergency	1	Stillwell, KS
Tulip	12	Holland	Happy Camper	1	Charlotte, NC
Cheezy	9	Chicago, IL	Lamb Chop	11	Scarborough, ME
Bovine	7	Kansas City, MO	Pollinator	1	Key Biscayne, FL
PI	5	Miami Beach, FL	Free Bird	64	Italy
Tasmanian Devil	1	Australia	Etch-A-Sketch	2	Byron, OH
Classic Deluxe	284	Ohio	Flying Crane	1	Miami, FL
Bayou	135	Baton Rouge, LA	Ghetto Girl	1	Detroit, MI
Eco Man	7	Hermosa Beach, CA	Dizzy***	1894	Cuba
Sphere	5	Tarrytown, NY	Changeling	272	Miami Beach, FL
Mormon	1	Seattle, WA	Spinner	111	Spain
Cyclone	1	Crystal River, FL	Cholita	71	Peru
Joker Man	5	Huntington Station, NY	Extractor	34	Canada
Pumpkin Soup	1	Evanston, IL	Hardware	13	Miami, FL
Insurance Man	1	Winter Park, FL	Groupie	13	Miami, FL
Redneck Preacher	1	Alabama	Sapphire	112	Miami Beach, FL
Jingle Jogger	1	Young Harris, GA	Gypsy	71	Spain
Belly Dancer	1	Miami, FL	Chilanga	9	Mexico
Bleeding Heart	1	Miami, FL	Jammin'	6	Jamaica
Black Label	8	Miami, FL	Pigeon	3	De Funiak Springs, FL
Skimmer	2	Miami, FL	Hershey Bar	2	Harrisburg, PA
Cadet	1	Bowling Green, KY	Guardian Angel	1	Puerto Rico
Lady Bug	39	Sweden	Hollywood Flasher***	487	Miami Beach, FL
Jazz Man	3	Montclair, NJ	Creve Coeur	409	St. Louis, MO
Buffalo Shuffler	1	Buffalo, NY	Popeye	60	Miami, FL
Full	1	Los Angeles, CA	Steel Man	2	Cuba
Tuna	1	Argentina	Oxygen	1	Mexico
Troublemaker	426	Los Angeles, CA	Oil Canvas	1	Mexico
Bad News	6	Colombia	Walk Away	1	Miami, FL
Philly Rock	224	Philadelphia, PA	Brimstone	1	Cuba
Director	23	Salt Lake City, UT	Lion	36	Coral Gables, FL
Toggle Switch	16	Huntsville, AL	Running Back	35	Miami Beach, FL
Symphony Girl	4	Centennial, CO	Mallard	5	Eugene, OR
Bhakti Babe	3	Puerto Rico	Human Factor	2	Townsend, MA
Buddhist	1	Trinidad	Peach	2	Augusta
Follower	159	Poland	Energizer	1	Argentina
Shady McCrady	2	Pittsburgh, PA	Last Laugh	1	Miami Beach, FL
Heavy Breather	1	Redondo Beach, CA	Jaguar	1	Miami, FL
Fire Ant	38	New York, NY	Bale	55	Italy
Race Walker	29	Chicago, IL	Feather	41	Italy
Celtic Dealer	29	Boston, MA	Orchid Man	20	Lebanon
Stroker	24	Chicago, IL	K-Lo	1	Panama City, FL
Slow Hand	24	Chicago, IL	Speed Writer	6	Miami, FL
Trapper	11	Philadelphia, PA	Serpentine	1	Washington, DC
Yoga Goddess	4	Dallas, TX	Phantom	1	Haiti
Oarsman	4	Tucson, AZ	Guacamole	1	Portsmouth, NH
Long Distance	1	Miami Shores, FL	Handlebar	118	Beaver Creek, OH
Paddler	1	Hialeah, FL	Chili Pepper	43	Chile
Cruiser	1	Los Angeles, CA	Abdul	36	Kent, WA
2005–Present			Fearless	9	Israel
GPS	52	Boston, MA	Karma	1	Canada
Plain Talker	1	Painesville, OH	New Balance	1	Boston, MA
Refund	1	Canada	Freshman	262	Germany
Mr. Sensitive	2	Yardley, PA	Farmer's Daughter	8	Canada
Candy Man	1	Cuba	Tin Foil	4	Minneapolis, MN
Slammer	1	Miami Beach, FL	Major	3	New Hampshire

Chastity Belt	3	Bolivia	Sandpaper	1	Switzerland
Swingin' Doors	2	Bakersfield, CA	Elite	1	Sweden
Lethal Yellow	2	Goldsboro, NC	Forceful	1	Sweden
In Vitro Girl	2	Miami, FL	Fatima	1	Douglas, WY
Lava	2	Miami, FL	Poutine***	1417	Canada
Margaritaville	2	Sarasota, FL	Moon Pie	2	Miami, FL
Revlon Lady	2	Philadelphia, PA	Impatience	12	Ithaca, NY
Circuit Breaker	2	Rogersville, AL	Patience	6	Asheville, NC
Impala	1	Belgium	World View	4	Washington, DC
Heron	1	Maryland	Candlestick	4	Irvine, CA
Pea Pod	1	Great Barrington, MA	Orion	3	Seattle, WA
Gadget	21	Freehold, NJ	Nutrasudical	1	Hemet, CA
Leap Frog	13	Titusville, FL	Bottle Washer	1	Hemet, CA
Action	6	River Grande, TX	Born Free	1	Washington, IL
Woolly	2	Gastonia, NC	Hooky	1	Cleone, CA
Brooklyn Bull	2	Brooklyn, NY	Nightingale	1	Mount Vernon, VA
Fancy Pants	1	Hannibal, MO	Amnesia	1	Miami, FL
Mile High	3	Denver, CO	Lunch Break	1	Canada
Ranger	2	Akin, SC	Anthropologist	1	Miami, FL
Dragon Fly	1	Seattle, WA	Cartwheel	1	Miami Beach, FL
Popsicle	33	Middlefield, CT	Triple B	1	Nicaragua
Jersey Surfer	19	Freehold, NJ	Intern	1	Nicaragua
Economist	2	Washington, DC	48 Cent	112	Woodmere, NY
Romeo	1	Venezuela	K Pod	32	Potomac, MD
Elevator Man	17	Miami, FL	Polar Orange	15	Luxemburg, WI
Boot Camp	8	Shaker Heights, OH	Bean Sprout	11	Asbury Park, NJ
Wilderness	4	Spain	Amazing	7	Hollywood, FL
Wet T-Shirt	3	Spain	String Bean	7	Asbury Park, NJ
Meatballs	2	Sweden	Trendsetter	3	Roanoke, IN
Ruby Tuesday	1	Cincinnati, OH	Consistent	3	Roanoke, IN
Hot Mama	1	Miami, FL	Pixie	1	Fort Wayne, IN
Jack Rabbit	1	Long Beach, CA	Bean Counter	1	Fort Wayne, IN
Baby	38	Peru	Panther Mom	1	North Miami Beach, FL
Extrapolator	30	Seattle, WA	Value Pak	1	Norway
GI Jane	6	Colombia	Snacker	14	Beaufort, SC
Pike's Peak	1	Belington, WA	Supernova	6	Cuba
Courageous	19	Venezuela	Bear Claw	6	Canada
Twizzler	3	Los Angeles, CA	Sacred Heart	2	Colombia
Yogi	2	Ecuador	Detention	2	Miami, FL
Sgt. Comic	185	Union City, NJ	Jet Stream	1	Lancaster, PA
Stakeout	135	Miami Beach, FL	Good Vibrations	1	Colombia
Lollipop	36	Miami, FL	Madd Max	1	Turkey
Deuces Wild	10	Milton, FL	Rainier	8	Seattle, WA
Siren	2	Miami, FL	Molecular	1	Minnesota
Refuel	1	Colombia	Tango Ray	1	Ocean Shores, WA
Medicine Man	1	Miami, FL	Hydration	1	Newport Beach, CA
Cliffhanger	1	Homestead, FL	Science Geek	1	New York, NY
Cooker	139	Seattle, WA	Myth	20	UK
Tonka	61	Minnetonka, MN	Gymnast	1	Japan
Monster-in-Law	6	Italy	Grey Matter	1	Biddeford, ME
Pocket Rocket	3	UK	Power Surge	1	Philadelphia, PA
Submarine	14	Wilmington, NC	Bourbon Street	1	New Orleans, LA
Bouncing Czech	11	Czech Republic	Sausage Man	132	Canada
Blood Sugar	8	Baltimore, MD	Pink Salmon	2	Cleveland, OH
Glow	1	Fredericksburg, VA	Schoolfish	1	Scaggsville, MD
Toddler	1	Baltimore, MD	Safety Man	1	Colombia
Sexy	50	Canada	Lost Newlywed	1	Spain
Copernicus	22	Canada	Thunder	114	New Haven, CT
YYZ	16	Canada	Cocktail	5	Tampa, FL
Cotton Candy	5	Bronx, NY	Coastal Intelligence	3	Cincinnati, OH
Strikeout	4	Roanoke, IN	Eye Focus	2	Italy

Name	No.	Location	Name	No.	Location
Jockette	2	Chicago, IL	Mr. Know-No	10	Greenwich, CT
Pushin'	1	Miami, FL	Smoochee	1	Sharon, MA
Bubbly	5	New York, NY	Smoocher	1	Sharon, MA
Barbie Doll	3	Winston-Salem, NC	Protector	1	Washington, DC
Alamo	3	San Antonio, TX	Cold Feet	1	Washington, DC
CC Rider	2	Canada	Thin Ice	1	Denver, CO
Fiction	2	Pensacola, FL	Empty	1	France
Huckleberry	1	Boise, ID	Ad-Add Man	11	Cleveland, OH
Chow Hound	1	Virginia Beach, VA	Of-Darkness	4	Hoover, AL
A-Pod	1	Panama	Reckless	1	Holland
Stork	23	Miami, FL	Dead Funny	1	Holland
Cheerleader	12	Danbury, CT	Abnormal	1	Boca Raton, FL
Architect	7	Columbus, OH	Amigo	1	Akron, OH
Scarlet Fever	7	Canada	Great Dane	45	Denmark
Source	2	Puerto Rico	Lateral Drop	20	Chicago, IL
Tex Mex	2	Houston, TX	Honey Bee	14	Dodge City, KS
Black Mouth	1	Miami, FL	Scissors	13	Manhattan, NY
Authentic	1	Venezuela	Nigerian Queen	3	Nigeria
Rejuvenate	1	Haiti	Reformed	2	Mexico
Riunite	117	Ithaca, NY	Cornerback	1	Syracuse, NY
Famished	74	Colombia	Tomgirl	1	New York, NY
Wells Fargo	3	Seattle, WA	Baby Doc	1	Medford, NJ
Rockin' Doc	3	Woodmere, NY	Brick	1	UK
Biggest Loser	2	Harrison, AR	Hermit Crab	11	Mexico
Producer	1	Canada	Granite	6	Boulder, CO
Salt Shaker	418	Berkshire County, MA	Zydeco	2	Milton, FL
Socialite	26	Switzerland	Beer Man	2	Boston, MA
Destroyer	19	Poospatuck, NY	Kidney Stone	1	Colombia
Pony Express	3	Nicaragua	3 Legged Antelope	1	Canada
Super Groovy	3	Miami, FL	Viking	1	Denmark
Summer Morning	2	Colombia	Drago	26	Sweden
Camelback	2	Venezuela	Ice Cream	3	Northfield, NJ
Maltese Doctor	2	New York, NY	Strong Bean	3	Asbury Park, NJ
On-line	2	Canton, OH	Big Spender	2	Northfield, NJ
Schnauzer	1	Miami, FL	Texas Democrat	2	Dallas, TX
Beantown Bandit	1	Newton, MA	Sunfear	2	Decatur, GA
Orbea 300	1	Puerto Rico	Designer	1	Boston, MA
Wonder Woman	1	Hollywood, FL	Tinkerbell	1	Northfield, NJ
Peer Pressure	1	Roanoke, IN	Big Sur	1	Monterrey, CA
Happy	1	Minnesota	Little Pig	1	New York, NY
Egyptian	1	Jamaica	Trek	1	Miami Beach, FL
Sand Dollar	8	Finland	Heavy Metal	1	Sweden
Strategist	401	Phoenix, AZ	Hitter***	771	Miami, FL
Bucket	40	Madison, WI	Seaside Sparrow	466	Palatine, IL
Asphalt	37	Naugatuck, CT	Flaca	82	Nicaragua
Floorboard	37	Orlando, FL	Bedrock	55	Suriname
Tinker 600	5	Ireland	Beast	33	Athens, GA
Structure	4	Kansas City, MO	Star Trader	10	Madison, CT
Strawberry Muffin	4	Poland	Smoking Ace	7	Deerfield Beach, FL
Spike	4	Syracuse, NY	Foreigner	7	Spain
Jayhawk	3	Kansas City, MO	Linebacker	5	Provo, UT
Gorilla	3	Oshkosh, WI	Mini Texter	3	Duluth, MN
Isotope	1	Panama	Drastic	3	New Jersey
Chelsea Boy	1	UK	7 & 7	2	Denver, CO
Blue Boy	1	Boston, MA	Red Bull	1	Canada
Power Fit	1	Roanoke, IN	Rappeller	1	Los Angeles, CA
Piper Cub	1	Roanoke, IN	LuLu Lemon	83	Miami, FL
Scallop	1	Roanoke, IN	Regulator	29	Miami, FL
Cabinet Maker	1	Roanoke, IN	Juju Doll	17	Peru
Server	1	Roanoke, IN	Swoosh	14	Santa Rosa, CA
Political Peanut	8	Washington, DC	Rush Hour	13	Miami, FL

Gunner	9	Virginia Beach, VA	Fructose	16	Omaha, NE
Training Partner	8	New York	Downhill	15	Salem, OR
Communicator	7	Singapore	Cloud Burst	8	New Haven, CT
Shield	3	Cleveland, OH	Door Kicker	7	Argentina
Country Roads	2	Enterprise, WV	Pontiac	7	Clarkston, MI
Churasco	1	Dominican Republic	Groundhog	5	Punxsutawney, PA
Bar Maid	1	Sweden	Scarlet Knight	3	Saddle River, NJ
Grizzly Bear	9	Las Vegas, NV	Hot Dawg	3	Canada
Reality	1	Clinton, NJ	Thruster	3	Marina Del Rey, CA
Solitude	1	Miami, FL	Splinter	2	Washington, DC
Emotional	1	Miami, FL	China	2	Peru
Tortuga***	521	Tarboro, NC	Zip Lock	2	Atlanta, GA
French Connection	6	France	Weatherman	1	Long Island, NY
Medic	4	Miami, FL	DR. Pink	1	Miami, FL
Graveyard	2	Manhattan, NY	Whupper	1	Philadelphia, PA
Dr. Ole	1	Sioux Falls, SD	Hell's Kitchen	1	Coral Gables, FL
Unrestricted	1	Seattle, WA	Goldfinger	1	Orlando, FL
Infantry Man	1	Honduras	Armour All	1	Baltimore, MD
K-9	17	Mexico	Maple Leaf	1	Canada
Teknic	8	Los Angeles, CA	Band Aid	1	Wilmington, NC
Cimarron	8	Uruguay	Mover	162	Buffalo, NY
Demolition	7	Springfield, MA	Black Hawk	113	Miami Beach, FL
Moonstone	6	Philadelphia, PA	Crazy Cabbie	22	Yonkers, NY
Neon Shoes	6	Cambridge, MA	Golden	8	Thailand
Aqualung	2	Tampa, FL	Hacker	8	Goldsboro, NC
2-Face	1	Canada	Tracks	5	Naranja, FL
Connector	1	St. Louis, MO	Blue Moon	5	Naranja, FL
Maniac	1	Allamuchy, NJ	Editor	3	Bolivia
Hound Dog	211	Warren, OH	High Performance	2	Canada
All American	174	Los Angeles, CA	Sweet Tea	1	Duluth, GA
Wine Taster	73	Miami Beach, FL	Froggy Squat	1	Dallas, TX
Valium	23	Canada	Trumpeter	1	Sweden
Figure Skater	3	Los Angeles, CA	Drill Bit	1	Winston-Salem, NC
Chiquita	3	Guatemala	Fear Factor	1	Colorado Springs, CO
Appleseed	3	Coral Gables, FL	Dewey	1	Elizabeth, NJ
Spirit Dancer	2	Puerto Rico	Cleanser	1	UK
Turkish Delight	1	Turkey	Natural Fiber	1	Boston, MA
Gizmo	1	Turkey	Locksmith	1	St. Louis, MO
Udon	1	Boston, MA	Shoe Guy***	694	Wausau, WI
Captain Shrink	1	Cambridge, MA	Major Taco	217	Mexico
El Dorado	1	Madison, CT	Pin Stripes	45	Newark, NJ
Icy Hot	100	Long Branch, NJ	Skitzo	38	Kossuth, MS
Advocate	98	Hungary	Piano Man	32	Long Island, NY
Illustrator	8	Phoenix, MD	Halo	29	Miami Beach, FL
Chef	6	Mexico	Rabbit	22	New Jersey
Textbook	5	Miramar, FL	Campaigner	10	Berkshire County, MA
Drizzle	5	Miami, FL	Planner	7	Miami, FL
Hungry Detective	3	Miramar, FL	Promoter	6	Miami, FL
Rock Climber	2	Argentina	Bar Fly	5	Argentina
Interrogator	2	Cleveland, OH	Pork Chop	4	Boston, MA
Light Headed	1	UK	Marketer	4	Cleveland, OH
Heavy Handed	1	Albuquerque, NM	Under Par	4	Miami, FL
Just Run	1	Monterey, CA	Monarch	4	Miami, FL
Pedi Cab	1	Boston, MA	Sgt. Major	3	Syracuse, NY
Zot	1	Boston, MA	Aloha	3	Hawaii
Fiction Reader	1	USA	Fortune Cookie	3	Long Island, NY
Collage	1	Miami Beach, FL	Someday	3	Philadelphia, PA
Deep Dish	236	Chicago, IL	Gabster	3	Los Angeles, CA
Crest	56	Mexico	No-Tell	2	Miami, FL
Wonderer	45	Dothan, AL	Chaos	2	Miami, FL
Dutch Treat	17	Netherland Antilles	Johnny B-Bad	2	Miami, FL

Reefer	2	Miami, FL
Lobster Claw	2	Phoenix, AZ
Good Grief	2	Alliance, NE
T-Bone	2	Miami, FL
B-Note	2	Schwenksville, PA
2nd	2	Puerto Rico
Cordinator	2	Boston, MA
Cholisha	2	Mexico
Passenger	1	Bangor, ME
Charger	1	Irvine, CA
Maddness	1	Irvine, CA
Catalyst	1	Texas
Badger	1	Indianapolis, IN
Indio	1	Atlanta, GA
Tiny Stepper	1	Miami, FL
Sound Guy	1	Lancaster County, PA
Cool Breeze	1	Jamaica
Mountie	1	Canada
Cartilage	1	Miami, FL
Aero	1	Ohio
Natasha	1	Romania
Running Nutritionist	1	Miami, FL
Over Friendly Ghost	1	Miami, FL
Soldier Girl	1	Venezuela
Great White	1	Georgia
Floater	157	Cuba
Fraud	44	Parma, OH
Uptown Girl	32	Long Island, NY
Fashionista	18	Venezuela
CAG	13	Miami, FL
Contractor	12	Chile
Underwriter	11	Nicaragua
Shoe Lace	8	Miami, FL
Passover	8	Los Angeles, CA
Relay	6	Miami, FL
T-Square	4	Los Angeles, CA
Wasabi	3	Washington, DC
Stilts	3	Washington, DC
Diplomat	3	Los Angeles, CA
Stretcher	2	Hawaii
Styrofoam	2	Miami, FL
Machupichu	2	Peru
Bullett	1	Martinsburg, WV
Red Leg	1	Dayton, OH
Grape	1	Dayton, OH
Rubber Ducky	1	Milwaukee, WI
Foxy Lady	1	Michigan
Pops	1	Baltimore, MD
Nueron	1	Miami, FL
Evictor	170	St. Louis, MO
Landscaper	10	Chicago, IL
Eraser	7	Pittsburgh, PA
Cross	6	San Jose, CA
Finisher	5	Miami, FL
Muscles	5	Long Island, NY
Red Back	4	Long Island, NY
3rd Coming	4	Aventura, FL
Risky Business	3	Boston, MA
Jabcys	3	Philippines
Euclid	2	Boston, MA
Shuttle Runner	2	Jersey City, NJ

Oakley	1	Philadelphia, PA
Otter	1	Miami, FL
Braid	1	Maitland, FL
Liason	1	New Jersey
Angio	1	Ann Arbor, MI
Diva	1	Ecuador
Ripper	1	Australia
Undecided	1	Australia
Calabria	1	Wayne, NJ
Anxious	1	Long Island, NY
Crunchy	1	Dayton, OH
Karaoke	149	Bronx, NY
Apollo	55	Miami, FL
Transporter	11	Germany
Tactical	8	Carlinville, IL
Chicken Fricase	5	Miami, IL
Device	4	Syracuse, NY
Pastor	3	Sharpsburg, GA
Sober	2	Miami, FL
Bone Saw	2	Sacramento, CA
Photo Genic	1	Kendall, FL
Chill	1	Miami, FL
Incognito	1	Hollywood, FL
Long Term	1	Minneapolis, MN
Homework	1	Miami, FL
Go Lightly	1	Richmond, VA
Strong Finish	1	Columbus, OH
Shark Soup	1	Denver, CO
Spa Man	1	U.S. Virgin Islands
Scoreboard	1	Augusta, GA
Preservationist	203	Denver, CO
Saturn	38	Czech Republic
E.R.	12	Ocean Township, NJ
Union Lady	10	Miami, FL
Suiza	7	Miami, FL
Combat Finance	5	Pittsburgh, PA
Meter Maid	4	Colombia
Rocket Man	4	Cocoa, FL
Lamp Light	3	Miami, FL
Sunflower	3	Kansas
Hobbit	2	Cuba
Subway	2	Sacramento, CA
Pontificator	2	Los Angeles, CA
Contagious	1	Las Vegas, NV
Baylor Bear	1	Waco, TX
Devilish Saint	1	Waco, TX
Full Monty	1	Dallas, TX
Right Wing	1	Canada
Manayunk	1	Philadelphia, PA
Senior Green	1	Miami, FL
Poppy Seed	1	West Palm Beach, FL
Snake Eyes	1	Las Vegas, NV
Sheik	387	Nigeria
Don Quixote	13	Coral Gables, FL
Big Sky	13	Glacier Park, MT
Lifeline	6	Miami Beach, FL
Streetcar	6	Austin, TX
Queen of Sheba	4	Ethiopia
Straight A's	3	Hot Springs, AR
Gazelle	3	Canada
Brewer	2	Milwaukee, WI

Dominator	1	Irvine, CA	Colgate	2	Miami, FL
Philly Phanatic	1	Philadelphia, PA	Eggman	1	Miami, FL
Titlest	1	Ridgefield, NJ	GQ	1	Miami, FL
Frenchy	106	France	Beaver	1	Miami, FL
L Train	22	Warsaw, IN	Rusher	1	Lancaster, PA
3D	9	Colombia	Detcord	1	Jamaica
Chex Mix	9	El Paso, TX	Melon Head	1	Tampa, FL
B.B.Gun	7	Miami, FL	Oiler	1	Dallas, TX
Cutter	7	France	Wildcat	1	Dallas, TX
Punk Rock	5	Coconut Grove, FL	Paisa	1	Miami, FL
Understatement	4	Canada	Mr. Canada	22	Canada
Paddle Head	4	Canada	3rd Time Charm	11	North Bay Village, FL
Deceiving	3	Miami Beach, FL	Mouth Piece	9	Chapel Hill, NC
No Direction	3	Cuba	Cooter	7	Tallahassee, FL
Louisville Slugger	3	Louisville, KY	Airforce 1	6	Springfield, OH
Ka-Ching	2	Canada	Stair Climber	6	Philadelphia, PA
Girl Watcher	2	France	TNT	5	Nicaragua
Mattress King	1	Seal, CA	Karo	5	Omaha, NE
Fro Yo	1	Coronado, CA	Hauler	4	Buffalo, NY
Telecom	1	Alexandria, VA	D.J.	4	France
Explorer	1	Peru	Tropical Smoothie	4	Fayetteville, NC
Choo Choo	1	Soddy Daisy, TN	Expression	3	Italy
Spokes	1	Soddy Daisy, TN	Teal Blue	3	Miami Beach, FL
Paris	1	France	Prose	3	Mexico
Courier	217	Peru	Sleepless Bear	2	Miami Beach, FL
Labrador	14	Spain	Soca	2	Trinidad
Shalom	7	Brooklyn, NY	Woobster	2	North Bay Village, FL
Rubberband Man	7	St. Louis, MO	Front Porch	2	Mexico
Galaxy	4	Minneapolis, MN	Persuasion	2	Nashville, TN
Turbo Prop	4	Jacksonville, FL	Henchman	2	Miami, FL
Big River	3	St. Louis, MO	Alligator Alley	2	Pembroke Pines, FL
Ragged Shoe	2	New Jersey	Styx	1	Miami, FL
Trimmer	2	Italy	Diesel	1	Houston, TX
Fine Design	2	Long Island, NY	Soybean	1	St. Louis, MO
Holistic	2	New York	BestMan	1	St. Louis, MO
Jungle Boy	2	Colombia	Theologian	1	Salem, VA
Levitra Lady	1	Cleveland, OH	Epic	1	Brazil
Meticulous	1	France	Play It	1	Alexandria, MN
Porpoise	1	Switzerland	Cat Napper	1	Miami Beach, FL
Concierge	1	Canada	Carnival	1	Trinidad
Dis-Able	1	Coral Gables, FL	Video Dude	1	Manhattan, NY
Bluff	1	Poplar Bluff, MO	Waterproof	1	Reston, VA
Bay Breaker	1	San Francisco, CA	Pacer	1	Chicago, IL
Eroader	1	Marion, NY	Ark	1	Washington, DC
Dictator	133	Coconut Grove, FL	Woodwork	1	Baltimore, MD
Nettles	41	Delmar, NJ	Velcro	1	East Royalton, VT
Safe Landing	9	Annapolis, MD	Acrylic	1	Canada
Wahoo	7	Richmond, VA	Enlightenment	1	Miami, FL
Agent Utah	7	Miami, FL	Demential	1	Philadelphia, PA
Take Charge	7	Coconut Grove, FL	Enchantment	1	New Mexico
Buffet	7	Peru	Mayflower	1	Miami, FL
Old School	6	Egg Harbor Township, NJ	Patriot	100	Derry, NH
Starbucks	5	Dayton, OH	Curly	8	Miami, FL
Thumper	4	Japan	Lead Off	7	Harrisburg, PA
Freestyle	4	Orange County, CA	Concept	6	Rockland County, NY
Knife	3	Miami Beach, FL	Polo	5	Wausau, WI
Steel Magnolia	3	Pittsburgh, PA	Above 9	4	Bosnia
Strudal	2	Lakeland, FL	Bio Feedback	4	Boise, ID
Temple	2	Lafayette, LA	Room Service	3	Rhode Island
Motley	2	Coconut Grove, FL	Beehive	3	St. George, UT
Slaughter	2	Brooklyn, NY	Infectious	2	Muncie, IN

No-Do	1	Ithaca, NY	
Banana Peel	1	Detroit, MI	
Fiber Optic	1	Kendall, FL	
HawkEye	1	USA	
Logger	1	Seattle, WA	
Nutcracker	51	Germany	
Defiant	42	Miami, FL	
Moccasin	20	Wausau, WI	
X-Ray	4	Canton, OH	
Stellar Foot	3	Brattleboro, VT	
Tornado	3	Newton, KS	
Free Diver	2	Vineland, NJ	
Regga Specialist	2	UK	
Cinnamon Roll	1	Brazil	
Ramblin' Man	1	Corpus Christi, TX	
Body Art	1	Miami, FL	
Swiss Miss	1	Switzerland	
Tamaqua	1	Sheepshead Bay, NY	
Mighty Red	1	St. Louis, MO	
Lil Sis	1	St. Louis, MO	
Pee Pipe	1	Phoenix, AZ	
Puka	1	Fort Wayne, IN	
Tonic	1	China	
Toll Booth	1	Miami Beach, FL	
Hump	1	Massachusetts	
Meken Ubai	26	Ithaca, NY	
Twin Fish	13	Dominican Republic	
Topolino	12	Italy	
Keystone	5	Pennsylvania	
Iron Horse	4	Montclair, NJ	
Exel	4	Dale, VA	
GoGo Sox	4	Chicago, IL	
Cornbread	3	Jacksonville, FL	
Common Man	2	Saint Paul, MN	
Lab Rat	2	Massachusetts	
Panama Jack	2	Panama	
Nice N Easy	2	West Chester, PA	
Ravioli	1	Miami, FL	
Ali Baba	1	Pittsburgh, PA	
Forensic	1	Riverside, CA	
Killer Tomato	1	Canada	
Kilometer	1	Canada	
Barrel Racer	1	St. George, UT	
Minister	1	Childress, TX	
Backpacker	1	Ithaca, NY	
Greek Olives	1	Greece	
Slide Rule	1	Wausau, WI	
Cheeky	4	Cleveland, OH	
Spicy	4	India	
Freckles	4	Carlyle, IL	
Quatro	3	Germany	
Ragnar	3	New York	
Dancing Gator	2	Palm County, FL	
Carb Loader	1	Orlando, FL	
NittyGritty	1	Minneapolis, MN	
Salami	1	Manhattan, NY	
Ticket Master	1	Stanford, CT	
Radar Love	1	Philadelphia, PA	
Nasty Nude	1	Philadelphia, PA	
Fire N Rain	1	Miami, FL	
Dirty Dog	1	Atlanta, GA	

Vaca	1	Ecuador
Easy Street	1	Cleveland, OH
Expresso	131	Brazil
Palladium	111	Jacksonville, FL
Opener	107	Edison, NJ
Covers	24	Germany
Wallabi	18	Australia
Junkyard	7	Cape Canaveral, FL
Hash Bitch	4	Miami, FL
Logistic	3	Los Angels, CA
Pressure Clean	3	Detroit, MI
Quid	2	UK
Bazooka	2	Philadelphia, PA
Yelp	1	Lexington, KY
Marielito	1	Cuba
Shimmy	1	Westchester, PA
Hokey Pokey	1	Harrisburg, PA
Greasy	1	Venezuela
Glacier	1	Pensacola, FL
Scrappy	1	Chicago, IL
5th Amendment	136	New York, NY
Insane Asylum	36	France
Mohawk	17	Miami Beach, FL
Greyhound	7	Amherst, NH
HandyMan	4	Miami, FL
Aqua	4	Germany
Pro Bono	3	Dallas, PA
Trinity	1	Canada
Golden State	1	Novato, CA
Sweat Rag	1	Wilmington, NC
Ink	1	Miami Beach, FL
Wee Gee	1	France
Saving Grace	1	Chicago, IL
Flapjack	28	Puerto Rico
Million Dollar Baby	21	Brazil
Illusion	6	Italy
Suave	4	France
Blind Sugar	3	Stuart, IL
Coconut	2	Coconut Grove, FL
Shocky	2	Miami Beach, FL
Gerbil	1	UK
Blue Motion	1	Switzerland
Speakeasy	1	Neenah, WI
Footprint	1	Elmont, NY
Efron	1	Port Jefferson, NY
Alion	1	Venezuela
Pink Panther	1	Manhattan, NY
Ice-T	8	Bergen County, NJ
Normandy Liberty	2	France
Swamp Thing	2	Winfield, LA
Red Fox	1	Houston, TX
Tolken	1	Italy
Rib Tickler	1	Canada
Radiation	1	Wayland, MA
Weevil	1	Denver, CO
Assessor	1	San Diego, CA
Unwind	1	Orange County, CA
Strawberry China	1	Tallahassee, FL
Yankee Clipper	1	Bronx, NY
Water Shoes	1	Cuba
Jockey	1	New Orleans, LA

Deacon	1	Los Angeles, CA	
Eveangeline	1	Gainesville, FL	
Tank Commander	2	Danville, IL	
Conversation	2	Kansas City, KS	
Thriller	2	Washington, DC	
Mushy Peas	2	UK	
Assertive Girl	1	Canada	
Rouge-miami	1	Miami, FL	
Hedge Hog	1	Northbrook, IL	
Granola	1	USA	
Aussie	7	Australia	
Bolt Cutter	3	Seattle, WA	
Star Fish	2	France	
Trampoline	2	Miami, FL	
Cupcakes	1	South Korea	
Shutter	1	Ithaca, NY	
Springboard	1	Gainesville, FL	
Alley Oop	1	Miami Lakes, FL	
Bendicoot	1	Australia	
Achy Breaky	1	Boston, MA	
Aqua Viva	1	Morocco	
Mad Scientist	1	Switzerland	
Blue Suede	1	Italy	
Asian Kobe	1	Laguna Niguel, CA	
Yellow Rose	222	Dallas, TX	
Juris Prudence	117	Belgium	
Warrior	84	Lancaster, PA	
Baker's Dozen	18	Trinidad	
Psychic	4	Connecticut	
Stockjock	3	Waterville, ME	
Options	3	Long Island, NY	
Sapporo	2	Tarboro, NC	
Memo 6	2	Chicago, IL	
Wireless	2	Southborough, MA	
Sauna	1	Brazil	
Kitchen Sink	1	Ohio	
Analyst	1	Virginia	
Palm Island	1	Miami Beach, FL	
Bruin	1	Boston, MA	
Newfie	1	Canada	
1040	1	Coral Springs, FL	
Hurry Up	1	Germany	
Starlight	1	Chile	
Burgers n Beer	1	Germany	
Black Dynamite	1	Miami, FL	
Dozen Dews	1	Apple Valley, MN	
New York Minute	84	New York, NY	
Death March	35	Minnesota	
Road Kill	26	Ithaca, NY	
4 String Slinger	14	Seattle, WA	
Nolita	8	Miami Beach, FL	
YoYo	7	UK	
Hummingbird	7	Alexandria, VA	
Trinket	5	Riverton, NJ	
Goa	5	Belgium	
Top Gun	4	Saddle River, NJ	
Recovery	3	New York, NY	
NO Ho Tango	3	No Ho, NY	
Tarheel	2	Charlotte, NC	
Portobello	2	Cuba	
Green Machine	2	Minneapolis, MN	
Tofu	2	Canada	
Tennis Whites	2	Woodcliff Lake, NY	
Laughter	1	Italy	
Conquistador	1	Washington, DC	
Transition	1	Chicago, IL	
Sweet Wine	1	Canada	
Hot Mess	1	Miami, FL	
Pelican	1	Pittsburgh, PA	
Flanker	1	Pittsburgh, PA	
Handover Hangover	1	Germany	
Jager Meister	1	Germany	
Pomegranate	1	Boston, MA	
Caterpillar	1	Peoria, IL	
Cool Cucumber	1	Norway	
Synergy	1	Manhattan, NY	
Jeter-2	1	Woodcliff Lake, NJ	
Encourage	1	Puerto Rico	
Gummy Bear	22	Long Island, NY	
Triple	19	Westchester County, NY	
Kitty	17	Meriden, CT	
Enforcer	15	Sea Isle, NJ	
Ram	12	San Antonio, TX	
Oriole	8	Baltimore, MD	
Mule	7	Brooklyn, NY	
Kindergarten	6	Costa Rica	
Stop Sign	5	Miami, FL	
Bones	5	Gulf Stream, FL	
Matzo Ball	4	Miami Beach, FL	
Short Fuse	4	Miami, FL	
Shoe Horn	4	Wausau, WI	
Slipper	3	Asheville, NC	
Tiny Dancer	3	Boston, MA	
Pad Thai	2	Argentina	
Treble Clef	2	Livonia, IL	
Not Guilty	1	Muskegon, MI	
West Plains	1	Midland, TX	
Organized Chaos	1	Boston, MA	
Sad Story	1	Cambridge, MA	
Blocker	1	Georgia	
Nightclub	1	Milwaukee, WI	
Short Stories	1	Boca Raton, FL	
Tracker Trailer	1	Atlanta, GA	
Self Hazard	1	Miami, FL	
Dirt Cheap	1	St. Louis, MO	
Quint	1	Miami, FL	
Chowder	1	Lowell, MA	
Cheers	1	Miami, FL	
Mai Tai	1	St. Jacob, IL	
Moth	1	Cocoa Beach, FL	
MC Square	1	South Africa	
Silver Nike	1	Tampa, FL	
Acupuncture	1	Pottstown, NY	
Compression	1	Philadelphia, PA	
Baby Moocher	1	Lake Tahoe, CA	
Responsible	1	Poughkeepsie, NY	
Bluegrass	1	Lexington, NY	
Search Engine	1	Miami Beach, FL	
Mascot	1	Canada	
Northern Dancer	1	Canada	
Visibility	1	Dedham, MA	
Replacement	15	Wausau, WI	

Type A	12	Terre Haute, IN	Koochie	2	West Chester, PA
Rascal	6	Truckee, CA	Chesapeake	1	Omaha, NE
Scraper	5	Terre Haute, IN	Squash	1	Sweden
Prophylactic	5	Ithaca, NY	Gellin	1	Sarasota, FL
Striker	4	Binghamton, NY	Encyclopedia	206	Coconut Grove, FL
Suspension	4	Coral Gables, FL	Judge	192	Bradford, VT
Sanitizer	3	Indianapolis, IN	Hot Potato	31	Short Hills, NJ
Framed	3	Miami, FL	Air Mail	19	Charleston, SC
Pagan	3	Iowa City, IA	Discreet	19	Miami, FL
Accountable	2	Aventura, FL	Rattle	3	Chicago, IL
Sisu	2	Wausau, WI	Dade	2	Miami, FL
Sooner	2	Oklahoma	Fantasy	2	Germany
Fenway	2	Boston, MA	Stogie	2	New York, NY
Dispatcher	2	Colombia	Spurs	1	Dallas, TX
Wairton	1	Canada	Pack Man	1	Honolulu, HI
Snow Dip	1	Canada	Radioactive	1	Green Bay, WI
Rational	1	Chicago, IL	Car 11	1	New York, NY
Indy Mom	1	Terre Haute, IN	Kite Man	1	Germany
Straight N Narrow	1	Indianapolis, IN	Kibbutcnic	1	Israel
Lemonade	1	Miami, FL	52 Aces	1	Germany
Ollie	1	Arlington, VA	Vice	24	Italy
Nole	1	Ithaca, NY	Rehab	2	Miami, FL
Bull Runner	1	Orlando, FL	Impaler	1	Medford, OR
Stiletto	1	Boca Raton, FL	4 Leaf Clover	1	Michigan
Green Thumb	553	Boston, MA	Low Maintenance	1	Canada
Vivacious	178	Vietnam	Grim Reaper	1	Miami, FL
Overcover	27	Germany	Ocean 9	1	Tunisia
Zebra	7	Baltimore, MD	Long Tall	1	Oklahoma
Ya Ya	4	Elizabeth, NJ	California Orange	1	Los Angeles, CA
Beautician	3	Modoc, IN	Alchemist	1	Tiburon, CA
Par Shooter	3	Centerville, OH	Panache	1	Hyannis, MA
B.B.Q.	2	Ocean Springs, MS	Magical Mystery Man	1	Shark Valley, FL
Plant Man	2	Homestead, FL	Ranter	86	San Francisco, CA
Ghirdelli	2	Modoc, IN	Bootsy	37	Cincinnati, OH
Wildlife	1	Miami, FL	Sprinkles	11	Panama
Saddleback	1	Lexington, KY	Amplifier	4	Detroit, MI
Lil Bro	1	Miami, FL	Stubs	4	Kingsport, TN
Kardio Dash	1	Modoc, IN	Dubs	3	Kingsport, TN
Lady Bass	1	Ann Arbor, MI	Slapshot	2	Minneapolis, MN
Decapitator	1	France	Grey Goose	1	Newark, NJ
Carpenter	1	Providence, RI	Vizcachita	1	Peru
House Plant	1	Kankakee, IL	False	1	Atlanta, GA
Aerospace	1	Dallas, TX	Dreams	1	Romania
Ryno	1	Chicago, IL	Fed Ex	1	Miami, FL
Greenwich Time	45	France	Breast Stroke	1	Springfield, NJ
Espionage	11	New York, NY	Buco	1	Springfield, NJ
Freshwater	8	Plymouth, MI	Beetle Bailey	1	Indianapolis, IN
Dimples	6	Marlton, NJ	Hammer	65	Honduras
Inappropriate	2	Miami Beach, FL	Front Flip	8	Westboro, MA
Anesthesia	2	Arlington, TX	Harbour Pilot	7	Fort Lauderdale, FL
Air Gun	2	Hialeah, FL	Seedling	6	Boston, MA
Transit	1	Grand Rapids, MI	Phaser	3	China
Mason Jar	1	Grand Rapids, MI	Mediterranean Dish	2	Jordan
Lukewarm	1	Germany	Frontseat	2	Dominican Republic
Bender	1	Sacramento, CA	Clarity	2	Canada
Gembo	1	Phoenix, AZ	Pathfinder	2	Lake Worth, FL
Jack Ina Box	1	Buffalo, NY	Red Rig	2	Cincinnati, OH
White Lightning	140	Atlanta, GA	Package Delivery	2	Brazil
Calculus	13	Cuba	Tabbouleh	1	Jordan
Eye Pupil	9	Long Island, NY	BMX	1	Richmond, VA
Dazzle	4	Hoboken, NJ	Protein	1	Tampa, FL

Name	No.	Location	Name	No.	Location
Game Juice	1	Miami, FL	P.M.	4	Kendall, FL
Close Call	533	Finland	Nibbler	3	Mexico
Totem Pole	29	Spain	Deer Hunter	2	Riverton, NJ
Crawler	14	Boston, MA	Perculator	2	Phoenix
Sculpturer	7	Denmark	Long Root	2	Fort Worth, TX
Metal Man	5	Honduras	Pain Killer	2	Fort Worth, TX
Defensive End	3	San Diego, CA	Gipper	2	Colorado
Windy City	3	Chicago, IL	Renewal	2	Baltimore, MD
Organizer	2	Canada	Bread	2	Portland, OR
Mr. Positive	2	Baltimore, MD	Butter	2	Portland, OR
Raybo	2	Miami, FL	2 Wheeler	1	Moorestown, PA
Problem Solver	1	Oklahoma	Hog Fish	1	Key West, FL
Prankster	1	Woodbridge, VA	Buriti	1	Littleton, CO
Reservations	1	Piedmont, SC	Ether	1	Orlando, FL
Anchor	1	Boca Raton, FL	Stable Girl	1	Czech Republic
Air Man	1	Wausau, WI	Rhymer	1	Kansas City, KS
Sure Thing	1	Baltimore, MD	Pickle	1	Chicago, IL
Matter of Fact	1	Baltimore, MD	Cherry Cherry	1	New Rockford, ND
Fireplug	1	UK	Copper Penny	1	Saint Paul, MN
Extinguisher	1	UK	Committed	1	Saint Paul, MN
Macro	1	Washington, DC	Rolling Flow	1	Charleston, WV
Fried Egg	1	New York, NY	Taurus	1	Pittsburgh, PA
Hanger	1	Tucson, AZ	Counya	1	Lafayette, LA
Sicilian	7	Canada	Pabst Blue Ribbon	1	Philadelphia, PA
Internal Affairs	6	Canada	Doubleheader	1	Smyrna, DE
Rollyball	5	Germany	Equity	1	San Francisco, CA
Voltage	5	Miami, FL	Deli	1	Saint Paul, MN
Smooth Operator	3	Chile	Canvas	1	Loganville, GA
Happy Ending	3	Colombia	Palette	1	Loganville, GA
Bon Voyage	3	Belgium	Underground	1	Coral Gables, FL
Sun Colors	2	Germany	Smarty	1	South Miami, FL
MTV	2	Los Angeles, CA	Hubris	35	Scranton, PA
Peppermint	1	Dayton, OH	Wild West	10	Warsaw, WI
Plaster Caster	1	Baltimore, MD	Zulu	7	Australia
Cholesterol	1	Poland	Hehrewer	5	Milwaukee, WI
Blue Cross	1	Covington, IN	Manifesto	3	New York, NY
Corn Flake	1	Covington, IN	Quince Quince	3	Chicago, IL
Dome Master	1	Newark, NJ	Lake Front	3	Chicago, IL
Hit and Run	1	Panama	So Fi Social	2	Milwaukee, WI
Adopter	1	Indianapolis, IN	Long Snapper	2	New Jersey
Licensor	1	Raleigh, NC	Duper	2	Grand Rapids, MI
Turbine	1	Italy	Valuable	1	Pennsylvania
Simplicity	1	Providence, RI	Ghost Distance	1	Milwaukee, WI
Bull Ony	1	Providence, RI	Mid South	1	Memphis, TN
Trombone	1	Nicaragua	West Nile	1	Noblesville, IN
Grouper	1	Cuba	Zuko	1	Princeton, NJ
Footworks	1	Minnesota	Rumza	1	Lincoln, NE
Klitch	1	New Jersey	Mid Sole	1	Warsaw, WI
Padre	1	Chicago, IL	Yuengling	1	Colombia
Sputnik	1	Russia	Cochlea	1	Austria
Knuckler	1	Ridgewood, NJ	Probation	1	North Wildwood, NJ
Weapons	39	Milwaukee, WI	Electric Hair	1	North Wildwood, NJ
1st Sgt.	19	Union City, NJ	Dart	1	New Jersey
Pill Pusher	19	Miami Beach, FL	Big Bird	1	Tampa, FL
Independence	17	Sharon, MA	Fathom	1	South Africa
Leap Year	10	Philadelphia, PA	Mr. White	43	Cuba
Thermometer	8	Kendall, FL	Frodo	42	Grant, AL
Chlorine	7	Nicaragua	Sappy	40	Cuba
Bag Pipe	7	Boston, MA	Kenetic	22	Manhattan, NY
Fig Newton	7	Milwaukee, WI	Equator	5	Ecuador
Tough Cookie	6	Baltimore, MD	Papa Eyebear	3	Woodmere, NY

Name	Count	Location	Name	Count	Location
Ball Park	2	Los Angeles, CA	Derby Day	1	Jackson, NJ
Didymus	2	Cincinnati, OH	Hodag	1	Tempe, AZ
Special Delivery	2	Pittsburgh, PA	Dirty Dancer	1	Ukraine
Halloween	2	Memphis, TN	Mags	1	Newburgh, NY
Unconscious	2	Milwaukee, WI	Digits	1	Atlanta, GA
Grasshopper	2	Milwaukee, WI	Pepperjack	1	Wausau, WI
Snow Monkey	1	Germany	Grout	1	Wausau, WI
Cle Dawg	1	Cleveland, OH	Burger Queen	1	Peoria, IL
Innovator	1	Chicago, IL	ROTC	1	Weston, FL
Muzzy	1	Chicago, IL	5 Fingers	1	Highland Park, IL
Tuber	1	Indiana	Mountaineer	1	Charleston, WV
Long Dress	1	Chicago, IL	Whole Grain	1	Brookline, MA
Red Light	1	South Miami, FL	Instant Karma	1	Puerto Rico
Snow White	1	Germany	Continental Divide	1	South Africa
Tequila Sheep	1	Mexico	Brownie	2	UK
Baby Steps	1	China	Infringement	1	Atlanta, GA
Mongoose	1	Detroit, MI	Broadway	1	Edison, NJ
Kidney Bean	1	Philadelphia, PA	Everydata	1	Yorkville, IL
Pulp	1	San Jose, CA	Heineken	1	Australia
Bumbela	1	Canada	Fixer	21	Melbourne Beach, FL
Process	23	Germany	Doomsday	12	Omaha, NE
Lucky	5	Brooklyn, NY	Rum Raisin	3	Colombia
Archer	3	Warsaw, WI	Re Vasc	3	Miami Beach, FL
Conn	3	Honduras	Lily Pad	2	Peru
Eclipse	2	Ecuador	RPM	2	Wellington, MA
Blond Bombshell	2	Sweden	Amp	2	Melbourne Beach, FL
Reconstruction	2	Shreveport, LA	Hallucination	2	Charlotte, NC
4 on the floor	2	Jackson, MS	Criminal Justice	1	Madison, WI
Wobegone	1	Duluth, MN	Furrier	1	Colorado
Terp	1	Washington, DC	Recon	1	Junction City, KS
Daisy	1	Chicago, IL	Scratch	1	White Bear Lake, MN
Ferment	1	Boston, MA	Supplement	1	Portland, OR
Icebox	1	Germany	Alarm Clock	1	Miami Beach, FL
Bulk	1	Kendall, FL	Butcher	348	Miami Beach, FL
Double Rainbow	1	Portland, OR	Aspen	2	Great Bend, KS
Ultra Pump	1	Portland, OR	More Less	1	Charlotte, NC
Swany	1	Michigan	L.A. Blue	1	Los Angeles, CA
Door	1	Germany	Latina 54	29	Puerto Rico
Next Door	1	Germany	Corona	11	Washington, DC
Intangible	43	Atlanta, GA	Picadillo	6	Miami, FL
Purple Planner	31	Brazil	White Belly	4	Biloxi, MS
Palindrome	16	Manhattan, NY	Imagination	3	Tampa, FL
Sea Horse	10	UK	Golden Ray	3	Tampa, FL
Nerd	4	Prince George's County, MD	Toy Soldier	3	Terre Haute, IN
Beet Reporter	4	Pennsylvania	Livestock	3	Portland, OR
Samsonite	4	Pittsburgh, PA	Sockless	2	Shelton, CT
GMC Pickup	3	Newburgh, NY	Hip Hop	2	Franklin, NC
Rosebud	3	Fort Lauderdale, FL	Kiki	2	Miami, FL
Sugarland	2	Sugarland, TX	Nester	2	Willington, FL
Tanker Surfer	1	Galveston, TX	Accommodating	2	Willington, FL
C-Note	1	Memphis, TN	Quiet Madman	2	Fall River, MA
10%	1	Eastern Shore, FL	Tres Leches	2	Hazlet, NJ
Compartment	1	Guatemala	Fox Den	2	Fairfax, VA
Artillery	1	Panama	Deer Slayer	1	Houston, TX
Wood Knocker	1	Seattle, WA	Double Sign	1	Jersey City, NJ
Discovery	1	Bulgaria	Percocet	1	Blue Belle, PA
Willpower	1	Morocco	Condiment	1	Pittsburgh, PA
Entertainer	1	New Britain, CT	Mountain Air	1	Abington, VA
Kappy	1	Philadelphia, PA	Naan	1	India
Manger	1	Israel	Yardley	1	Trenton, NJ
Tamarind	1	Austin, MN	Tiger Cub	1	Colorado Springs, CO

Name		Location	Name		Location
Roof Bolt	1	Toronto, OH	T.J. Mini	1	Finland
Stress Reliever	1	New Jersey	Gizz	1	Brazil
Luxury Seat	1	Fall River, MA	Kelp	1	Monterey, CA
Friendly Shy	1	Chicago, IL	Fuel	1	Brazil
Watch Out	1	Palm Harbor, FL	Naccatoni	1	Missouri
Sidewalk	1	Tarpon Springs, FL	Turron	1	Spain
Hales Owen	1	UK	Bell Hop	121	Serbia
Happy Bubbles	1	UK	New York Second	4	Wilkes-Barre, PA
Lobotomy	293	Mexico	Mid Wife	4	Butte, MT
Hot Rod	48	Miami Beach, FL	Karolina K	4	South Carolina
Bomb Squad	27	Portugal	Punisher	2	Miami, FL
Extra	22	Tallahassee, FL	Top Chef	2	Saddle River, NJ
Boy Next Door	16	Philadelphia, PA	Finger Wolf	2	Orlando, FL
Headhunter	16	Castleberry, FL	Sight Unseen	1	Salem, VA
Metal World	2	Concord, NC	Crimson	1	Dallas, TX
Skyscraper	2	Monterey, CA	Pyramid	1	New York, NY
Chontalena	2	Nicaragua	Without Limits	1	Wilmington, NC
Pun	1	Los Angeles, CA	Aspire	1	Wilmington, NC
9 Yards	1	Williamsburg, NY	Wasp	1	Sweden
Saxy	1	Philadelphia, PA	Rank'n file	1	Miami, FL
Daddy-O	1	Michigan	Mobilizer	1	Orlando, FL
Sadlands	1	Milwaukee, WI	Mad Cow	118	UK
Chill Red	1	Evansville, IN	Witch's Brew	6	Puerto Rico
Global	1	Brazil	Book Fair	5	Miami, FL
Rushin	1	Russia	Pheasant	4	Heron, SD
Museum	1	Belgium	Trustee	3	Garfield, NJ
Ole Tanger	1	Columbus, OH	Herocious	2	Miami Beach, FL
Raw Bar	1	Honduras	Coffee Buffalo	2	Blue Belle, PA
Flopsy	18	Germany	Ghanja	2	Jamaica
Tugboat	15	Biscayne Bay, FL	Mixed Breed	2	Portugal
Milonga	15	Argentina	Thirsty Dog	2	New York, NY
Stroganoff	8	Brazil	Sol Pedal	1	Thomaston, GA
Conqueror	5	Spain	Scandic	1	Sweden
Viper	5	Ocala, FL	Runday	1	Sweden
Unpopular	4	Brazil	Praying Mantis	1	Orlando, FL
Tu Tu	2	Argentina	Saab Story	1	Sweden
Fish Hook	1	San Diego, CA	PBC	1	Baltimore, MD
NPR	1	Washington, DC	Soft Shell	1	Baltimore, MD
Mad Hatter	1	Miami, FL	Chaser	1	Puerto Rico
Witch Doctor	1	Chicago, IL	Resurface	1	Cleveland, OH
Nice Guy	1	Chicago, IL	911	1	Kalamazoo, MI
Turquoise	1	Brazil	RV	1	Elkhart, IN
Picanha	1	Brazil	Pollo Fargo	1	Fargo, ND
Twirler	1	Aventura, FL	Iron Girl	1	Sweden
Ybor	1	Ybor City, FL	Parking Meter	1	Vero Beach, FL
Palmeiras 17	1	Brazil	Quaker Oats	1	Philadelphia, PA
Expiration	1	Brazil	Striped Bass	1	Garfield, NJ
Ant	1	Sweden	Spine Guy	1	San Diego, CA
Close Encounter	1	Ann Arbor, MI	Portogee	1	San Diego, CA
100%	1	Brazil	Clownfish	1	Norwalk, CT
Frosty	43	UK	No Preservatives	1	Connecticut
Navy Brat	5	Miami Beach, FL	Orca	1	Detroit, MI
Molder	4	Union City, NJ	Study	1	Washington, DC
Oily	3	Brazil	Full Court	1	Myrtle Beach, SC
Empanada	3	Hungary	Hypnosis	1	Wake Forest, NC
Dan-O	2	Hernando Beach, FL	Sibling Rivalry	1	Portugal
Thumbelina	2	Princeton Junction, NJ	Tame Hair	1	Wildwood, NJ
Believer Achiever	1	Silver Springs, MD	Media Tracker	1	New York, NY
Red Wing	1	Detroit, MI	Guinness	1	New York, NY
Turkish Taffy	1	Chicago, IL	Dos Equis XX	44	Miami, FL
Danalize	1	Harrisburg, PA	Bev	7	Delaware, OH

Name	#	Location	Name	#	Location
Brokenheart	3	Mexico	Glyphics	1	Miami, FL
Unsettled	2	Charleston, SC	Distributor	1	Brazil
Warehouse	2	Miami, FL	Point Guard	1	San Diego, CA
Trance	2	Miami, FL	Disco	6	Arlington, TX
Baked Alaska	2	Anchorage, AK	High Resolution	5	Chicago, IL
Pecan	2	Princeton Junction, NJ	Immunity	2	Germany
Thursday Dog	1	Atlanta, GA	Microcirculation	2	San Diego, CA
Scrum Cap	1	Saratoga, NY	Tasker	1	West Point, NY
Otto	1	Livingstone, MT	Hometown Prodigy	1	Miami, FL
Gorginho	1	Brazil	Good N Plenty	1	Dominican Republic
Metabolism	1	New York, NY	Kentucky Woman	1	Louisville, KY
Rushmore	5	Heron, SD	Biscuits N Gravy	1	Jacksonville, FL
Orange Slice	4	Serbia	F-150	1	Baltimore, MD
Pleasure Seeker	3	France	Fish Slayer	1	Cuba
Gluten Free	1	Tucson, AZ	Bitch's Brew	1	Oakland, CA
38 Special	1	Laramie, WY	Airborne	1	Mexico
Doctor Laser	1	Tucson, AZ	Airsat	1	Homestead, FL
Legally Blond	1	St. Louis, MO	Caracas	1	Brazil
Sustainable	1	Branson, MO	Backpacking Beaver	1	Miami, FL
Dingo	1	Ashland, KY	Foos	1	Germany
Penalty Box	1	New York, NY	Congas	31	Washington, DC
Kickboard	1	Springfield, MO	Sushi	4	Canada
Cover Girl	1	Bronx, NY	Giving Back	2	Hancock, MI
Astro Babe	1	Houston, TX	Multi	2	Cameron, WV
Coated Shell	1	Nicaragua	Intervals	2	Miami, FL
Repocheta	1	Dominican Republic	Wildflower	2	Tampa, FL
Homebody	1	Madison, WI	Dirty Laundry	1	Los Angeles, CA
Correspondent	1	Chicago, IL	Hat Trick	1	Miami, FL
Sleeve	1	Miami, FL	Meter Reader	1	Baton Rouge, LA
5th Street Circle	1	Chicago, IL	Backup Plan	1	New York, NY
PH Balance	1	Venezuela	English Pub	1	UK
Sketchy	36	Switzerland	Redvelvet Cupcake	1	Miami, FL
Cyber Dragon	5	Colombia	Army Bratt	1	Fort Stewart, GA
Caterer	4	Peru	Strawberry Shortcake	1	New York, NY
Pelican Girl	2	Sugarloaf Mountain, MD	Triple Threat	1	Tampa, FL
Cleats	1	Wausau, WI	Genetics	38	Lakeland, FL
Goosy	1	Glendale, WI	True Story	16	Italy
Bachelorette	1	Atlanta, GA	Splitter	2	Thailand
Family Bible	1	Reno, NV	Star Wars	2	UK
Junk Mail	1	Wilmington, NC	Fire Ax	2	Charlottesville, VA
North Woods	1	Wausau, WI	Chelada	2	Alexandria, LA
Backburner	1	Miami Beach, FL	Hot Furnace	2	Alexandria, LA
Forever Bluejeans	1	Germany	Double	1	Westchester County, NY
Petri	1	Duluth, MN	Horchata	1	Kinnelon, NJ
Offwhite Pearl	1	Duluth, MN	Little Sky	5	Colombia
Swati	1	Canada	Moisturizer	3	Fort Worth, TX
Euchre	1	Plymouth, MI	Wiggles	2	Edgewood, KY
Wallstreet	1	Garfield, NJ	Practical	1	Miami, FL
Baby Strokes	1	Saint Paul, MN	Universal Love	1	New York, NY
Maat	1	Los Angeles, CA	Etiquette	1	New York, NY
Lotus	3	Germany	Whammy	2	Miami, FL
Shampoo	2	Yonkers, NY	Sonar	2	Rochester, NY
Bajah Boy	2	Tampa, FL	Fly Girl	2	Portugal
Duvel	1	Belgium	Havoc	2	Charlotte, NC
Latin Lion	1	Philadelphia, PA	Acorn	2	Milford, CT
Ma$e	1	San Francisco, CA	Night Jar	1	Napa Valley, CA
Dead Pool	1	Pittsburgh, PA	Direct Connection	1	Dallas, TX
Roulette 13	1	Pittsburgh, PA	Pickett	1	UK
Banff	1	Spokane, WA	Wickett	1	UK
Mountain Dog	1	San Diego, CA	By the Book	1	Mozambique
Yokohama Mama	1	Japan	Olarfies	1	Austin, TX

Merger	1	Austin, TX	
Botox	1	Daytona Beach, FL	
Red Bandit	184	Boston, MA	
31 Kilo	59	Miami, FL	
Conveyor Belt	7	Italy	
Quinoa	5	Washington, DC	
High Tolerance	4	Germany	
Redheaded Stepchild	2	Fort Wayne, IN	
Mexican Horseshoe	2	Mexico	
Caesar Salad	1	Brazil	
World Traveler	1	Farmingdale, NY	
Insulin	1	Bloomington, IN	
Bad Day	1	Miami, FL	
Unoffendable	52	Saint Paul, MN	
Lutefisk	32	Norway	
Sound Check	8	Miami, FL	
Water Survival	3	Pennsylvania	
Ducky	2	Atlanta, GA	
Ladrona	2	Tallahassee, FL	
Hookem Horn	1	Houston, TX	
Aggie	1	Dallas, TX	
Re Curve	1	Lawton, OK	
Bang Buster	1	Manhattan, NY	
Grilled Chicken	1	Miami, FL	
Category 5	1	Homestead, FL	
Arm Drag	1	New York, NY	
Almond Joy	1	Chicago, IL	
20,000 Leagues	1	North Salem, NH	
Double Joint	1	Fillmore, CA	
Targa	1	Chicago, IL	
10th Avenue	1	Canada	
Deep Thinker	1	Miami, FL	
Special Ed	1	Canada	
Wind Up	1	Canada	
Overpriced	26	Houston, TX	
Weekend Warrior	12	Miami Beach, FL	
Diamond Calfs	6	Russia	
T-Rex	4	Miami, FL	
Zen	4	Queens, NY	
Yoga Toes	4	Lafayette, LA	
Justice	3	New York	
Lugnuts	3	Nashville, TN	
Permission	2	Eagle, ID	
Custard	2	Ann Arbor, MI	
Electro Glide	2	Washington, DC	
Tao	2	Richmond, VA	
No Ice	1	Riverton, NJ	
Posthumous	1	Switzerland	
Hoot Owl	1	Washington, DC	
Pooh	1	Boston, MA	
Hills	1	Jackson, MS	
Page Turner	1	Salt Lake City, UT	
Dandelion	1	New Jersey	
Humanity	1	Manchester, CT	
Blue Valentine	1	Chicago, IL	
Silly Pants	1	Poland	
Scribner	1	Milwaukee, WI	
Church Singer	1	Delaware, NJ	
Fire Monkey	1	Rochester, NY	
Proxie	1	San Diego, CA	
Bosley	1	Phoenix, AZ	
Stone Cutter	1	Oakland, CA
Paddy O Prado	1	Iowa
Cup O Joe	1	Iowa
Blow Dry	1	Connecticut
Sir Loin	1	Twin Falls, ID
Cayuga	1	Washington, DC
Passport	1	UK
Cold Cuts	1	Canada
Frozen Potatoes	1	Alexandria, VA
Pup	1	Brazil
Nash Vegas	3	Nashville, TN
Cajun Man	3	Brusly, LA
Drawbridge	2	Philadelphia, PA
Pebbles	2	Cape Cod, MA
Thurxton	2	Greenville, SC
About 18	2	Canada
Dirt	2	Buffalo, NY
Suefro	2	Coral Gables, FL
Spiked Grass	2	Germany
Forget me not	2	Cranston, RI
Y2K	2	Birmingham, AL
Vida Vegas	1	Las Vegas, NV
Space Rocket	1	Houston, TX
Laser Zone	1	Springfield, VA
El Ponte	1	Italy
Ice Pack	1	Canada
Creepy Money	1	Raleigh, NC
Tulsa Time	1	Tulsa, OK
Senseless	1	Lancaster, PA
Twig Newton	1	Baltimore, MD
Screener	1	St. Louis, MO
Grully	1	Lancaster, PA
Wakeboard	1	Lancaster, PA
Pilsner	1	Holland
Bronze	1	Atlanta, GA
Get Smart	1	Atlanta, GA
Pussycat	1	Durham, NC
Narrative	1	Philadelphia, PA
Shagsly	1	North Carolina
Manual	1	Puerto Rico
Wayward Bear	1	Texas
Pink Flamingo	1	Miami, FL
305	17	Miami, FL
Surf N Turf	5	Newport, RI
Traction	4	Washington, DC
Zentrick	3	Belgium
Pyro Mahn	2	Miami, FL
Mirimichi	2	Wilmington, NC
Open Book	2	Miami, FL
Browmian in Motion	2	Stony Brook, NY
Best Option	2	Miami, FL
Chain Champ	2	Miami, FL
Fizz	2	Manhattan Beach, CA
Hoop	2	Manhattan Beach, CA
North Star	1	Baltimore, MD
Clean Dirt	1	Philadelphia, PA
G6	1	Chappaqua, NY
Mind Face	1	Raleigh, NC
Yorkshire Pudding	1	UK
Muse	1	Troy, NY
BMW	1	Germany

Name	Count	Location	Name	Count	Location
Spring Song	1	Fredericksburg, VA	Beer Nuts	1	Plano, TX
20/20	1	Ireland	Sacred Fire	1	St. Augustine, FL
Cranberry	1	USA	Iron Monkey	1	Chattanooga, TN
Ritalin	1	St. Cloud, MN	Wild Pig	1	Chattanooga, TN
Sound Effects	1	Derby, CT	Long Engagement	1	New Brunswick, NJ
Special K	1	Miami, FL	Comic Book	1	Miami, FL
Wam Bam	1	UK	Carmel Swirl	22	Lewisburg, WV
Volcano Lightning	1	Worcester, MA	Cross Examiner	3	Flanders, NJ
Morning Dew	1	Boston, MA	Conundrum	3	Miami, FL
Jazz Dancer	1	Manhattan Beach, CA	Dutch Oven	3	Billings, MT
Chuli	8	Bolivia	Princess Leia	3	Portugal
Killer Milkshake	4	Gainesville, FL	Country Slim	2	Athens, GA
Philly Cheesesteak	4	Philadelphia, PA	Rip Writer	2	New York, NY
Dove Bar	3	Brooklyn, NY	Loaner	2	France
Butterscotch	3	Philadelphia, PA	Pillbox Hat	2	UK
Walk On	2	Lincolnshire, IL	Roma	2	Canada
Albatross	2	San Jose, CA	Oyster Shell	2	Chicago, IL
White Sea	1	Russia	Country Cousin	1	Ocala, FL
Flash 29	1	Jacksonville, FL	Airbus 330	1	Italy
Twin Timber	1	Big Timber, MT	Irish Postcard	1	Fort Lauderdale, FL
Low Single	1	Grand Rapids, MI	Pink Ceiling	1	Sublimity, OR
La Bottom	1	Milwaukee, WI	7 Walls	1	Opelika, AL
Water Wiggle	1	Crowley, LA	Island Spice	1	France
Shazam	1	Denton, TX	Musical Bath	1	France
Sign In	1	New York, NY	Twitter	1	Miami, FL
Tramson	1	Memphis, TN	Jaffa Juice	1	Ukraine
Nemesis	1	Tampa, FL	Jedi	1	Portugal
Mohave	1	Norco, CA	Bloody Wolf	13	France
Rye Bread	1	Philadelphia, PA	Mantra	12	Buffalo, NY
Soila	1	Miami Beach, FL	Ruby Ruby	5	St. Louis, MO
Royal View	1	Springfield, IL	Elliptigo	3	Decatur, IL
Golden Globes	1	Miami, FL	Child Bride	3	Decatur, IL
More or Less	1	Brazil	Proof Reader	3	Norway
Pink Rock	1	Baltimore, MD	Kudos	2	Canada
Stucco	1	Canada	Catch Up	2	Canada
Language Doctor	1	Canada	Rikers Island	1	New York, NY
Blue Devil	1	San Jose, CA	On Point	1	New York, NY
Day Tripper	1	Myrtle Beach, SC	Supply Officer	1	Tampa, FL
Overboard	1	Bryson City, NC	Quality	1	Belgium
Hype	16	Venezuela	Norco	1	Corpus Christi, TX
Freshie	9	Canada	Beems	1	Saint Paul, MN
On Time	5	Boston, MA	Blue Cheese	1	Switzerland
Harlem Shuffle	5	Nigeria	Clemson	1	Hartsville, SC
Frequent Flyer	4	Brazil	Maple Pie	1	Canada
Dork Kord	4	Italy	Green Juice	1	Washington, DC
Rum Runner	3	UK	Messiah	1	Miami, FL
61 Degrees	2	Austin, TX	West Ham	1	UK
Grumpy	2	Peoria, IL	Fresca	1	Columbus, OH
1/2 Full	2	Philadelphia, PA	Wine Stop	1	Moorhead, NC
South Beach Rat	1	Miami Beach, FL	1 Eye	1	Durham, NC
Lights Out	1	Germany	Slapshooter	1	Bradford, VT
Late Bloomer	1	Portland, OR	Art Byte	1	Newton, MA
Tae Kwon Do	1	Kaneohe, HI	Ridgeback	1	Albuquerque, NM
Prepper	1	Natrona Heights, PA	Boiler Maker	50	Ann Arbor, MI
Mahhala	1	Mountain Vale, NJ	Chopper	12	Canada
Stray Talk	1	Orlando, FL	Flo Rider	7	Los Angeles, CA
Hospice	1	Charleston, SC	Magnet	3	Italy
Antarctica Romance	1	New Rochelle, NY	Kettle Balls	3	Norway
Finger Style	1	Indianapolis, IN	Northern Lights	3	Norway
Immortal Jellyfish	1	Indianapolis, IN	Dunkin Coffee	3	Decatur, GA
1/2 Empty	1	Philadelphia, PA	Dog Rescue	3	Washington, DC

Name	#	Location	Name	#	Location
Chop Sticks	1	Canada	Perfume Man	1	Norway
Cubbie Bear	1	Miami, FL	Koi Fish	1	Miami, FL
Forward Shot	1	West Palm Beach, FL	Full Plate	1	Miami, FL
Chick Pea	1	Vero Beach, FL	Old New England	1	Concord, NH
Seal Call	1	New York, NY	Auburn	1	Tuscaloosa, AL
Database	1	Charlotte, NC	Serendipitous	1	Los Angeles, CA
Hamster Wheel	1	Miami, FL	Fraudstr	1	Portugal
Sugar Beet	1	Boise, ID	Extended Family	1	Stockton, CA
Wake Up Call	9	Chicago, IL	Fiberglass	1	Stockton, CA
Sgt. Tiburon	2	Brazil	Pinky Promise	1	Stockton, CA
Caca	2	Spain	25 Caliber	1	Los Angeles, CA
Beginner	2	Surfside, FL	Watch Band	16	Belgium
Playlist	2	Fayetteville, NC	Mugz	10	Miami, FL
Enchilada	2	Fayetteville, NC	Lion Hair	5	Honduras
Jaybird	2	Winston-Salem, NC	Shirley Temple	3	UK
Manu	1	Brazil	Pressures On	2	Manson, IA
Happy Heart	1	Miami, FL	Rag Brie	2	Manson, IA
Freedom Defender	1	Miami, FL	Blue Crab	2	Maryland
Red Lobster	1	San Antonio, TX	Platano	2	Dominican Republic
Clavicle	1	Mexico	Army Scout	2	Sunrise, FL
Gremio	1	Brazil	Frisky	2	Livingston, MT
Dirt Maker	1	Canada	Snowflake	2	Fayetteville, NC
Talking Machine	1	Canada	4 Winds	2	Azerbaijan
Fraulein	1	Germany	Pennies from Heaven	2	Pennsylvania
Tuna Fish	1	Dominican Republic	Pop Tart	2	Sykesville, MD
Behind the Scenes	1	Greenfield, MA	Tundra Star	2	Rochester, NY
Tidal Wave	4	Manhattan, NY	Special Needs	2	Flanders, NJ
Uncle Saltflats	4	Bolivia	Toffee Chip	2	UK
Yabba Dabba Do	4	Chicago, IL	Alternative Art	1	Cleveland, OH
Rockin' Robbin	3	Guatemala	Extra innings	1	Manhattan, NY
Vie	3	Pittsburgh, PA	22 Twice	1	Bronx, NY
Barefoot Economist	2	Albuquerque, NM	Antique	1	Germany
Miss Bolivia	2	Bolivia	Choices	1	San Jose, CA
27 Ideas	1	Mexico	Tail Slide	1	Boise, ID
Foquito	1	Mexico	Inauguration	1	Washington, DC
Burpee	1	Kansas City, MO	Nestee	1	Wellington, FL
Hard Going	1	Miami, FL	Catholic	1	Lexington, KY
Brie	1	Midland, TX	Sherlock	1	Lexington, KY
Bumper	1	Italy	Yellow Jacket	1	Dunwoody, GA
Waterfall	1	Venezuela	J Trigger	1	John's Creek, GA
Mr. Curious	1	Elkhart, MD	Farm Mom	1	Crawfordsville, FL
Action Law	1	Yonkers, NY	Forbes	1	Bulgaria
Minimalist	1	Connecticut	Heavy D	1	Cape Coral, FL
Green Papaya	1	Laos	Mail Sweetie	1	Broussard, LA
Elvi	1	Anoka, MN	Mr. Wonderful	1	Riverton, NJ
Chera	1	Highlands Ranch, CO	Purple Panda	1	Riverton, NJ
No Shortcuts	1	Eden Prairie, MN	Showtime	69	Forest Hills, IL
City Attorney	1	Coral Gables, FL	Backwards Propell	11	Washington, DC
Broken Water	1	Coral Gables, FL	Propell Forward	9	Washington, DC
AK 47	1	Miami, FL	Medical Tourist	5	Canada
Fonda Honda	1	Brazil	Vee Fish	3	Bosnia
Rogaine	1	Brazil	Snots	3	Greenwich, CT
Latenight Libra	1	Los Angeles, CA	Bar Code	3	Philadelphia, PA
Laszie	1	Washington, DC	Death Defier	2	Clarksville, TN
Cranker	1	San Jose, CA	Asthma	2	Ocean, NJ
Pony Girl	16	Chicago, IL	Swiss Fries	2	Switzerland
Flip Flop	11	Chicago, IL	Brick Top	1	Canada
Blue Water	10	Baltimore, MD	Mahi Mahi	1	Canada
Mizzou	5	Columbia, MD	Blind Guy	1	Canada
Oak Tree	2	Oak Park, IL	Colorist	1	Canada
Maytag	1	Galesburg, IL	Shakespeare Love	1	UK

Zini	1	UK	Vinegar	3	Italy

Name	Count	Location
Zini	1	UK
Phish Bonez	1	Saratoga, FL
Bloodwork	1	Wellington, FL
Base Pace	1	Miami, FL
Salsa Brown	1	Washington, DC
Data Center	1	Miami, FL
Inmate Runner	1	Greensborough, PA
Blue Law	1	Miami, FL
Cobber	1	Philadelphia, PA
Tuxedo	1	Miami, FL
Chicken Market	1	Long Island, NY
Brownie Points	1	France
Major Minor	1	Indianapolis, IN
4 AM	1	Miami, FL
Keystone Cop	1	USA
Tchako	1	Chicago, IL
Surface Man	1	Loveland, CO
Fathead Daddy	1	Greenwich, CT
Dancing Queen	1	Connecticut
Pingu	1	Finland
Motor Man	1	Bolivia
Captain Charter	4	Solomons Island, MD
Let's Play 2	3	Chicago, IL
Thin Lizzy	3	Tampa, FL
Duckwood	1	Marietta, GA
Listing	1	Indianapolis, IN
Kiko	1	Germany
Polar Pineapple	1	Appleton, MD
Polar Raspberry	1	Appleton, MD
Pot Shop	1	Denver, CO
World Trotter	1	Germany
Mowed Grass	1	Germany
Woodworker	1	Cleveland, OH
Hog Shooter	1	Miami, FL
Open Shell	1	Philadelphia, PA
Morning Kool-Aid	1	Annapolis, MD
Oregano	1	Annapolis, MD
Dizard	1	Boston, MA
Gypper	1	Philadelphia, PA
Fear Buster	1	Miami, FL
Sweedheart	1	Sweden
Balsamic	14	Italy
Tan Thru	6	Dartmouth, MA
Ferris Wheel	3	Switzerland
Book Face	2	Canada
Price Tag	2	Homestead, FL
Nutella	2	Homestead, FL
One Way Ticket	2	New Jersey
Mystic Pizza	2	Miami, FL
Wire Boat	1	Dartmouth, MA
Rubs	1	Kingsport, TN
Mountain Kid	1	Canada
Prairie Kid	1	Canada
Generac	1	Canada
Millennium	1	Canada
Broller	1	Shawnee, KS
Vi Andi	1	Hungary
Fix It	1	Colombia
Thermal	1	UK
Hoagan's Heroes	21	Portland, OR
Roses N' Guns	13	Colombia

Name	Count	Location
Vinegar	3	Italy
Fiddle Sticks	2	Bloomington, IN
Chucky Smooth	2	Jamestown, NY
Suburban Spy	1	Nashville, TN
Banana Slug	1	Chapel Hill, NC
Somebody	1	Oakland, CA
Wilas	1	Louisville, KY
Turk	1	Albany, KY
Pacific Sunset	1	San Diego, CA
Wicked Pissa	1	Boston, MA
Correspondent	1	Dallas, TX
Soft Pillow	1	Colombia
Red Nebraska	5	Grand Island, NE
Zool	2	Chicago, IL
Chest Pounder	2	Highland Beach, FL
Brother Curly	1	Charlotte, NC
Turning Point	1	Tampa, FL
Princess Jasmine	1	South Brunswick, NJ
Loosely Grounded	1	UK
Lemon Drop	1	Hudson River, NY
Link	1	Jackson, MS
Orange Mormon	1	Mims, FL
Wamps	1	Charlottesville, VA
Cinnamon Crunch	1	Rome, NY
Carry On	1	Rome, NY
Porsche	1	Germany
Stone Man	32	St. Louis, MO
Esmerald Hunter	5	St. Louis, MO
Wood U	2	Kendall, FL
Heart n Roses	1	Dallas, TX
Morning Chirper	1	Dripping Springs, TX
Presser	1	Bolivia
Nephew Suspension	1	Bolivia
Bitter Hops	1	Ronkonkoma, NY
Blooper	1	Toms River, NJ
PG Tips	1	UK
Dullsville	1	Fort Wayne, IN
Cow Horn	1	Ventnor, NJ
Scaler	1	Ventnor, NJ
Vegemite	1	Australia
Cattle Rancher	1	Austin, TX
Currency Exchange	1	Chile
Ground Fire	1	Brazil
Dessert Mold	1	Breaux Bridge, LA
Craw Lady	1	Breaux Bridge, LA
U Could	1	Kendall, FL
Wind Farm	1	Tiburon, CA
Ox Lady	3	Germany
Power Tool	2	Richmond, VA
Blackberry Circus	2	UK
Phone Booth	1	Richmond, VA
Splicer	1	Richmond, VA
7 and 1	1	Denver, CO
Prescription Fill	1	Charlotte, NC
Water Fowl	1	Charlotte, NC
Yorvick	1	UK
Lights On	1	Pinehurst, NC
Ice Gnat	1	Argentina
Lake Erie Monster	1	Cambridge, OH
Blockhead	1	Portugal
Pool Cage	1	Bradenton, FL

Name	#	Location	Name	#	Location
Tiger Eye	1	Bradenton, FL	Public Corruption	1	Ezel, KY
Zanna	1	Italy	Purdue Wings	1	Hazard, KY
Jetlag	1	Pleasanton, CA	Mint Recovery	1	Brooklyn, NY
Fashion Reader	1	Terre Haute, IN	Right Hook	1	Slovenia
Xbox	1	Terre Haute, IN	Turbulance	1	Slovenia
Forehand	1	Finland	Cabernet	1	New Orleans, LA
Backhand	1	Finland	Young Sole	4	Weston, FL
Crappie	1	Terre Haute, IN	Frozen Rope	3	Weston, FL
Psyched	4	West Palm Beach, FL	Mended	3	Tampa, FL
Home Stretch	3	Dallas, TX	Farm Funk	2	Canada
Cookie Monster	1	Indianapolis, IN	Glorious	2	Tampa, FL
Mooster	1	Indianapolis, IN	Checkpoint	2	Puerto Rico
Peelstr	1	Indianapolis, IN	Shooting Star	1	Bolivia
Do Something	1	Port Charlotte, FL	Pick	1	Madison, WI
Kumquat	1	Germany	Fish A Runi	1	Germany
Hussy	1	Dayton, OH	Snow Ski	1	Austria
Gender Traffic	1	Collingswood, NJ	Downs	1	Austin, TX
Patuau	1	Bolivia	Fun Puns	1	Philadelphia, PA
Banana Smoothie	1	Ireland	Boat Coach	1	Ridgefield, CT
Newster	1	UK	Minnow	1	Ridgefield, CT
Bee Sting	2	Germany	Lottery 44	1	Nashville, TN
Spinal Tap	2	San Francisco, CA	Pub Crawl	1	Milwaukee, WI
Beet Red	1	Omaha, NE	Peak	1	Tampa, FL
AC/DC Electrical	1	Nicaragua	Drumlyn Charity	1	Sansbury, CT
Powerless Vincent	1	Poland	Nerd Master	1	Washington, DC
Rouge	1	Poland	On Tap	2	Lascolinas, TX
Conductor	1	Houston, TX	Pimento	1	Baldwin, KS
Litter Box	1	Sioux City, IA	Astra	1	Endora, KS
Pies of Gato	1	Spain	Double Stuffed	1	Lascolinas
Capper	1	Cincinnati, OH	Surrogate Mom	1	Canada
Green Bean	1	Santa Barbara, CA	Transmitter	1	Canada
Agent Bunchie	1	Somerset, KY	Cruisin' Car	1	Westin, FL
Titos	1	Weimar, TX	Mind Finder	1	Denmark
White Cloud	3	Sacramento, CA	Pint Glass	2	Lemmon, SD
Hay Ride	3	Eldersburg, MD	Baltimore Chop	1	Baltimore, MD
Wall Blocker	2	Eldersburg, MD	Dirt Collector	1	Canada
Mars Man	1	Orlando, FL	Paleo Blue	1	Kirkwood, WA
German Mule	1	Germany	Twitchy	3	Miami Beach, FL
Hungry Dog	1	Buffalo, NY	Initiative	2	Greenwich, RI
Lovin' Life	1	Colombia	Top Shelf	1	Irving, TX
Dr. Fun	1	Miami Beach, FL	Mover Maneuver	10	Schenectady, NY
Mood Swing	1	Miami Beach, FL	Sovereign	1	Milwaukee, WI
6 Seater	1	Houston, TX	Peanut Butter Cup	2	Japan
Extra Points	1	Hialeah, FL	Chile Flamingo	1	Hungary
Cut Splitter	1	Utah	Strawberry Smoke	1	England
Buick Electra	1	Johnson City, TN	F-Stop	1	England
Rattler	1	Johnson City, TN	Chicago Brick	1	Chicago, IL
Noche	3	Spain	Easy Exit	1	Fall River, MA
Papillon	2	Miami, FL	Equilibrium	1	Lowell, MA
Outside the Box	2	Miami, FL	Black Honey	1	New Zealand
Cat Ears	1	UK	White Russian	1	Belarus
Gruyere	1	UK	Former Fat Guy	1	Tampa, FL
Train Track	1	Miami, FL	Juice Cleanse	1	St. Paul, MN
Rollover	1	Atlanta, GA	Wonder Fit	1	St. Paul, MN
Battlefield	1	Germany	Two Way Radio	1	Lutz, FL
Asbestos	1	Aberdeen, MD	Buffalo Jack	1	Buffalo, NY
Sunday School	1	Aberdeen, MD	Shave Club	2	Chicago, IL
Salt Pan	1	Curacao	Epic Shooter	1	Miami, FL
Fahrenheit 69	1	Sykesville, MD	Aerial Yoga	2	Jonesburo, GA
Dear Jerky	1	Richmond, KY	Slummer	1	York, Maine
Traditional Country	1	London, KY	Squirrel Fish	1	Argentina

Gold Rush	1	Nevada City, CA	
Gingko	1	Germany	
Nalgene	1	Baltimore, MD	
Disastrous	1	Portland, OR	
Ponch	1	Columbus, OH	
Nu Skin	1	Spain	
Rubber Face	1	Norway	
Auto Pilot	2	Owings, MD	
Pugs	2	Columbus, OH	
Crazy Dater	1	Manhattan, NY	
Pebble Hill	1	England	
No Need	1	Thailand	
Magneto	1	Italy	
Alba	1	Italy	
Dryer	1	Brooklyn, NY	
El Bruce	1	Russia	
KGB	1	Russia	
Squeed	1	Russia	
Exploser	3	Portugal	
Defuse	3	Portugal	
Sea Dragon	2	Yonkers, NY	
Summer Slammer	1	Austria	
Curly Girly	1	Hialeah, FL	
Hopeful	4	Red Lodge, MT	
Advance Man	2	Pleasanton, CA	
Dabbler	3	Russia	
Lo Lo	1	Venezuela	
Openness	1	Rome, NY	
Dreamness	1	Rome, NY	
Hold 'Em	2	Marietta, GA	
Empire State	1	New York, NY	
High Steppin'	1	Italy	
Dabs	1	Miami, FL	
Ring Tone	1	Miami, FL	
Playah	1	Canada	
Octane	1	India	
Sopah	1	India	

Kooshe	1	Slovakia	
Sweet and Sour	1	Philippines	
Realization	1	Lithuania	
Slither	1	Atlanta, GA	
Lychee	1	Atlanta, GA	
Green Paper	1	Italy	
Cuna	1	Italy	
Crème Brulee	1	France	
PPA	1	Jacksonville, FL	
Geometry	1	Franklin, NC	
Mzungu	3	St. Paul, MN	
Orienteer	1	Poland	
Applicator	21	Cuba	
Risky	1	New York, NY	
Dog Paddle	1	Rio Grande, CA	
Iron King	1	Rio Grande, CA	
Golden Boy	2	Cambridge, MA	
Golden State	1	Wilmington, DE	
Mixed Berry	1	Colombia	
Early Bird	1	Russia	
Apple Vodka	1	Poland	
Yolo	1	Canada	
Choker	1	Washington, DC	
Loaded Dice	1	Long Island, NY	
Roasted	1	Phoenix, AZ	
Vocalizer	1	Phoenix, AZ	
Boiling Over	1	Columbus, IN	
Saber	1	St. Louis, MO	
Eighteen Moons	1	Italy	
Grappa	1	Italy	
Roundabout	1	Phoenix, AZ	
Aggressively Boring	1	Miami, FL	
Scarlett Carnation	1	Brooksville, OH	
Snook	1	Troy, OH	
River Pader	1	Germany	
Peaceful Mind	1	France	

ACKNOWLEDGMENTS

I WOULD LIKE TO THANK the diverse collection of human beings that make up the Raven Run family for each one's individuality and genuine spirit—particularly, the man himself, Robert "Raven" Kraft, who trusted me with his story and always did what he said. Every mile getting to know you all has been an honor, and I hope you recognize our stories within these pages.

There were many Raven Runners who absorbed my questions with exceptional grace and good humor. I want to especially thank Gringo, Hurricane, Dizzy, Hitter, Chocolate Chip, Giggler, Teen Idol, Poutine, Butcher, Hurdler, and Taxman. For opening the Raven Run up to anyone with a computer, Carlos "Spinner" Alvarez deserves praise and thanks for his work on RavenRun.net. For always asking how you can help and being a bright light everywhere you travel, I thank Bieke "Juris Prudence" Claes. To Miracle, for your wisdom, insight, and photography, thank you for helping me understand the world you share with Raven. Miracle once told me she imagined putting a book together to be like that scene in *Sorcerer's Apprentice*, where Mickey is beginning to try his own sorcery powers. "He begins to direct the mop and the buckets and before you know it, there's a million buckets of water, and they're dancing, it completely gets away from him," she recalled to me. "Is that how you feel writing this book?"

It is, sometimes, how I feel. But I am lucky to have friends who are also terrific readers and editors. For their commitment to me in person and for making me sound better in print, I'm grateful to Kaitlyn Gentile, Jocelyn Lebow, Annie McNamara, Lindsay Eriksson, Heather Kamins, Corey Ginsberg, Tanya Bhatt, and—as always—Theodore "Dr. Ted" and Dale Rosengarten. For his generosity in sharing his internal library that encompasses the history of South Florida, I also thank Paul George.

For her immense talent to capture an entire world between a camera's shutter, I am in awe of Mary Beth Koeth. Together, we navigated the fantastic bizarreness of Miami Beach and found creative ways to afford the city and remain ourselves. One day we may be able to go to a restaurant outside of the happy hour menu but for now and forever, I am grateful for her friendship, kindness, and vision.

I am thankful to the authors of many works that have provided helpful context to our common elusive character, Miami Beach. Among them, I'd like to acknowledge John Rothchild's *Up for Grabs,* Marty Stofik's *Saving South Beach*, Marvin Dunn's *Black Miami in the Twentieth Century*, Howard Kleinberg's *Miami Beach: A History*, Mirta Ojita's *Finding Mañana*, *This Land Is Our Land: Immigrants and Power in Miami*, by Alex Stepick et al., Gerald Posner's *Miami Babylon*, Joan Didion's *Miami*, Polly Redford's *Billion Dollar Sandbar*, and Norman Mailer's *St. George and the Godfather*.

For creating the space that first made Miami feel like home to me, I want to thank Mitchell Kaplan for his wonderful Books & Books and the Miami Book Fair International. You have made so many writers feel worthy, and I am fortunate to be but one beneficiary of your confidence and positive thinking. Every good thing that people say about Mitchell is true.

It was in the author's lounge at the Miami Book Fair, in fact, that I happened to sit next to Ronald Goldfarb, who became my literary agent and *Running with Raven* champion. Thank you, Ron, for making me believe the sagacity of your old barber, Carmine from New Jersey, who said, "Ever ting gonna be more better soon." Thanks to you and Gerrie Sturman, it is more better now.

Ron had the idea to send this book to Michaela Hamilton at Kensington's Citadel Press, where Raven's story has been respected and valued from page one. In my first conversation with Michaela, she promised me that, at Kensington, "We never let our authors go out with spinach in their teeth." To you and Lulu Martinez and the entire Kensington team, thank you for your thoughtful and sensitive improvements to and care of this work.

Every day reminds me of how lucky I am to have three best friends whose DNA is linked to mine. To my brothers, Pat Huttenbach and Eric Huttenbach, and to my sister, Marisa Huttenbach Crawford, thank you for making sure I am never more than myself and for making me believe that myself is enough, or maybe sometimes a little too much. Thank you also for making me a grateful in-law to Yve and Chas and proud aunt to Steven, Amanda, Greg, Emma, and Charlie.

To my father, Dirk Huttenbach, for never tiring of my questions and instilling a deep interest in how history happens and is recorded, thank you. You were my original search engine, and I appreciate every meal that I share with you and Barbara. Last, but likely most valuable to my efforts, I thank my mother, Muriel Patterson Huttenbach, whose love and belief make me think I can accomplish anything in this big world.

Many people contributed in diverse and significant ways. Among them, I want to acknowledge a few generous Kickstarter Backers: John Edwin Mason, Anneke Strachan Herman, Marijke Strachan, Brent Shinall, Carolina Boechat Raimondi, Maxwell Bonnie, Hadi Irvani, Ben Tan, Carlos "Sergeant Comic," Edward "Thunder" James Murphy, Amy "Preservationist" Tancig, Anne Marie and Billy Parker, Andrew Savysky, Laura and James Sheppard, Priscilla "Miracle" Ferguson, Ruth

Van Maldegem, Terry Smith and Abby Bender, Jason Setchen, the Miami Ad School, Mike and Marlene Koeth, Mike "Boy Next Door" Czabator, Mark "Espionage" Macaluso, The Worley Family, Randy Eng, The Hurdler, Burger "Petroleum Man," Jonathan Rosenthal, Robert Nelms, and John and Laurie Huseby.

I'll end these thanks where I started, with Raven, who sings a song called "The Road Is Long." The road is long, indeed, Raven, and I'm so glad you invited me and twenty-five hundred friends to run it with you.

ABOUT THE AUTHOR

LAURA LEE HUTTENBACH, a graduate of the University of Virginia, has been a serious athlete since her older brothers taught her how to slide tackle in soccer when she was four. In high school as a four-sport star, she was named Female Athlete of the Year for the state of Georgia. She moved to South Beach in 2011 after finishing her first book—*The Boy Is Gone,* the life story of a Kenyan independence leader whom she met while backpacking in Africa. During her evening runs in Miami Beach, she met Raven and became fascinated by his story. While running with Raven, she learned Miami Beach history and met characters of the past and present who were unlike any she'd ever known. Currently, she lives in New York City, and her website is lllhuttenbach.com. To find out more about the Raven Runs, visit www.ravenrun.net.